RED CENTRE, DARK HEART

Evan McHugh's previous books include award-winning travel guides to Sydney, *The Rot Stuff, Pint-Sized Ireland* and *1606: An Epic Adventure*. He writes a weekly column, 'Dry Rot', in the *Sunday Mail* and has written for television and radio. He is married and lives in Sydney. More great Australian stories appear in Evan's *Shipwrecks: Australia's Greatest Maritime Disasters* and *Outback Heroes: Australia's Greatest Bush Stories*.

EVAN McHUGH

RED CENTRE, DARK HEART

VIKING
an imprint of
PENGUIN BOOKS

VIKING

Published by the Penguin Group
Penguin Group (Australia)
250 Camberwell Road, Camberwell, Victoria 3124, Australia
(a division of Pearson Australia Group Pty Ltd)
Penguin Group (USA) Inc.
375 Hudson Street, New York, New York 10014, USA
Penguin Group (Canada)
90 Eglinton Avenue East, Suite 700, Toronto, Canada ON M4P 2Y3
(a division of Pearson Penguin Canada Inc.)
Penguin Books Ltd
80 Strand, London WC2R 0RL England
Penguin Ireland
25 St Stephen's Green, Dublin 2, Ireland
(a division of Penguin Books Ltd)
Penguin Books India Pvt Ltd
11 Community Centre, Panchsheel Park, New Delhi - 110 017, India
Penguin Group (NZ)
67 Apollo Drive, Rosedale, North Shore 0632, New Zealand
(a division of Pearson New Zealand Ltd)
Penguin Books (South Africa) (Pty) Ltd
24 Sturdee Avenue, Rosebank, Johannesburg 2196, South Africa

Penguin Books Ltd, Registered Offices: 80 Strand, London, WC2R 0RL, England

First published by Penguin Group (Australia), 2007

1 3 5 7 9 10 8 6 4 2

Text copyright © Evan McHugh 2007
Illustrations copyright © Michelle Havenstein and Nick Charalambous 2007

The moral right of the author has been asserted

Design by David Altheim © Penguin Group (Australia)
Cover photograph by Rob Penn/Getty Images
Typeset in Fairfield LH Light by Post Pre-press Group, Brisbane, Queensland
Printed and bound in Australia by McPherson's Printing Group, Maryborough, Victoria

National Library of Australia
Cataloguing-in-Publication data:

McHugh, Evan.
Red centre, dark heart: true stories of mystery, drama and death in remote Australia.

1st ed.
Bibliography.
ISBN 978 0 670 07078 7 (pbk).

1. Crime – Australia – Case studies. 2. Rural crimes – Australia – Case studies.
3. Criminals – Australia – Case studies. 4. Criminal investigation – Australia – Case studies.
5. Bushrangers – Australia – Case studies. I. Title.

364.994

penguin.com.au

CONTENTS

INTRODUCTION

A lonely road. A secluded homestead. A remote landscape.

'Mummy and Daddy are asleep,' the little girl on the telephone said. 'I've tried shaking them but they won't wake up.'

The operator in the outback New South Wales town of Jerilderie suspected something was terribly wrong. She rang the police and kept five-year-old Tania Lewis talking while two officers drove out to the property. There they found Tania and her three-year-old brother alive and well, but the body of her father, shearer Mick Lewis, lay in a pool of blood on the kitchen floor. He'd been shot in the head. His wife Sue was found in bed. She too had been killed by a .22 calibre gunshot to the head.

In the two centuries since Europeans first settled the outback (and, indeed, during the millennia that indigenous Australians have inhabited it) it has remained a sparsely populated frontier, an environment most urban dwellers struggle to comprehend. Little wonder the 1978 murder of Mick and Sue Lewis attracted widespread media attention, not least because of the heart-rending image of two small children left to fend for themselves. Sensational headlines like 'Outback House of Horrors' reflected the belief that remote Australia is a wild place inhabited by outlaws who can kill in cold blood, then disappear without trace.

The Australian landscape is challenging at the best of times but add a criminal dimension and it has a menace that has few rivals anywhere else in the world. There's no denying the morbid fascination that crimes in remote locations exert. Not only do they occur in isolated places, they're often isolated from other crimes. In cities, one day's grisly murder is rapidly overtaken by the next day's shocking slaying, but in the outback, crimes often occur where 'nothing ever happens'. This factor alone throws outback crime into sharp relief.

Then there's the influence exerted by the outback itself. Its sheer size and the fact that it's largely uninhabited creates an environment that presents challenges to criminal investigations rarely encountered in other countries. Where do you begin to look for the suspect, clues or even the victim? How do you cope with the logistics of an investigation that encompasses vast areas?

These aspects and characteristics of outback crime were the criterion applied when considering stories for inclusion in this volume. Many cases involved seeking the tiniest needle in the biggest haystack. Yet the answers to the question 'Where do you start?' produced extraordinary stories of tenacity, endurance, determination, luck and sometimes pure genius. There have, of course, been less auspicious investigations, and these have been included as well.

The selection follows something of a historic arc, starting in the days when 'the outback' began on the edge of the first settlements and the European occupation of the land was disputed by the indigenous population. It covers the 'glory days' of bushrangers and cattle duffers, whose bush skills and lawlessness combined in bold exploits that evoked admiration, despite the criminality involved, and created a romanticised view of the outlaw and the outback. And it encompasses the present day, when the outback has become a major tourist attraction, but one where visitors often fail to understand just how thin the veneer of civilisation can be.

The journey to the dark heart of Australia's red centre begins in an unlikely place, as chapter 1 reveals. It was in Tasmania's south-west wilderness that a most disturbing aspect of the wide brown land's 'beauty and terror' was first laid bare – a tale of cannibalism so horrific that at first it was disbelieved.

At the same time, squatters were claiming parts of the outback, carving out immense holdings over which they exercised flimsy control, leaving themselves wide open to cattle and sheep duffers. The most notorious of these was Harry Redford, the subject of chapter 2. In his case, though he stunned the country with his crime, he also helped extend the frontiers of settlement beyond what was thought possible.

Bushrangers are synonymous with the outback and in chapter 3 the relationship between crime and the bush was fully realised. Ned Kelly was more than a criminal. He was a consummate bushman able to use his skills to turn a corner of Victoria into his personal domain. Kelly's defiance, and the bush itself, became a menace to the government's authority.

In the rampage of revenge killings by Jimmy Governor and his brother Joe described in chapter 4, menace turned into outright dread. Governor, part Aboriginal, was such a skilled bushman that he eluded the immense manhunt which pursued him, and even turned and hunted the hunters. Meanwhile, whole communities became refugees, as the bush acquired an aura of malevolence that lingers to this day.

Chapter 5 demonstrates both how easy and how hard it is for someone to disappear in the outback, in the now little-known, but at the time famous, murder of an unremarkable farm labourer, Bill Groves. His unexpected departure from Boorara Station, in the far south-west of Queensland, was quite plausible but the suspicions of his mates prompted an investigation that covered thousands of hectares of hot, dry, shadeless country.

Outback life is often tough and uncompromising, and nowhere is that more evident than in the rugged mining towns, the subject of chapter 6. Life is often lived by a different set of rules, but, even taking that into account, nothing could have prepared Kalgoorlie for the reign of terror that erupted when a series of bomb blasts killed fifteen people in 1942. At the time it was the biggest mass murder in Australia's modern history. What could drive a man to commit such a crime? The answer may well lie in the kind of landscape that can break a man's spirit and drive him to despair.

In chapter 7, the missing person, Larry Boy, was suspected of murdering his tribal wife on Elsey Station in the Northern Territory. He set police and Aboriginal trackers the ultimate test of their bush skills during a forty-day hunt through the crocodile-, snake- and mosquito-infested jungles and swamps south of Arnhem Land.

Once again, the advantage lay with the fugitive, but the combination of relentless determination and incredible tracking skills finally tipped the balance.

No compilation of outback crimes would be complete without reference to the Azaria Chamberlain case in chapter 8, easily the most controversial investigation in Australia's history. Here the outback presented a tantalising mystery: could a dingo have done it? The question was debated far and wide by an insatiable public, while the dead baby's parents became the victims of a trial by media. The case exacted a terrible toll on Azaria's family and in the process revealed there was much about the outback that we still didn't understand.

As the backpacker phenomenon gained momentum in Australia in the 1980s, the temptation for innocent young adults, looking for freedom and adventure, to hitchhike was irresistible. However, when seven bodies were found in the Belanglo State Forest, just south of Sydney, it soon became clear that backpackers were being preyed upon by a serial killer – the subject of chapter 9. The killings were on the doorstep of one of the country's largest cities, yet they had all the characteristics of outback crimes – victims meeting their end in lonely, rarely visited places at the hands of an 'outlaw'. It was a case that shifted the boundaries of the outback and revealed them to be disturbingly closer than we thought.

The final chapter describes the disappearance of Peter Falconio, easily the most publicised investigation of recent years. Completing the historical arc of the selection, it embodies the nightmare scenario of the outback – coming face to face with evil and all you can do is run. However, it also demonstrates the tenacity of an investigating team that, with very little to go on (again there was no body), carried out its work under the scrutiny of an international media frenzy. The investigation spanned half a continent, stretching the investigators to the limit, yet ultimately they overcame the challenges the outback presented.

There is something deeply compelling in the tragedy, mystery and drama of crime, and while it's all too easy to dwell on the criminal mind and the macabre details of their behaviour, there are also benefits to be found in seeking a deeper understanding of the context in which crime occurs. If nothing was ever learned, the victims would have suffered in vain.

As *Red Centre, Dark Heart* reveals, from the dark forests of the Tasmanian wilderness to the shifting red dunes of the central deserts, the outback of Australia is a mixture of beauty and danger that both beguiles and confronts. It's a place of many secrets where evil deeds can go unnoticed and unpunished for years. However, against all odds, justice can prevail.

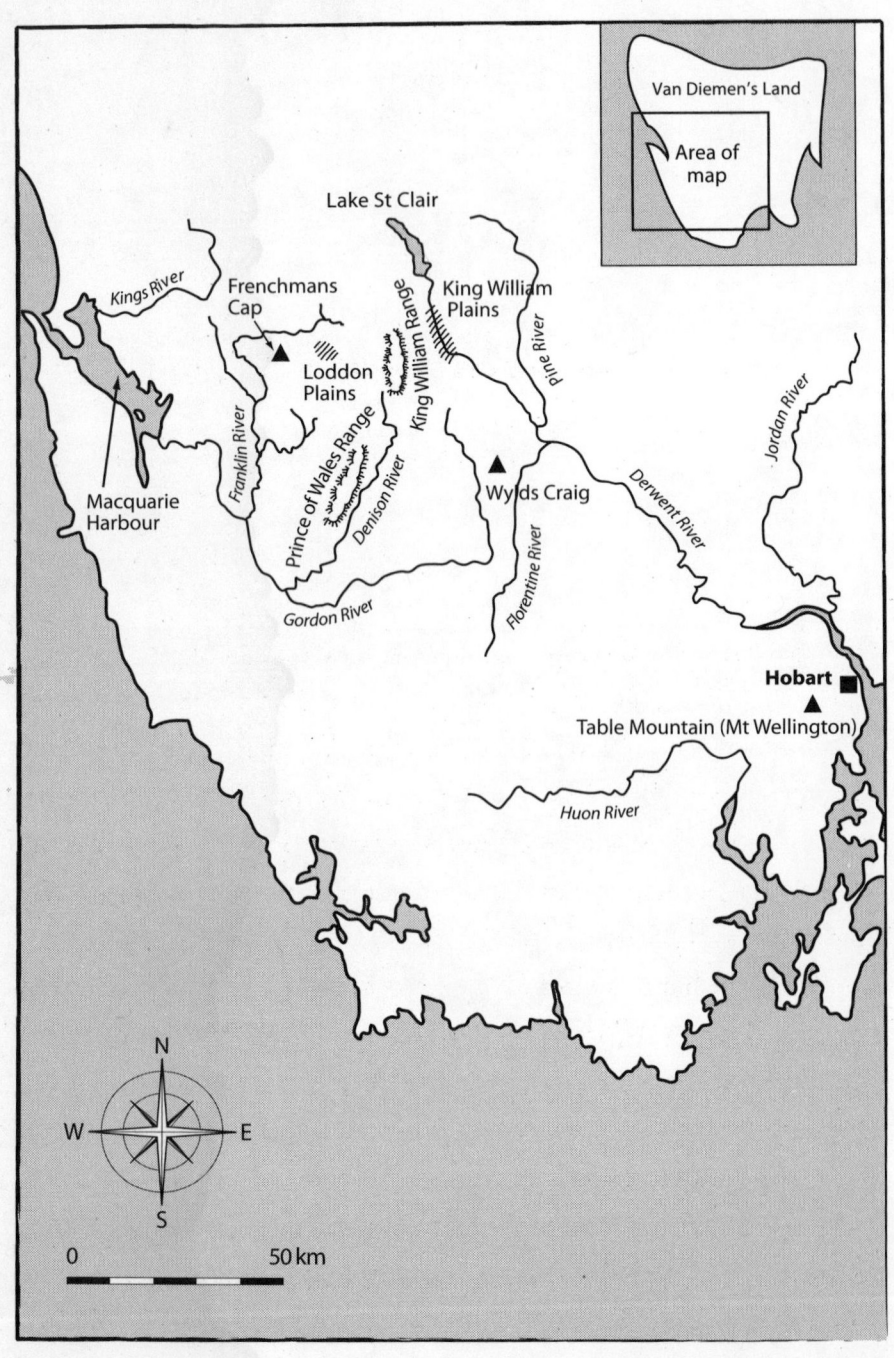

Van Diemen's Land

Area of map

Lake St Clair

Kings River

Frenchmans Cap

King William Plains

King William Range

Loddon Plains

Pine River

Franklin River

Prince of Wales Range

Denison River

Wylds Craig

Jordan River

Macquarie Harbour

Derwent River

Florentine River

Gordon River

Hobart

Table Mountain (Mt Wellington)

Huon River

N
W   E
S

0   50 km

1

CANNIBALS

For the first seven days the escape of eight convicts from Tasmania's notorious penal settlement at Macquarie Harbour in south-west Tasmania was completely unremarkable. Then, as the forlorn band struggled through thickly forested and mountainous terrain that yielded so little sustenance it was shunned even by Tasmania's Aboriginal population, the cold, wet and starving men began talking about eating each other.

'I'm so hungry, I could eat a piece of a man,' William Kennerly muttered when the men bedded down for the night in the wind- and rain-swept vicinity of the 1443-metre mountain called the Frenchman's Cap, a bare thirty kilometres from the place they'd fled, on 28 September 1822. The escapees – Alexander Pearce, Alexander Dalton, Thomas Bodenham, Matthew Travers, William Brown, John Mather, Robert Greenhill and Kennerly – were finding out the hard way why the impenetrable, inhospitable and uninhabited forests were regarded as a more effective barrier to escape than any prison wall. Even today, few roads penetrate the region that extends 150 kilometres from the settled districts around Hobart across to the south-west coast. It remains a virtually track-less wilderness.

The subject of cannibalism was raised again the next morning, by Robert Greenhill. 'I've seen the like done before,' he said. 'It tastes very like pork.'

At least one of the men, John Mather, objected: 'It would be murder to do it. And then perhaps we won't be able to eat it.'

'I'll warrant you,' said Greenhill, 'I will eat the first part myself but you must all lend a hand that we may be equally guilty of the crime.'

The ethical debate (such as it was) ended there, but the con-sequences were to add a new and unsettling edge to the way we regard the often hostile Australian landscape. In the gloomy forests of south-west Tasmania, these men were about to become subject to one of the grim realities of survival in remote and isolated places, where the rule of law and the notion of justice cannot penetrate.

It didn't take the convicts long to select their victim. Greenhill's eye fell on Alexander Dalton, who he maintained had volunteered to flog his fellow prisoners. There's no evidence that this was so; however, when the forlorn band stopped that night, Dalton, Brown and Kennerly's suspicions about the others' intentions prompted them to camp by themselves.

It wasn't enough. At 3 a.m. Greenhill made his move. He took up an axe and crept towards his sleeping victim. Dalton never saw him coming. A single blow split his head, and he died without uttering a sound. Even if he had, it would have made no difference. There was no one outside the immediate circle of grim-faced men who was remotely within hearing, let alone able to act to save his life.

After they'd killed him, the men removed Dalton's clothes, disembowelled his body and decapitated him. Mather, Travers and Greenhill put his heart and liver on the fire, but were so hungry that they took them off before they were properly cooked. They offered some to the others, but none had the stomach for it. However, the next morning, the body was cut up and distributed among the party to carry as they continued their journey.

It was too much for Brown and Kennerly. Brown, in particular, could have felt that, in a macabre interpretation of 'survival of the fittest', he was the most vulnerable. He'd been lagging behind for some days, having been in bad shape even before he'd escaped, due to the floggings and poor food of the penal settlement. That morning he and Kennerly turned his slow progress into an opportunity to escape their companions. They vanished not 500 metres from the previous night's campsite.

The remaining five escapees – Pearce, Bodenham, Mather, Travers and Greenhill – coo-eed but got no answer. They debated searching for the two, who had a cooking pot and tomahawk between them. If Brown and Kennerly made it back to Macquarie Harbour, their story of cannibalism would hang them all. However, the chances of them making it back to the penal settlement were practically nil, and it was eventually decided not to bother.

As it happened, on 12 October, Brown and Kennerly did manage to stagger back to the Gordon River, near Macquarie Harbour, where they signalled a passing boat. The surgeon at Macquarie

Harbour battled to save the pair from the ravages of extreme starvation and exposure but Brown died three days later and Kennerly died on the 19th, apparently taking the secret of what had happened to Dalton to their graves.

According to some accounts that Alexander Pearce later gave concerning his escape from Macquarie Harbour, Dalton had also escaped with Brown and Kennerly. In other accounts, Pearce described Dalton's death in great detail. If he did escape, Dalton didn't reach Macquarie Harbour, which prompted historian James Bonwick to imagine what his fate might have been. In 1856 he wrote in *The Bushrangers*:

> *His faltering steps were numbered; and, as the dreary wind howled his requiem, and the dim twilight rested upon his famine-stricken countenance, the sternest advocate of the penal code would have said that justice was satisfied. Lying upon the wet ground, forsaken by his comrades in sin, with the dew of evening mingling with the chilly damp of death upon his brow, had he no mother, wife, or child in the far distant land, who, with love for even his degraded soul, might have soothed his last hours, and received his last sigh in the kiss of forgiving affection?*

The remaining felons pressed on through scrub so thick that one of them went ahead to break a trail for the others to follow. At times they had to burrow through the undergrowth on hands and knees, and, in pouring rain, ascend mountains of over 1000 metres. In some accounts the men forded two large rivers; in others, it was just one river, which they thought was the upper reaches of the Gordon. In fact, it was more likely to have been the Franklin, as they were endeavouring to reach the settlements to the east, using the sun and moon to guide them.

Around 9 October they crossed a river. The two non-swimmers, Travers and Bodenham, used narrow tree trunks laid between rocks to drag themselves across. It was the second month of spring in the southern hemisphere, and in the highlands of south-west Tasmania immersion in an icy stream must have put all the men in extreme danger of hypothermia. Maintaining their body temperature taxed their reserves of energy even further, and there was only one way to replace them. All too soon, the last pieces of Thomas Dalton were consumed.

The bedraggled band of convicts struggled on, until on 15 October they reached another broad stream. The remains of Dalton were long gone and they were again famished. For the second time, the talk turned to sacrificing another life. There was an effort to retain at least an illusion of civilisation in justifying their actions, as an account attributed to the Reverend Robert Knopwood describes: '[They] began to intimate to each other that it would be much better for one to be sacrificed as food for the rest than the whole of them to perish for want.'

This time they cast lots to see who would die. The depths of the men's exhaustion was evident in the reaction of the man who lost the lottery of life and death, Thomas Bodenham. He didn't beg for his life, nor did he try to dissuade his companions; he only asked for a few minutes to pray and make peace with his God before he died.

Greenhill and Travers sent Pearce and Mather to gather firewood.

'Killing Bodenham might not be agreeable to you,' Greenhill told them, 'and I doubt you'd volunteer to be the executioner. As I've been placed by fortune in a similar situation before when I've acted as executioner, I've no objections to fulfilling the same office.'

Indeed, he'd had no qualms about killing the hapless Dalton, and again Greenhill took his axe and killed Bodenham with a single blow to the head. Then they began the bloody butchering of the still-warm corpse. When Pearce and Mather returned, a fire was kindled and they cooked pieces of the freshly killed Bodenham, 'which they soon devoured very greedily'. The four remaining men spent a day recuperating and gorging on the remains. The murder scene was undisturbed until ten years later, when the first 'explorer' to visit what are now known as the Loddon Plains, surveyor William Sharland, found human bones. He suspected he'd come across the probable site of Bodenham's demise.

The escapees' journey had brought them to the western tier of the mountains that lay west of the settled regions around Hobart, from where they could see some way to the east. They came to a river (either the upper reaches of the Derwent or the Gordon), which they traversed for three days looking for a place to cross. According to Pearce's confession to John Barnes, a former surgeon at Macquarie Harbour: 'Our provisions were all out again and we said that we would all die rather than any more should be killed.' (Reported to the Select Committee on Transportation in 1838.)

In fact, the opposite seemed to have been the case. They were still in country that provided them with nothing in the way of sustenance, let alone anyone who could help them. Under the circumstances, there was no choice but to continue their practice of preying on each other to survive, and protestations that they should not kill any more of their party only meant that the thought had returned to the forefront of their minds. Mather suspected he was next.

In the Select Committee account, Mather is reported to have taken Pearce aside and said, 'Pearce, let us go on by ourselves. You see what kind of a cove Greenhill is. He would kill his father before he would fast one day.'

Pearce's confession, together with a handwritten deposition held in Sydney's Mitchell Library (generally attributed to Macquarie Harbour Commandant, Lieutenant John Cuthbertson), suggest the possibility that only at this stage did Mather succumb to the cannibalism of the others. The two accounts vary slightly. The Select Committee version stated: 'We boiled some of Bodenham and drank it.' The Cuthbertson version read: 'We boiled some fern and drank it.' Both accounts continue: 'Mather took his first, and it made him so sick he begun to vomit.'

Whether it was his first experience of cannibalism or the fern tea that made him ill, Greenhill took advantage of Mather's vulnerability and made his move. He struck him on the head with the axe, but Mather survived the blow.

'Murder!' he shouted. 'Will you see me killed?'

Mather was stronger than Greenhill and managed to overpower his assailant, grabbing hold of the axe. However, instead of pressing home his advantage, he showed the merciless Greenhill compassion. He threw the axe to Pearce and told him to keep it, an action Mather was soon to regret.

Mather had thought Pearce his ally. Pearce had sworn his friendship and agreed to expose any plan to take Mather's life. Yet, as
their hunger pains increased, Pearce started to align himself with
Greenhill and Travers. Two days later, camped by a small creek,
the fire that kept them warm also served to remind them that they
had nothing to cook. Mather was in considerable distress, having
discovered Pearce's betrayal, and was sitting apart from the other
three. He was in an impossible position. If he tried to escape, he
would certainly perish alone. If he stayed, it was only a matter of
time before his companions made a meal of him.

Sitting separately allowed the others to hatch their plans. When
the fire died down, one of them set off to get more fuel. As he
passed near Mather he pounced, holding him down while the others
swooped in for the kill. The axe smashed down on the head of the
struggling man. With one against three, Mather stood no chance.
In Knopwood's narrative, Greenhill then told his companions they'd
done society a service by taking Mather's life. To this the others
agreed, but it was more likely that Travers and Pearce knew better than to disagree with a man who had an axe and an insatiable
appetite for his fellow man.

While he dined on Mather, Pearce had other almost-as-difficult
things to digest. In particular, the close relationship between Travers
and Greenhill meant he was likely to be the next item on their grim
menu. He had as long as it took them to consume Mather before
it would be his turn.

For the next four days the three journeyed over several ranges
of hills, surviving on the remains of Mather that they had taken
with them. On the fourth day Travers was bitten on the foot by a

snake. According to Knopwood it 'so affected his leg as to make him despair of ever reaching the summit of his wishes'. Tasmania has three land snakes, all venomous, especially the lowland copperhead (*Austrelaps superbus*) and the tiger snake (*Notechis scutatus*), which has a bite that, while neurotoxic, can also cause muscle damage and affect blood clotting.

The bite didn't kill Travers but his leg swelled so much (suggesting the bite was from a tiger snake) that he was unable to travel. Realising his injury made him particularly vulnerable, he begged the others to leave him. Greenhill and Pearce would have none of it. Greenhill in particular believed his friend would recover, so they stayed with Travers for the next five days. By the end of that time, Travers was almost mad with fear. He was prepared to be abandoned to a solitary death, but the thought of being eaten was something entirely different.

Travers was particularly fearful that Pearce would turn Greenhill against him, but Greenhill stood by his long-time friend. He boosted Travers's spirits by telling him he was sure they were close to the eastern settlements, that they would soon be dining on fresh mutton. He said he would sooner carry Travers than leave him. It was just the encouragement the injured man needed, although Greenhill neglected to mention that they had finished all of Mather and the further Travers managed to drag himself, the easier it would be on his two hungry companions. And, with the assistance of the other two, Travers struggled on, his progress painfully slow.

All day Greenhill and Pearce helped him climb the steep hills and make the tortuous descents to the streams. They laid saplings across the water to help him cross, then supported him again as he hobbled onward. Travers pushed himself to the limit of his endurance and at the end of their day's journey collapsed into an exhausted sleep.

Despite Greenhill and Pearce being almost as tired, having all but carried Travers in their severely weakened condition, they still took time to discuss what to do about their companion. It was while they were discussing his fate that Travers was woken by the pain in his leg. He realised they'd been talking about him, and again begged them to leave him. However, when the pain in his leg abated, he was unable to stay awake and keep watch over his companions.

No sooner was he asleep than the pair agreed that Travers's time had come. None of the historical accounts name the person who struck the fatal blow, but on this occasion it may have been Pearce. According to Knopwood:

> Greenhill was much affected by this horrid scene and stood quite motionless to see one who had been his companion throughout the whole of troubles – compelled to be slaughtered as food for to subsist on – for had he been fortunate enough to have escaped from being stung there was such a strong tie of affection between him and Greenhill that Pearce would most evidently have fallen the first victim, after Mather's carcass was disposed of.

However, the terrible fate of his friend didn't stop Greenhill eating him. It served to emphasise how the uncompromising wilderness had stripped the men of any remaining vestige of humanity. For the next two days Greenhill and Pearce stayed where they were, feeding on the body of Travers. They 'protested to each other the greatest fidelity and friendship' while discussing the likelihood that they were close to the settled districts, and that what remained of Travers would be sufficient to last whatever distance remained to be covered.

They carefully packed up all of Travers that they were able to carry, both men knowing that when this food ran out they would be facing a final showdown – whoever survived would be left alone in the wilderness. They would then face their fate, haunted by the horrors strewn throughout the dark forests stretching back to Macquarie Harbour.

As luck would have it, they soon came upon an open plain that had all the look of a superb stock run, approximately sixty kilometres long by twenty kilometres wide. Although they searched all day, they found no cattle, sheep or other signs of European habitation (the site was most likely the King William Plains, now mostly submerged beneath a lake). Their search appeared to be rewarded when they caught sight of a column of smoke. They cautiously approached, discovering an Aboriginal camp of some fifty men, women and children.

Sure that the camp would have a good store of food, they decided to attack, hoping the element of surprise would work in their favour. Greenhill prepared to attack with his axe; Pearce took hold of a stick. Both men crept close to the camp, then leapt from cover, wild and ragged, howling like demons and flailing their weapons about them as they ran forward. Terrified by the monsters that had suddenly sprung up before them, the people ran for their lives, leaving everything in the camp behind, including pieces of kangaroo and possum.

At this point of his account, Knopwood makes the unintended ironic observation that: 'They would not have had the least shadow of chance of escaping without being dreadfully hurt if not cruelly murdered – for although these natives are not cannibals, there have been several instances of people being barbarously murdered by them in several parts of the colony.'

Since the European settlement of Australia, the indigenous population has been accused of cannibalism, more often than not on scant evidence or mere hearsay. Here is a thoroughly documented case of cannibalism; however, the perpetrators weren't Aboriginal, they were Europeans.

Greenhill and Pearce knew they had only a moment before the people recovered from their fright and returned in sufficient numbers to retaliate. They grabbed what food they could, threw the abandoned spears into the fires and bolted. When they felt safe from pursuit, they quickly cooked and hungrily ate the stolen food. The next morning they ate well once more, before proceeding on their way.

By this stage their clothes were reduced to rags. They were barefoot and carried numerous cuts from falls and from pushing through dense undergrowth. Some of their wounds had ulcerated. The good news was that the weather was becoming warmer, and the terrain was becoming easier to traverse. However, they were beginning to fear they were lost. Thinking they should have reached civilisation by now, they worried their attempts at navigation by the sun and moon had failed.

Yet, all they could do was press on. The days passed until they again found themselves without food, and the torments of hunger began to grow once more. Greenhill became increasingly mindful of having the axe, and Pearce grew more alert to his own danger. At night, when they camped, Pearce kept well away from Greenhill, far enough to have ample warning of his approach. Any pretence of friendship was forgotten as the one warily regarded the other.

There was a brief respite when they came upon another Aboriginal camp. Again the two wild-looking men – ragged and filthy and bellowing madly – so startled the indigenous people that they fled. That night Greenhill and Pearce dined on kangaroo once more. Knopwood noted: 'They then lay themselves down to sleep – nearer to each other than they had done for several days. They began to converse with each other in the mutualest manner they possibly could – apparently on the strongest terms of friendship.'

The next day their prospects brightened even further when they sighted what they thought was Hobart's Mount Wellington. Pearce had lived and worked on the slopes of the mountain as a shepherd, and he was sure that he recognised it. It lay in the direction they were intending to travel, confirming that their navigation had been correct all along.

Calculating that it would take just two days' journey to reach (about thirty kilometres away), Greenhill and Pearce set off with as much speed as they could muster. Thinking themselves near to civilisation, they ate most of the kangaroo that remained. They continued just as eagerly the next day, reaching the foot of the mountain around midday. It was then that they discovered they were mistaken. There were no flocks of sheep grazing on its slopes nor any sign of European habitation. It was yet another peak among the many they'd struggled over. They'd probably reached Wyld's Craig (1339 metres), eighty kilometres from Macquarie Harbour and still seventy or so from Hobart.

Approaching the brink of despair the two pressed on, hungry once more. Greenhill in particular was despondent and said he would 'never get to any port with his life'. Pearce was more optimistic, believing they had to be getting close, considering how far they thought they'd come. Not long after, their appetites once more got the better of them.

In the submission to the Select Committee, Pearce is reported to have said: 'I watched Greenhill for two nights as I thought he eyed me more than usual. He always kept the axe under his head when he laid down and carried it on his back when walking.'

At night when they made their campfire, Pearce made sure he sat opposite Greenhill. As the situation between the two men deteriorated, despite their exhaustion from walking each day, they slept fitfully, on guard for any move by the other. Pearce had good reason to be cautious, as the Knopwood account relates:

One evening when we were both lay down he pretended to be asleep and I just in the act of slumbering when I perceived him raise himself up taking the axe with him in his hand. On discovering this I immediately rose as though out of a slumber appearing as I had not perceived him. Fortunate it was for me that I was not asleep for had I been I should have shared the same fate as the others. This piece of treachery on the part of Greenhill so much affected me that I was determined to embrace the first opportunity of leaving him, but he having possession of the axe at this time made me form a resolution of getting possession of the axe.

They travelled on, ever watchful. Pearce maintained that Greenhill made several attempts on his life, but he was always ready to defend himself. Then, according to the Select Committee submission, Greenhill let his guard down. Pearce said:

> *One night we came to a little creek between two hills where we kindled a fire, our provisions had been out some days before this. I thought Greenhill had determined to kill me for his looking at me and watching me so narrowly. Near day break he fell asleep. I instantly seized the opportunity, took the axe from under his head and struck him with it and killed him. I cut off part of his thigh and arm which I took with me.*

It was pure luck that Pearce had been the one to survive the gruesome showdown deep in the wilderness. He was now the only surviving witness to the fate of seven of his fellow escapees, five of whom had been murdered and devoured, their bones strewn over 100 kilometres of wilderness. Now alone, Pearce pushed on, still making his way to the east. All the remains of Greenhill that he was able to carry lasted just a few days, after which Pearce went hungry.

Two days later, despairing of ever reaching civilisation, and perhaps haunted by the horror in which he was a central character, Pearce took off his leather belt and tried to use it to hang himself. It seems he thought better of the idea. Shortly after, happening on a deserted Aboriginal camp, he fed on some morsels of kangaroos and possums left behind, taking what he couldn't eat with him. Several days later, he was fortunate to come upon a duck and ten of her young. He leaped into the water, the mother flew off, and he managed to capture two of the ducklings.

The following day he ascended a hill from where he saw another peak that looked like the hoped-for Mount Wellington (all historical accounts refer to Table Mountain, as it was known until 1822, when it was renamed for the Duke of Wellington to commemorate his victory at Waterloo). This time it was the real thing. With renewed hope Pearce pressed on, and two days later, in mid-November, he finally heard the sound that told him his appalling six-week odyssey was at an end: the bleating of a flock of sheep.

On finding the flock, the starving man drove the sheep into a confined area of rocks and scrub until they were piled on top of each other. He then rushed at them and caught one, but he was so wasted and thin that the animal dragged him twenty or thirty metres over the rocks, leaving him so battered that he was forced to let go. He repeated the exercise, but this time he chose a lamb. He was so hungry he started to eat the creature raw. He was still gorging when he heard dogs barking. His marauding hadn't gone unseen. A voice shouted, 'Leave that sheep alone or I'll blow your brains out.'

Pearce turned and saw a shepherd levelling a musket at him. Pearce's condition had deteriorated so much it was only when he spoke that the shepherd realised he knew him. Knopwood's account supplies additional details: 'I being almost naked, my clothing being torn from my back, my flesh being almost torn from my bones by the brush. My beard was three or four inches [7.5 to 10 cm] in length. In short my figure was actually distressing and would have moved the hardest heart to pity me.'

The shepherd was a fellow convict named McGuire (described in some accounts as Tom Triffett), and while it may seem remarkable that a convict was armed, it was common practice in Van Diemen's Land. The shepherds needed a gun to protect themselves and their flocks, plus it provided the means to supplement their diet. McGuire took Pearce to his hut where he cooked what was left of the lamb and fed him. He looked after Pearce for several days 'with the tenderness of a saint' before the still terribly weak escapee moved on to stay with another shepherd.

Just as he and his fellow escapees had hoped, Pearce received help from the convict workers and former convicts in the more remote areas of the settled districts. Eventually Pearce fell into company with a pair of bushrangers, William Davis and Ralph Churton. Their operation involved stealing sheep from large landholders and selling them at reduced prices to small farmers (many of them former convicts), who knew better than to ask any questions. They convinced him to go bushranging with them, arguing that if he went to Hobart and gave himself up he'd only be sent to Macquarie Harbour again. Pearce was taken to their well-armed and provisioned hideout, where they were holding some 180 sheep. They had re-marked their ears and were waiting for the marks to heal before trading them with the small landholders.

It was when they tried to move the sheep that things started to unravel. A campaign to suppress bushranging, sheep duffing in particular, was under way and the group was surprised by a patrol of the 48th Regiment (the colonial police force being still in its infancy). A pursuit ensued during which the bushrangers abandoned the sheep and their knapsacks, weapons and provisions. They managed to escape but two days later, while resting beneath a tree, they were surprised by the regiment a second time.

Davis saw the soldiers approaching and tried to run. He was promptly shot through the thigh and arm. Churton and Pearce hadn't even got to their feet when they were seized and taken into custody. All three men were taken to Hobart where Davis and Churton were charged with stealing a total of 500 sheep. They were tried, found guilty and hanged.

Pearce's case, however, took a decidedly unexpected turn when he confessed to the murder and cannibalism of four or possibly five of his fellow escapees, explaining in detail how he became the first convict to succeed in escaping from Macquarie Harbour by travelling overland. His admission of cannibalism was more than enough to put a noose around his neck, yet, no one believed him. His story was thought to be so unlikely, so utterly depraved, that the authorities suspected it was concocted to discourage them from searching for the other escapees. In 1838 the Select Committee on Transportation was told that: 'There being no proof against him except his own statement, which was not relied upon, he was returned to the penal settlement of Macquarie Harbour.'

He arrived back in February 1823. His reputation as an escapee saw him held in leg irons, and among his fellow prisoners he enjoyed considerable fame, both as a successful escapee and a man with a story beyond compare. But it wasn't to end there. On the 13th or 16th of November (accounts vary), Pearce knocked off his leg irons with an axe and escaped again, this time with one other prisoner,

Thomas Cox, who had apparently pressured Pearce for some time to make a second attempt. It was a very poorly judged idea.

The pair headed north, hoping to follow the coast to Port Dalrymple, the settlement on Tasmania's north coast near present-day Launceston. They didn't get far before they found themselves in the same predicament as the previous escapees. They had run out of food and were soon exhausted and hungry, many kilometres from help. When they reached the King River, Cox revealed he was unable to cross because he couldn't swim. For Pearce, who may have been planning to get as far as he could with Cox before killing and eating him, this was a major setback. In a fury he attacked Cox with an axe, hacking at his head three times before turning to leave the mortally wounded man.

'For mercy's sake,' Cox called out weakly, 'come back and put me out of my misery!'

Pearce obliged him and with a single blow of the axe Cox was no more. Pearce decided to make a meal of his dead companion. He cut a piece off his thigh, which he cooked on the fire and ate, then took another piece with him and swam the river.

However, he didn't get far into the wilderness before it became obvious even to Pearce that he had no hope of covering the distance to Port Dalrymple without food, with no prospect of getting any and with no companions to sustain him. He turned back, swam the King River and made his way along the shore of Macquarie Harbour. When he saw a schooner coming from the penal settlement, he made a signal fire and was picked up by a pilot boat.

Back at Macquarie Harbour, he admitted murdering Thomas Cox and said, 'I'm willing to die for it.'

This time, Pearce's version of what happened was able to be corroborated. Thomas Smith, coxswain to the Commandant at Macquarie Harbour, was ordered to return to the scene of Cox's demise (with Pearce) to collect his body. Smith later testified that Pearce hadn't just killed his companion: 'The head was away, the hands cut off, the bowels were torn out, and the greater part of the breech and thighs gone, as were the calf of the legs, and the fleshy parts of the arms.'

'How could you do such a deed as this?' the appalled coxswain had asked Pearce.

'No person can tell what he will do when driven by hunger,' Pearce replied. What he had done went beyond mere hunger. All that remained of the victim was stripped completely naked. This was the sixth murder that Pearce had been involved in and the extent of the mutilation suggests that he was starting to enjoy it.

The *Hobart Gazette* captured, in colourful terms, the revulsion that surrounded Pearce in prefacing its report of his trial, which took place on 20 June 1824:

The circumstances which were understood to have accompanied the above crime had long been considered with extreme horror. Report had associated the prisoner with cannibals; and recollecting as we did, the vampire legends of modern Greece, we confess, that on this occasion, our eyes glanced in fearfulness at the being who stood before a retributive Judge, laden with the weight of human blood, and believed to have banqueted on human flesh!

Pearce actually entered a plea of not guilty, and in opening for the prosecution, Attorney General Joseph Gellibrand (who would later disappear in mysterious circumstances near the newly founded Melbourne) made a plea to the jury 'to dismiss from their minds all previous impressions against the prisoner; as, however justly their hearts must execrate the fell enormities imputed to him, they should dutiously judge him, not by rumours – but by indubitable evidence.'

The jury, not made up of civilians but by seven commissioned officers, found Pearce guilty of murder. Judge Pedder, newly arrived to preside in the recently constituted Supreme Court of Van Diemen's Land, said he was prepared to refer Pearce to the only 'tribunal where mercy may be obtained'. He then delivered his judgment: 'Your sentence is that you be removed from this place to the gaol, and (when the supreme authority shall appoint) thence to the place of execution, to be hanged by the neck till you are dead; afterwards your body to be delivered over to the surgeons for dissection.'

The sentence was carried out the following month, and, as decreed, Pearce's body was dismembered after his death. Exactly what happened to his body after that isn't clear, but the head embarked on an extraordinary journey that saw it, thirty years later, become part of a collection of 1000 skulls belonging to an American phrenologist, Dr Samuel Morton. Phrenology – the study of the shape of the head – was supposed to be able to identify the mental powers and characteristics of the individual. It was also a 'science' used to demonstrate the superiority of the Caucasian over the Negroid. While debunked by Darwinian evolutionary theory and discredited after the American Civil War, several museums still retain collections of skulls in the interests of science, particularly those of Aboriginal Australians, despite the gross cultural affront that represents. Alexander Pearce's skull (missing the lower jaw) can still be seen in the Museum of the University of Pennsylvania.

From the moment Thomas Cox's horrifically mutilated body was discovered and the earlier confession was given credence, Pearce was destined to become one of the most infamous figures in Australian criminal history. He was soon to be immortalised in works of fact and fiction, and some that mixed the two.

Pearce's story may have inspired Magwitch, the terrifying convict in Charles Dickens's *Great Expectations* (published 1861). Magwitch was described as 'A man who had been soaked in water, and smothered in mud, and lamed by stones, and cut by flints, and stung by nettles, and torn by briars' who tells Pip, the young hero of the story, 'What fat cheeks you ha' got . . . Darn me if I couldn't eat 'em and I han't half a mint to't.' To which he adds, 'There's a young man hid with me, in comparison with which young man I am a Angel. That young man has a secret way pecooliar to himself, of getting at a boy, and at his heart, and at his liver.'

Pearce is more clearly revealed in Marcus Clarke's *His Natural Life* (1874), in the monstrous Gabbett, who is based by Clarke's admission on Pearce, and, to a lesser extent, on William Buckley (an absconder from the first attempt to settle Port Phillip in 1803, who was suspected of cannibalising two of the convicts with whom he'd escaped). Clarke wrote:

He was a spectacle to shudder at . . . Not only because, look-ing at the animal, as he crouched, with one foot curled round the other, and one hairy arm pendant between his knees, he was so horribly unhuman, that one shuddered to think that tender women and fair children must, of necessity, confess to fellowship of kind with such a monster. But also because, in his slavering mouth, his slowly grinding jaws, his restless fingers, and his bloodshot, wandering eyes, there lurked a hint of some terror more awful than the terror of starvation – a memory of a tragedy played out in the gloomy depths of that forest which had vomited him forth again; and the shadow of this unknown horror, clinging to him, repelled and disgusted, as though he bore about with him the reek of the shambles.

Through such figures, both factual and fictitious, the regions of Australia that lay beyond European settlements soon became imbued with fears that were scarcely able to be articulated. As explorers, and the settlers who followed, pushed the boundaries of the unknown back towards the red centre of the country, the outback regions that were outside the law inevitably shrank. Yet to this day the outback and its outlaws are still challenging those boundaries and the efforts to police areas so sparsely inhabited that infamous crimes can go unnoticed and undiscovered for years.

In their unrestrained lawlessness the crimes of Alexander Pearce and his colleagues marked the beginning of a criminal history that haunts the outback still. They infested the bush with a danger it hadn't known during 40 000 years of indigenous habitation. It started with brutal men who became cannibals in a harsh unforgiving land, and it didn't end there.

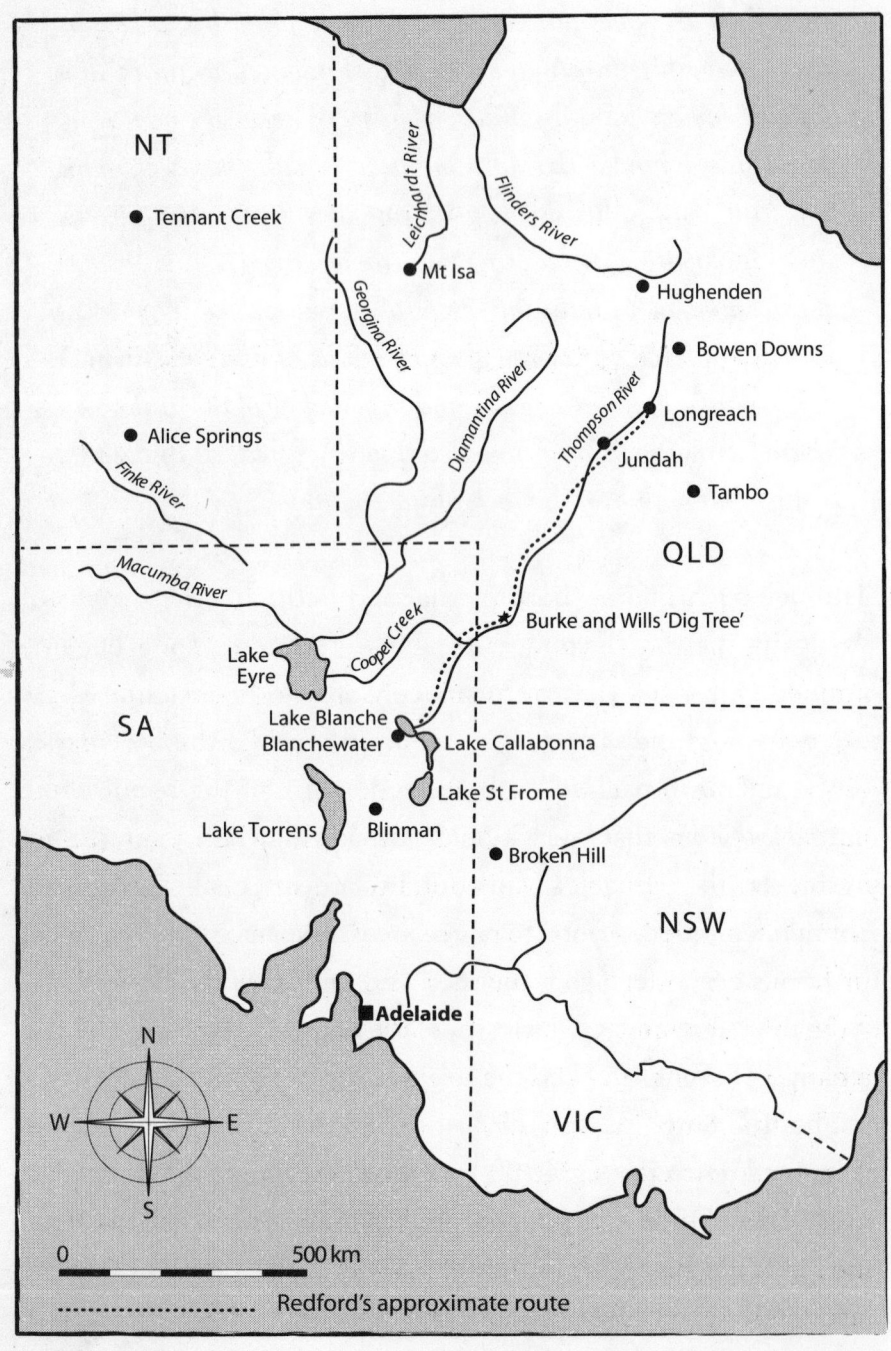

NT

● Tennant Creek

Leichhardt River

Flinders River

● Mt Isa

● Hughenden

Georgina River

● Bowen Downs

Diamantina River

Thompson River

● Longreach

● Alice Springs

Jundah

● Tambo

Finke River

QLD

Macumba River

Lake
Eyre

Cooper Creek

★ Burke and Wills 'Dig Tree'

SA

Lake Blanche
Blanchewater

Lake Callabonna

Lake St Frome

Lake Torrens

● Blinman

● Broken Hill

NSW

■ **Adelaide**

N
W   E
S

VIC

0   500 km

····················· Redford's approximate route

2

THE TYRANNY OF DISTANCE

One of the surest ways to commit the perfect crime is for the crime to go unnoticed. This usually takes some doing, but when the crime was committed in an outback region that had only been traversed once before by Europeans, you don't have to go to too much trouble to cover your tracks. Especially when most of that previous party of Europeans died in their attempt, and those who survived reported it to be so parched and barren that it discouraged further investigation. As it turned out, it was only the sheer scale of the crime committed in the far outback of western Queensland in early 1870 that led to its detection.

The first clue that something was amiss came in the middle of the year when a bushman, scouting new grazing land in the uninhabited south-western corner of the state, came upon a most unexpected sight. In the soft soil and verdure that had followed particularly good rains in that otherwise arid environment, the bushman, John Costello, discovered the tracks of a huge mob of cattle being driven into the desert towards South Australia. They were heading into country that just nine years before had killed the first explorers who clapped their blighted eyes upon it, Robert O'Hara Burke and William Wills. Whoever was driving the mob was either lost, insane or going to great lengths to avoid being noticed by anyone who might be interested in where the stock had come from or where they might be going.

Costello's suspicions were sufficiently aroused for him to tell police what he'd found. He estimated there were hundreds of cattle in the mob and suggested the most likely source of such a large number of beasts could only be the huge Bowen Downs Station, located in central-western Queensland between Hughenden and Longreach. However, when the police contacted the management of Bowen Downs, their story wasn't taken seriously.

There were several reasons for their disbelief. The Bowen Downs property was vast, covering 250 square kilometres (one of many immense holdings of the Scottish Australian Investment Company, whose properties covered large tracts of western Queensland), and it was controlled from Sydney. Bowen Downs was typical of outback properties run by absentee owners – overstocked and under-managed. Most were so big they were impossible to fence, which allowed stock to wander. Many of the stock were unbranded and left to their own devices, until the occasional muster revealed their condition and numbers to the property managers. Consequently, the station managers often had no definite idea of how much stock they had. So Bowen Downs had no way of knowing whether the report was true or not.

In any case, they weren't about to despatch stockmen into the wasteland of the red centre, where there was a good chance they'd perish in the pursuit of phantom cattle. The station managers already had their hands full dealing with cattle duffers operating closer to home. They were often from nearby small property holdings, and were a constant source of trouble, but typically they took only a few head of cattle at a time to supplement their herds. Never the hundreds as suggested by police.

As a result, Costello's report wasn't investigated, and over the ensuing months the distant trail grew colder and colder. Indeed, the mystery might have been forgotten completely except, when Bowen Downs did their annual muster, they came up well short of their expected total number of cattle. In particular, a prize stud bull, a pure-white shorthorn known as the Duke of Marlborough (Whitey for short), was nowhere to be found. It was only then, after almost a year had passed, that Bowen Downs contacted police and demanded immediate action.

There was a time when it would have taken weeks for a message from Queensland police to reach their colleagues in South Australia; however, by December 1870, the tyranny of outback Australia's enormous distances had in part been conquered by the introduction of telegraphic communications. Within hours, details of the theft, including descriptions of the brands used by Bowen Downs, were received in Adelaide. There were registers of brands in use at the time, but they weren't widely distributed, and South Australia didn't consider it necessary to keep details of Queensland brands because it was unthinkable that cattle could cross the harsh, dry expanse between the states.

All that changed in January 1871 when a drover from a South Australian station heading for Adelaide was arrested with cattle branded LC, a Bowen Downs brand that stood for Landsborough and Cornish. At the same time, Bowen Downs' stock agents, Elder Smith, reported that their Adelaide representative had seen LC-branded cattle in the Adelaide saleyards. Inquiries soon revealed that all the LC-branded cattle had come from just one South Australian property, Blanchewater Station.

Blanchewater Station lay in the extremely marginal cattle country of South Australia's north-east, on the edges of Lake Blanche and Lake Callabonna. The lakes are fed by the Strzelecki Creek, which flows (when it flows) down from Queensland. Included among its tributaries is the Thompson River that extends all the way to Bowen Downs. Here, it seemed, was a potentially well-watered route that the cattle duffers had followed through a landscape that was otherwise so dry the cattle would have died of thirst within days. The hapless explorers Burke and Wills had missed it, but it appeared that someone with less noble aspirations had not only found the route but turned it to their criminal advantage.

In February, Blanchewater Station was contacted by Boyd Morehead, manager of Bowen Downs, and Robert Barr Smith, a partner in Elder Smith, requesting to visit Blanchewater to see if any LC-branded cattle were still there. Blanchewater was owned by a South Australian MP, John Baker, who'd briefly served as Premier. Baker responded that he was perfectly happy for them to do so, but insisted that he wasn't giving any LC-branded cattle back, because he had a signed bill of sale and they were his. Despite agreeing to their visit, when it came to actually arranging a convenient time, Baker contrived a range of difficulties to thwart the Bowen Downs men.

A frustrated Morehead eventually sought a legal opinion on his rights if he went to Blanchewater to take back any cattle he thought were his. The conclusion was that if Baker really could prove he'd bought the cattle, then Morehead might be charged with duffing. Under the circumstances, Morehead thought better of it and in the end was forced to recover some of his own LC cattle (for use as evidence if the duffers were ever brought to trial) by buying them back at the Adelaide saleyards, where Baker and the butchers of Adelaide were turning them over just as fast as they could.

Morehead fared a little better when it came to getting information from Baker regarding how he'd come by the Bowen Downs cattle, although what he learned must have shocked him to the core. According to Baker, around June 1870 a man who called himself Henry Collins had arrived at Blanchewater with two other men, driving, not the hundreds of cattle thought to have been stolen, but a staggering 1000 head.

Collins met with Blanchewater Station's manager, J. Mules, and he couldn't have chosen a better time. The property was desperately short of cattle because its stock had been killed by a succession of droughts over the previous years. The rains that had helped the duffers bring the cattle down the rivers from Queensland had also helped Blanchewater, which was greener than it had been in years. Restocking, however, was a slow process. So when Collins appeared out of nowhere and offered to sell Mules his mob at the bargain price of between £3 and £5 a head, Mules jumped at the chance. Collins explained that the LC brands were those of his brother, Lawrence Collins, who owned a property in Queensland. Mules didn't know any better, or perhaps wasn't so foolish as to inquire further. So the deal was done.

Newspapers in Brisbane, Adelaide, Melbourne and Sydney reported the 'sensational' details and followed developments closely. By its magnitude, the theft surpassed any previous concept of cattle duffing. Other large landholders were horrified, realising that the loss of such large numbers of cattle could ruin them. If nothing else, it starkly demonstrated the inability of landholders (or sparsely distributed police forces for that matter) to keep track of their stock. Worse still, the exploits of Henry Collins and his fellow cattle duffers had increased the potential area where stolen stock could be hidden. There was little consolation that the duffers, by their extraordinary feats of overlanding cattle, had also pioneered a new stock route for western Queensland graziers to the potentially lucrative Adelaide market.

While the people of Adelaide digested both the news of the crime and the Bowen Downs cattle, South Australian police started to piece together Henry Collins's movements after he'd left Blanchewater. With a promissory note for a figure of between £3500 and £5000 (the figure varies depending on the source) that could be cashed in six months, Collins and his mates continued south to Adelaide. On the way, despite the risk of exposing the crime, he couldn't resist giving an interview to a small newspaper in which he boasted that his trip had taken four months. They'd had to make an eighty-kilometre detour to avoid floodwaters in what was supposed to be a desert; they'd encountered friendly Aboriginals (who wouldn't be friendly to men with such an immense source of protein?), six-metre-long snakes and alligators (most likely two-metre desert goannas).

By February 1871, information provided by Mules enabled police to issue notices in South Australia and Queensland for the arrest of Henry Collins for cattle stealing from Bowen Downs:

Collins, alias James Courtley, thirty-two years old, 6' 1" [185 cm] tall, with broad shoulders, large hands, high cheek bones, brown hair, dark whiskers, moustache, nose slightly hooked at the point; shows upper teeth when laughing.

The notices also mentioned that the management of Bowen Downs offered £200 for information leading to the arrest of the culprits. Inquiries soon revealed that shortly after Collins had arrived in Adelaide he'd cashed the promissory note with a money dealer and set sail from South Australia aboard the SS *Aldinga* on 20 July 1870, bound for Melbourne, Victoria.

While Boyd Morehead was scouring Adelaide, a party of stockmen, led by the Bowen Downs overseer, Edmund Butler, was following the still obvious trail of the stock from Bowen Downs to South Australia. They may have had an Aboriginal tracker with them, although even the greenest cityslicker could have followed the mass of hoof prints and cowpats extending south past the famous 'dig tree' where Burke and Wills had met their end. The stockmen found the desert transformed to a state of breathtaking abundance, brought on by the rains and flooding river systems. In fact, they believed they were looking at some of the finest grazing country they'd ever seen. The succulent grasses were so high you could lose your rapidly fattening cattle in them. All it needed was a season of good rains.

Unfortunately, the abundance also ran to a plague of rats that assailed the stockmen throughout their journey. However, their efforts were soon rewarded. At an incredibly remote outback store on the Strzlecki Creek they found Whitey, the prize bull from Bowen Downs. Whitey was in the possession of storekeeper Allan Walke, who produced a bill of sale for it signed by Henry Collins. Walke named the two men who were with Collins – George Doudney (actually Dewdney) and William Brooke (actually Rooke).

The names meant nothing to Butler but, in a lucky twist, the name Henry Collins meant plenty to one of his men. Stockman John Craigie had family connections in Adelaide and had been there on family business in July 1870 when he'd run into an acquaintance from Queensland. His name was Harry Redford (or Readford) and he was one of the small landholders notorious for duffing cattle from the bigger stations (especially Bowen Downs). During their chance meeting in a bar thousands of kilometres away from their remote Queensland properties, Redford mentioned that in Adelaide he went by the name Henry Collins. Months later and far away on the Strzlecki Creek, Craigie made the tenuous connection. The description of Collins matched Redford exactly.

Another hallmark of the perfect crime is not getting caught. Notices for the arrest of Redford were soon issued in Queensland, South Australia and Redford's home colony of New South Wales. The obvious place for a man of Redford's exceptional bush skills to hide out would be the remotest regions of the outback that he knew like the back of his hand. He was wanted in three of the biggest colonies in the country, which meant the police were faced with searching almost half the continent. However, while police scoured the most isolated corners of their respective jurisdictions, where any stranger in the empty landscape would immediately attract their attention, Redford decided to hide somewhere the police would never think to look – right under their noses.

Redford didn't bother to hide at all. Instead, the son of a freed convict returned to his native New South Wales and, having made his fortune, married his childhood sweetheart, Bessie Skuthorpe, in April 1871. He bought a pub near Gulgong, which required that his name, as the licensee, be notified in the *NSW Police Gazette*. In yet another coincidence in the Bowen Downs case, the notice relating to his publican's licence as well as the warrant for his arrest appeared in the same issue. It was a far easier connection to make than that made by John Craigie, but, incredibly, no one twigged.

Months passed and the law made no progress in catching up with the respectable publican Harry Redford. It may have been the belief that he really had committed the perfect crime that ultimately led Redford astray. Or perhaps he just wanted a little excitement. In October he gave a couple of his mates, Fred Howard and Bill Osborne, a tip about robbing a Mudgee store (near Gulgong) and stealing its safe. When the two men attempted the robbery they soon discovered the safe was too heavy to carry, so they went back to Harry and asked if they could borrow his horse. Then when they couldn't get the safe open they asked him for more help. Eventually the pair made off with £60 in cash and valuables. Bill Osborne was never seen again but Fred Howard was soon caught. Unfortunately for Harry, Howard confessed all.

Harry Redford was arrested for his part in the robbery on 7 November. He may well have beaten the charges because the only evidence against him was from a man testifying to save himself. Yet a background check on Harry finally revealed the warrants for his arrest for the theft of the Bowen Downs cattle. He was rearrested on 13 November and charged with cattle duffing. By the beginning of January 1872 he was on his way to Rockhampton, Queensland, aboard the coastal trader *Queensland*. He left behind his wife, who was pregnant and nearing full-term with their first child. Jemima Redford was born on 20 January.

The logistical difficulties of assembling evidence of a crime that spanned the outback meant that it took months to put together the case against Harry. The Bowen Downs stockmen had brought the white bull back from South Australia along the route Harry and his mates had pioneered. Storekeeper Allan Walke was brought to Queensland and accommodated at Bowen Downs for several months at the station's expense. One of Harry's accomplices in the initial theft, itinerant labourer James McPherson, had just been tried and convicted. He was convinced to provide evidence in the trial against Harry.

Other problems presented themselves to the prosecution. One was a lack of proof regarding how many cattle had actually been stolen, since most of the evidence had long ago swelled the bellies of the Adelaide populace. Another was the track record of duffing cases at the Roma District Court where Harry was to be tried. Most juries returned verdicts of not guilty, and the man who defended most of the cases, Ratcliffe Pring QC, was particularly effective in exposing the deficiencies in the prosecution cases.

Even the elements conspired to delay the trial. The case was about to go ahead when massive floods hit Roma and the surrounding country. It was impossible for many of the lawyers, witnesses and jurors to reach the court, and the case had to be rescheduled. Finally, the case went before Charles William Blakeney, a judge who'd been forced to leave his native Ireland after being financially ruined by a chronic gambling problem. His son, Queensland solicitor Charles John Blakeney, had helped his father get back on his feet. As it happened, Blakeney Jnr was instructing Harry's legal representative, George Paul QC. Harry hadn't been able to engage the capable Ratcliffe Pring because, in an effort to counter his demolition of previous duffing cases, he'd been hired for the prosecution.

The trial began at 9 a.m. on 11 February, according to Brisbane's *Courier-Mail* correspondent whose report is the only surviving firsthand record of proceedings. The old Roma courthouse has since burnt down, but it was a wooden building that did little to combat the ferocious heat of western Queensland in mid-February, especially as it was filled to capacity with eager spectators. Plenty more heat was generated from the start of the trial in which:

> *Henry Redford was indicted that he, in the month of March, 1870, at Bowen Downs Station in the colony, 100 bullocks, 100 cows, 100 heifers, 100 steers, and 1 bull, the property of Messrs Morehead and Young, feloniously did steal, take, and carry away, and in a second count for receiving the same knowing them to be stolen.*

The jury selection process rapidly degenerated towards farce. Out of a panel of forty-eight, forty-one were objected to by the prosecution or defence. That left only seven jurors, five short of the dozen needed. George Paul had used all twelve of his objections. The prosecution had rejected twenty-nine. Paul suggested they go through the forty-one dismissed jurors again, provided he could make more objections. Judge Blakeney proposed a different course: only those jurors rejected by the prosecution would be reviewed, and since Paul hadn't objected to them the first time round he wouldn't be allowed to object to them the second time. Paul wasn't happy, and he said as much, whereupon the judge informed him that if the law hadn't been applied correctly, then Paul could always apply for a mistrial.

The reason for all the objections was in part due to the fact that few people living in the outback identified with the 'big-end' of rural life, while plenty identified with the hardships of the small landholders. The pioneering men and women struggled to support their families on their small blocks; indeed, there weren't many who'd hadn't been tempted to make use of straying stock to put food on the table for their hungry kids. The countless challenges of the bush also encouraged the community to pull together when times were tough, particularly when fire and flood threatened, but the big stations tended to look after themselves. Consequently, finding an impartial jury was a matter of balancing the 'us' and the 'them'.

Eventually, five more men were selected, including one who'd been found guilty of cattle duffing in 1869, and others who were suspected of having been bribed by the defendants in previous duffing cases. However, as a counterbalance, jurors, such as the foreman

James Nimmo, had been on juries that had returned guilty verdicts.

Throughout the morning and into the heat of the afternoon the prosecution witnesses built a strong case against Harry Redford. The prosecution even went to the trouble of bringing the Duke of Marlborough to the trial as evidence. He was tethered outside the courthouse throughout the day. Much of the prosecution's case revolved around this distinctive animal, as Bowen Downs' manager Boyd Morehead, overseer Edmund Butler and stockman John Craigie all identified Whitey as the beast outside the court and the property of Bowen Downs.

The prosecution even presented expert forensic evidence. The bill of sale Henry Collins signed for Allan Walke and Henry Redford's signature on a recognisance of bail were both produced. The *Courier* then reported that J.K. Cannan 'was examined as an expert, and gave it as his opinion that the signatures "Henry Redford" to the recognisance and "Henry Collins" to the receipt were written by the same person.'

Allan Walke took the stand and testified that:

> He [witness] had no doubt whatever as to the prisoner being the man who sold him the cattle and signed the receipt, as he remained at his [witness's] place for some days afterwards; the bull he then purchased remained in his possession for over three months until delivered to the authorities, having been identified by Messrs Butler and Vernon [a Bowen Downs stockman] and claimed as the property of Messrs Morehead and Young, the owners of Bowen Downs in this colony.

Then the prosecution called James McPherson. The itinerant labourer testified that he, Redford, John McKenzie (a small landholder who'd previously been acquitted on charges of duffing), Dewdney and Rooke:

> *Went 25 miles [40 km] up the Thomson River, and there built cattle yards; when the yards were completed, he, with the others, mustered a large number of the Bowen Downs cattle, and filled the yards with them; the cattle were afterwards drafted off in mobs of two or three hundred at a time to Forrester's camp; the white bull outside the Court was amongst the cattle taken at that time, the object being that he would keep the cows and heifers quiet, of which there were a large number in the mob; ultimately the whole of the cattle were driven off by Redford, McKenzie [he probably meant Dewdney], and Brooke [actually Rooke], towards the southern colonies.*

Up to this point the prosecution case was formidable, if not unassailable. The evidence of Walke and McPherson in particular was crucial eyewitness testimony, as, to a lesser extent, was that of the expert signature witness Cannan. However, it was during George Paul's cross-examination of James McPherson that the cracks started to appear. The *Courier* reported: 'Mr Paul's examination of this witness occasioned some amusement. The witness stated that he was not a cattle stealer, although he might have stolen some, though not to his knowledge.'

Then Paul asked if McPherson had been charged with stealing cattle from Bowen Downs. Yes, he had to admit he had. Were they the cattle he'd just given testimony about? Yes, they were. What was the result of his trial? He'd been discharged on the grounds of insanity and sent to an asylum in Brisbane. (He'd actually pleaded guilty and turned Queen's evidence, but the police had locked him up in an asylum pending Harry's trial.) Was that where he remained? No. He'd escaped.

James McPherson, star witness for the prosecution, was literally an escaped lunatic. He'd been recaptured at Armidale in New South Wales then brought to Roma to give evidence in Harry's trial. As Paul continued his questioning, it just got worse. Was he offered anything if he testified? Yes, 'a promise of a free pardon if he gave fair evidence at the trial; that he was there trusting to the honour of the authorities respecting the free pardon to be granted to him.'

By now evening was falling but the trial continued into the night. The prosecution finished presenting its case and then the defence had its opportunity. Here there was another nasty surprise for the prosecution. George Paul didn't call any witnesses, not even Harry. Instead, after Ratcliffe Pring made his closing remarks for the prosecution in 'a very lucid and forcible manner', Paul got to his feet to speak. It's a great loss that his exact words have not survived (the court transcripts are thought to have been destroyed in the 1950s); however, the content was summarised by the *Courier* as follows:

> *Mr Paul addressed the jury and pointed out the many weak points in the case, and was particular in drawing attention to the evidence of the witness McPherson, who he designated as an approver seeking to escape the penalties of his own crimes,*

by giving evidence to convict his quondam mate. He argued that the Court should, under the circumstances, direct the jury to dismiss from their minds altogether the evidence given by the lunatic, or pretended lunatic, as being utterly unworthy of credit. He also pointed out the hardships his client had to endure for a period of twelve months since his arrest, during which time he was kept a close prisoner, and absolutely refused bail until an order had to be obtained from the Supreme Court for that purpose. His remarks occupied over an hour, and were listened to with marked attention by the jury.

Among the other weaknesses Paul may have pointed out was the lack of expertise of the 'expert' signature witness. J.K. Cannan wasn't a trained forensic specialist; he was a Roma bank manager. Another witness who'd testified to Harry's identity was an alcoholic who police had kept in a stable prior to the trial to keep him sober. Then there was Allan Walke. Paul may not have needed to point out that during his stay at Bowen Downs and Roma, Walke had earned quite a reputation, being described as 'a gentleman loafer' and 'a despicable character'. There was a story going around Roma that he'd suggested a way to deal with the case was to pay him a bribe or do the bull in.

Paul may have pointed out that even if the case was proven, Harry Redford had done western Queensland a great service in opening a new stock route to the Adelaide markets. The route had revealed vast areas that offered great potential for grazing (it's now referred to as the Channel Country). The way people regarded this large area of the outback had changed for all time. It operated by its own rules, its own cycles of drought and plenty. It could be soul-crushingly unyielding for years, then produce abundance beyond the wildest hopes and dreams.

Further clues to the content of Paul's address can be found in Judge Blakeney's summing up and directions to the jury as reported by the *Courier*:

> *He trusted that the jury would not be led away by the specious although clever address of the counsel for the prisoner; that they would dismiss from their minds the hardships said to have been endured by the prisoner, no doubt placed before them with a view to making him a martyr . . . He next would submit that, supposing that the jury accepted Mr Paul's recommendation, and gave no credence to McPherson, yet the case was plain against the prisoner. The bull had been identified beyond all question as the property of Messrs Morehead and Young; it is also identified as being the one sold by the prisoner to Mr Walke, and the evidence of that gentleman could leave no doubt on any reasonable mind that the prisoner at the bar and the person who sold that animal in South Australia were one and the same person. He would, with these remarks, request them to consider their verdict.*

The jury retired at 9 p.m., but none of the large crowd who had sweated throughout the entire day's proceedings left the building. No one wanted to miss a thing. An hour later, the jury returned. The court was called to order and the foreman was asked if they had reached a verdict. They had. James Nimmo rose to his feet to speak. An expectant hush fell over the multitude.

'Not guilty,' he said.

According to the *Courier*: 'Much surprise was evinced at the verdict, in which the Judge joined.' Blakeney was so disbelieving that he asked the foreman to repeat his verdict, in case he'd misheard. When Nimmo confirmed what he'd said Judge Blakeney was moved to observe, 'Thank God, gentlemen, that verdict is yours, not mine.'

The final hallmark of the perfect crime is not getting convicted. Harry Redford, a free man, rich and famous as well, returned to New South Wales, his wife and baby daughter. However, he left a devastated Roma legal system in his wake. Judge Blakeney wrote to the Queensland Attorney General attacking the jurors. The jurors wrote attacking the judge, saying his intimidating manner wasn't helping their impartiality as they were in fear of giving offence.

The *Courier*'s gossip columnist joined in the controversy with a column in late February 1873. According to 'A Bohemian':

Amusements are scarce about Roma, so an occasional diversion in the shape of a judge-and-jury trial for cattle-stealing is a delicious treat. The last sittings of the Roma Court were more than usually amusing as there were several cattle-stealing cases tried and the jurors enjoyed it much. They chaffed the prosecutors unmercifully and got rare old sport out of them.

On 4 April the government withdrew Roma's criminal jurisdiction for two years, which only enraged Roma's citizens further. Shortly after, Judge Blakeney was confronted by an angry mob. There are suggestions he may have been in considerable personal danger before he was assisted from the scene. As it turned out, state elections were to be held in 1874 and the jurisdiction was returned early as a certain vote winner.

Harry enjoyed considerable notoriety in the wake of his exploit. The route to South Australia pioneered by Redford and his companions Dewdney and Rooke (neither of whom were ever apprehended) was eventually dotted with vast outback stations. As a consequence, Redford was demonised by some, admired by others. He was eventually immortalised in Rolf Boldrewood's epic novel of bushranging *Robbery Under Arms*, published in 1881. By then, however, he'd been convicted and done time on another charge of duffing cattle and horses. Ironically, when he went before the court in Toowoomba, south-east Queensland, it was to find that George Paul had been called to the bench. When Harry was found guilty, Judge Paul gave him eighteen months' hard labour. Harry went on to pioneer a stock route from Queensland to the Northern Territory where he found work as manager of Brunette Downs. His reputation as one of the outback's finest bushmen – either on the right or the wrong side of the law – was well established. Unfortunately, his skill didn't extend to swimming and in March 1901 he drowned while trying to cross the flooded Corella Lagoon.

Postscript: Many large landholders didn't heed the deeper lesson that Bowen Downs had taught, when Harry Redford and his mates managed to make 1000 head of cattle all but disappear into the emptiness of the outback.

In the mid-1890s, when a severe drought forced many outback properties to be sold at rock-bottom prices, brothers Sidney and

Sackville Kidman moved in and bought many of them on deposit. They then went onto the properties (which they had closely examined on horseback during their pre-purchase inspections) and mustered the stock that the absentee owners didn't know existed. They fattened the stock on other properties that weren't drought affected, then used the windfall profits from selling the beasts to finalise the purchase. In gaining ownership of some properties for free, the only real difference from Harry Redford's exploit was that it was all legal. The tyranny of distance cost the absentee owners just as dearly. It's often said that ignorance is no defence in law. In the outback, it's no protection either.

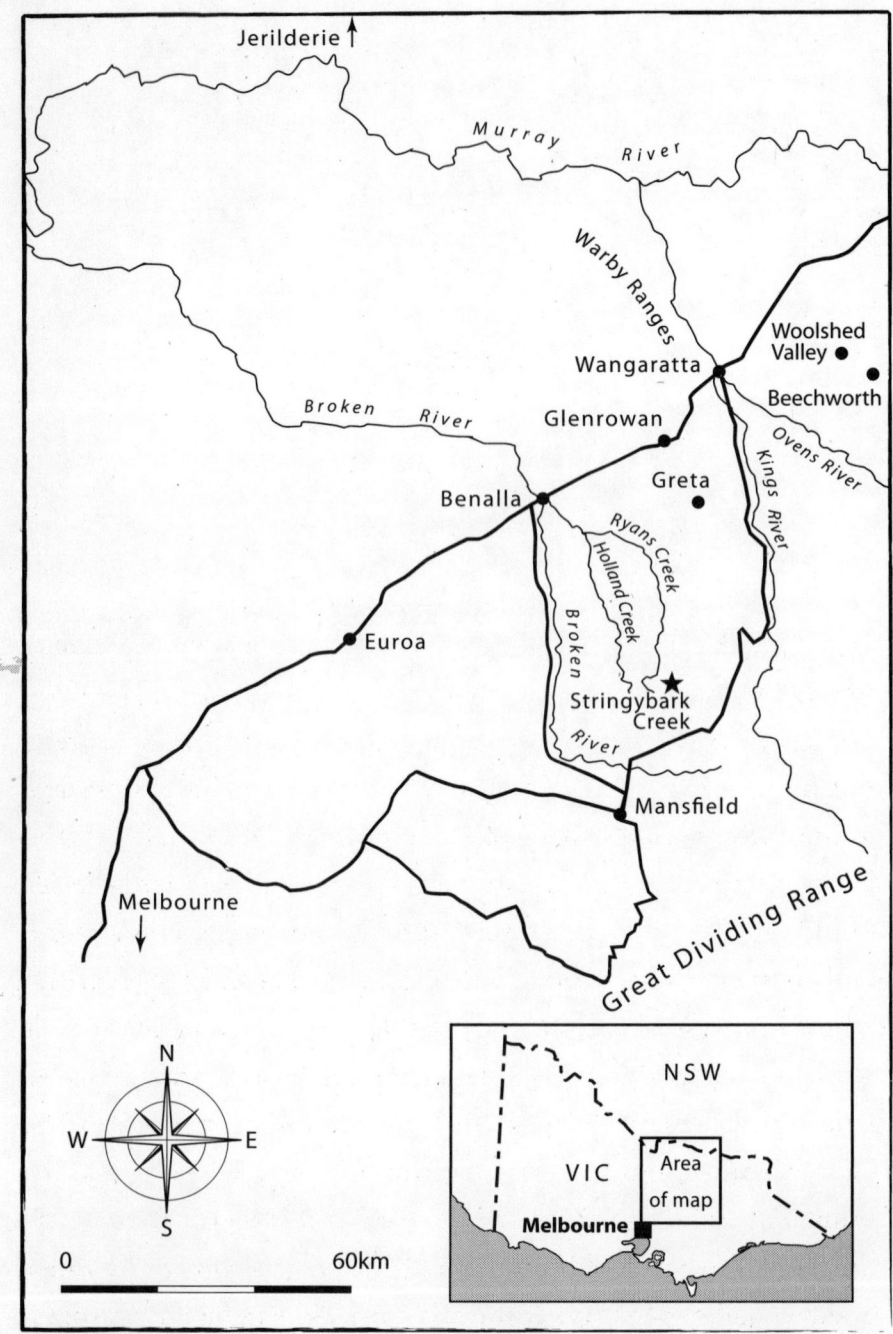

Jerilderie ↑

Murray   River

Warby Ranges

Wangaratta

Woolshed
Valley ●

● Beechworth

Broken   River

Glenrowan

Ovens River

Benalla

Greta

Kings River

Ryans Creek

Holland Creek

Broken

Euroa

Stringybark
Creek ★

River

Mansfield ●

Melbourne
↓

Great Dividing Range

N
W — E
S

0   60km

N S W

VIC   Area
             of map

Melbourne

3

KELLY

In the 1940s, Sidney Nolan created a now-famous series of paintings depicting the events of what had become known as the Kelly Outbreak. Nearly seventy years had passed since the Outbreak but the tale remained as potent as when it had made headlines around the world. During that time, from 1878 to 1880, the story of one of the last bushrangers became more than a series of crimes affecting the communities of north-eastern Victoria and southern New South Wales. Indeed, even then the central figure in the story seemed larger-than-life, and one of Nolan's works encapsulates that stature. It's an Australian landscape where, from behind a conical hill (recognisably Morgan's Lookout near Glenrowan in Victoria), a gigantic black figure looms. It's immediately recognisable as the man who not only ranged the bush but also haunted Victoria's police and government, at times openly challenging their authority. Nolan saw no need to explain the mythical figure he had portrayed. The painting goes by the simple title, *Kelly*.

On the afternoon of Saturday, 26 October 1878, 23-year-old Edward 'Ned' Kelly had no such reputation. To Victorian Police Sergeant Michael Kennedy and constables Michael Scanlan, Thomas McIntyre and Thomas Lonigan, he was just another petty criminal they wanted behind bars. Ned's horse-stealing operations had been seriously curtailed by a prolonged police investigation. He and his mates had been the bane of the region's large land-holders whose immense properties were in stark contrast to the tiny 'starvation blocks' where families like the Kellys struggled to make a living. Eventually, a highly irregular incident resulted in a policeman being shot in the hand and Ned's mother jailed with two others for attempted murder. Warrants for the arrest of Ned and his younger brother Dan were also issued over the same incident. Both went into hiding for six months with two other young men, Steve Hart and Joe Byrne. Now it was simply a matter of locat-ing Ned's mountain lair, somewhere in the foothills of the Great Dividing Range between Mansfield and Wangaratta, and bringing them in – as some police would have it, dead or alive.

The four policemen didn't know that they had established their depot – at Stringybark Creek, north of Mansfield – just two kilo-metres from Ned's hideout. Nor did they appreciate that they'd stumbled into the backyard of a consummate bushman, who'd spent most of his time on the run perfecting his skills with firearms.

Ned, on the other hand, had already been informed that the police were coming, through a network of friends, relatives and sympa-thisers, mainly small landholders who'd endured intimidation and harassment by the police and the large landholders. He was also aware of a second patrol that was working south from Greta, the nearest town to the Kellys' 32-hectare starvation block. The night before, Ned had seen the tracks of Sergeant Kennedy's patrol and located their camp. In deciding on a plan to deal with them, Ned was confident of his superior knowledge of the bush. It had been his home since childhood.

Barely in his teens, he'd gone bushranging with an old crim named Harry Power, perhaps inspired by the exploits of Jack Donohoe, Captain Thunderbolt, Ben Hall and Dan Morgan, which had given bushranging a veneer of adventure. The reality, Ned discovered, was long days in the saddle, cold and wet, living rough while being hunted by police and local volunteers. Food was so scarce that at one point Ned and Powers held up a delivery boy and took his lunch. Ned had matured since then and, when not being harassed by police, he was diligent and hard working, a born leader. Like many in the bush, he could turn his hand to nearly anything and faced life's challenges with an indomitable spirit. For Ned, living rough in the rugged north-east of Victoria was no longer something to suffer. It was a life he'd grown to love.

Now, with one patrol nearby and the other approaching, Ned was concerned that, if the two patrols combined and laid siege to his hut at Bullock Creek, he and his mates would be massively out-gunned. All they had was a carbine, shotgun and revolver between the four of them. So he decided to strike first — ambush the patrol at Stringybark Creek, then take their weapons and use the extra firepower to deal with the other party.

That afternoon, Ned took the carbine and revolver, Dan took

the shotgun, and with Steve and Joe they headed for the police camp. They crept as close as they could, given that the scrub was thin around the encampment. From behind cover, Ned saw two of the police, whom he mistook for two constables he knew – Flood (who'd had an affair with one of Ned's sisters, leading to her death in childbirth) and Strahan. Ned assumed the other two police were inside the tent. Covered by Dan, he moved in.

One of the policemen was seated on a log near the fire, the other was hobbling a horse.

Ned shouted, 'Bail up! Throw up your hands!'

'Flood' turned, saw Ned aiming his sawn-off carbine at him and did as he was told.

The other policeman, 'Strahan', leapt to his feet and ran. According to a later account by Ned, the policeman dropped behind a log six metres from where he'd been sitting. When he lifted his head from behind the log to shoot, Ned fired a single shot that struck 'Strahan' in the right eye.

'Oh, Christ, I'm shot,' cried 'Strahan'.

He came out from behind the log, his hands raised to surrender, then collapsed and died.

Ned quickly discovered that the policeman he'd shot wasn't Strahan but Thomas Lonigan, who'd once 'blackballed' Ned by grabbing his testicles in a fight in the town of Benalla. And the man he took to be Flood was actually Thomas McIntyre. As for the other two policemen, they were out on patrol but expected back soon.

Ned was to later claim that he'd known Strahan (who was, in fact, in the party working south from Greta) and Lonigan had made bold claims before leaving on the Kelly manhunt, which, mistaken identities aside, justified his actions.

'I won't ask him to stand,' Strahan had reputedly said. 'I'll shoot him first, like a dog.'

'If Kelly is to be shot,' Lonigan had remarked, 'I'm the man who will shoot him.'

The statements suggest that the patrol was in fact a death squad. However, immediately upon realising that the man he'd shot was Lonigan, in the shock of the moment Ned's reaction gave no indication that he was aware of Lonigan's vow. According to McIntyre, he said, 'Well, I'm glad of that for the bugger gave me a hiding in Benalla one day.'

Ned and his mates' search of the camp revealed a remarkable cache of weapons and ammunition. For four police there were seventy-two rounds for their revolvers, a shotgun with thirty-six shells and a large number of rounds for a Spencer repeating rifle, which was with Constable Scanlan.

Ned observed, 'You buggers came to shoot me, I suppose.'

Ned and McIntyre talked for about fifteen minutes. Ned said he would spare Sergeant Kennedy and Constable Scanlan if McIntyre could persuade them to surrender. Then they heard the approaching horses. Dan and Joe Byrne (armed with the police weapons) took cover in the thin scrub around the camp and Steve (also armed) slipped into the tent. Ned hid behind a log near the fire, telling McIntyre to sit and not try anything or he'd be shot. McIntyre complied, and, by one of his accounts, called out to the approaching officers, 'Oh sergeant, you had better dismount and surrender for you are surrounded.' However, in his first version of what happened, he didn't get a word out before Ned and the others sprang up shouting, 'Bail up! Hold your hands up!'

Instead, Kennedy dropped forward on his horse to make his body as small a target as possible, then dismounted so his mount was between him and danger. Scanlan tried to turn his horse and escape, but the animal took fright and circled instead. Scanlan had his rifle slung across his back but with one movement swung it under his arm and fired at Ned, the weapon still strapped to his body. The shot missed. Kennedy's first shot from his revolver, fired across the rump of his prancing horse, grazed Dan who had left his cover and was advancing.

Ned shot at Scanlan, causing him to fall from his horse. As his own horse skittered, Kennedy gained the cover of a tree and continued firing. In the confusion, McIntyre leapt on Kennedy's horse and tried to escape. Ned maintained he could have shot McIntyre, who was between him and Kennedy, but McIntyre had surrendered and Ned was reluctant to shoot an unarmed man. Scanlan was on the ground, alive but wounded, struggling to unsling his rifle. Dan and Ned had their attention on Kennedy; Joe Byrne was a dozen metres from Scanlan, on his right side. According to McIntyre, Scanlan tried to get up but fell on his hands and knees, and was shot under the right arm, probably by Joe Byrne.

'I saw him fall – I saw the blood spurt out from the right side as he fell,' McIntyre later said.

McIntyre galloped away. He maintained he was shot at while escaping, but he might have been hearing the continuing gunfight between the 'Kelly Gang' and the sole police sergeant, now outnumbered four to one and armed only with a revolver.

Kennedy managed to flee, on foot, through the scrub, with Ned in pursuit. The policeman's flight was a terrifying scramble through unfamiliar terrain. Ned was master of the situation, moving swiftly and easily through the bush as he'd often done while chasing kangaroos. When Kennedy tried to fire on his pursuer, Ned, absolutely lethal with his weapons, fired back and hit him in the armpit. Wounded, Kennedy again fled in desperation through the trees. Night was falling, and realising the hopelessness of his position Kennedy turned to Kelly and raised his arms.

In the fading light Ned didn't realise Kennedy had dropped his revolver. He thought Kennedy was about to fire at him, and so shot the unarmed man through the right side of his chest. Kennedy fell where he'd tried to surrender. Ned might have been able to claim he had killed in self-defence in the shoot-out with Lonigan and Scanlan, but in hunting Kennedy for over a kilometre, it was a different story.

Reports obtained from friends and relatives of the Kelly Gang suggest Kennedy did not die instantly, that he lingered, in great pain, talking to Ned about his wife and their eleven-month-old baby he'd buried just a few months before. It's possible he wrote a note to his wife and asked Ned to get it to her as some pages were torn from his notebook. If there was a message it was never passed on. These accounts also suggest that Ned, taking pity on Michael Kennedy, decided to end his suffering, but Kennedy begged him to spare his life. Ned shot him in the chest.

Back at the police campsite the clothing and bodies of the police were robbed and the tent was set alight. Joe Byrne took a ring from

Michael Scanlan's finger that he wore for the rest of his short life, a grim souvenir from the man he probably murdered.

With McIntyre about to raise the alarm, the Kelly Gang could no longer remain at their hideout on Bullock Creek. Armed with the weapons and ammunition taken from the police, and mounted on their horses, they put as much distance as possible between themselves and Stringybark Creek, riding towards a future where, as the killers of three policemen, they would be hunted as never before. Their plan was to head north towards the Murray River and New South Wales, knowing that, once news of their deed at Stringybark spread, the entire countryside would be on the lookout for them.

It took more than a day before word reached Mansfield. Thomas McIntyre had ridden his horse to a standstill, then turned it loose and headed in a different direction, hoping to throw off the Kelly Gang, who he feared were close behind. He crawled inside a wombat hole for the night, continuing on his way at first light. He reached Mansfield late Sunday afternoon and tried to raise the alarm, but the news didn't get far because the town's telegraph office was closed.

The Kelly Gang's flight was hampered by torrential rain. With one of Ned's cousins, Tom Lloyd, scouting ahead for them, they passed through Greta, getting dry clothes and a hot meal. Rather than risk the roads, they proceeded through the bush towards Beechworth, seventy kilometres south of the border. However, the rain got heavier and the creeks and rivers started rising.

During that time they were spotted by Constable Hugh Bracken, who recognised Ned and Dan as wanted men in relation to crimes prior to Stringybark Creek. Word hadn't reached him about the murders of three of his fellow officers. Nevertheless, he tried to raise the alarm. The Kelly Gang continued on to the home of Aaron Sherritt, in the Woolshed Valley west of Beechworth. Aaron, a close friend and neighbour of Joe Byrne, stood guard while the gang rested in a cave overlooking the Chinese camp where Joe, an opium addict, bought his drugs.

While the men regrouped, word of the killings at Stringybark Creek was finally spreading. On Monday, a reward for the capture of the Kelly Gang was set by the Victorian premier at £800 – £200 each. Superintendent Charles Nicolson was put in charge of the manhunt for Ned and the others. By Wednesday, the government had gathered enough details of what had happened at Stringybark Creek to realise the police were facing a formidable adversary. The Kelly Gang hadn't fled the approaching police. On the contrary, they'd emerged out of the mountain ranges and confronted them, shooting two. Then Ned had hunted down a third and shot him in cold blood. It was a terrible and terrifying crime. The apparition of a lethal gunman stalking his victim through the bush was the stuff of nightmares for the police and law-abiding citizens. The reward for the gang was raised to £2000 – £500 each.

The rain was falling so heavily that it threatened to thwart the gang's hope to cross the Murray and escape into the wide open spaces of western New South Wales. All that day and into the next, they picked their way through the floods, often finding the rising waters had cut off their line of retreat. On the Friday they called at the house of one of their horse-stealing accomplices, William Baumgarten. He had been arrested and his wife held the gang responsible. She told them where they could go, and when a police party arrived shortly after she set them on their trail. With the police close behind, Ned and the others abandoned their horses and took to the floodwaters, hiding among the reeds. Had the police spotted them, escape would have been impossible, but the rising waters forced the police to go a different way.

Ned's hopes of getting to New South Wales were defeated by the floods, which were approaching biblical proportions. He had no choice but to return to the country he knew well. It was three days before the official police pursuit really started, by which time the Kelly Gang had melted away into the bush, and the heartland of their friends and relatives.

In Melbourne, the politicians seemed to think that legislation would fix everything. At the end of October 1878, the state parliament rushed through a Felons Apprehension Bill that required the Kelly Gang to surrender at Mansfield police station by 12 November. To the astonishment of few, they didn't, thereby acquiring the legal status of outlaws – literally persons outside the normal protection afforded to all citizens by law – who could be shot on sight.

Meanwhile, in north-eastern Victoria, police patrols were facing the reality of trying to capture a group of armed and dangerous men who had an intimate knowledge of the country and a well-developed network of support. Many police were extremely wary of blundering into another deadly ambush; others were frustrated by their timid commanders. Weeks passed without so much as a sighting of the gang. There was no denying that Ned had the upper hand and it wasn't long before he used it.

On Sunday, 8 December 1878, Joe Byrne rode into the small town of Euroa and had lunch at De Boos Hotel. He learned that on the following Tuesday most of the town would be either at the funeral of a local boy who'd fallen from a horse or at a hearing of the Licensing Court. The next day, at lunchtime, the rest of the gang rode up to a homestead near Faithfull's Creek, five kilometres along the railway and telegraph lines out of town. Without any fuss, they drew their guns and took the station hands hostage. By nightfall, fourteen people were locked in a slab hut near the homestead.

On the Tuesday morning Ned and Joe Byrne worked on letters (Ned dictated to the better-educated Joe) to Victorian MP Donald Cameron, who'd been critical of the hunt for the Kellys, and to Benalla's Superintendent John Sadleir, presenting their side of the Stringybark Creek incident and the series of provocations that had led to it. Lunchtime came and went. In the early afternoon Ned, Steve and Joe left the homestead and crossed to the telegraph lines. They tore down the lines, chopped down poles, smashed insulators and twisted the wires into knots, effectively isolating the town from outside communication.

Leaving Joe to guard the prisoners, Ned, Steve and two helpers drove a hawker's wagon and a cart into town while Dan rode. They reached Euroa at around 4 p.m. and drove into the back yard of the Euroa branch of the National Bank. Dan, Steve and the others remained outside while Ned went to the front door, knocked and said he had a cheque to cash. When the bank's accountant opened the door slightly to say the bank was closed, Ned shoved his way inside and bailed him up, along with the teller. Steve entered the bank through the back door, where an old school friend was ironing in the bank's kitchen. They exchanged the usual country courtesies before Steve explained the nature of his visit and took her hostage.

Ned made his way to the office of bank manager Robert Scott, where he grabbed a revolver from the desk and shouted, 'Bail up.' Ned and Steve gathered up about £400 before turning their attention to the adjoining bank residence, home to the manager, his wife and seven children. Scott attempted to stop them but when Steve Hart aimed two revolvers at his head, his resistance evaporated.

In the residence, the manager's wife was surprised and impressed by the well-dressed bushrangers. While her husband continued to stall, she saved him the possibility of being shot and found the key to the strong room, which yielded over £2000 in currency and gold.

The whole family was herded out to the yard, loaded into their own buggy and the carts and driven to Faithfull's Creek, where a telegraph-line repairer had been dropped off by a passing train to fix the break in the line. Surveying the deliberate damage to the wires, he'd wandered over to the homestead to find out what was going on, and was promptly taken hostage.

There were now thirty-seven hostages (including sympathisers who had been planted among them). The gang were in no hurry to leave. They ate dinner and let the male hostages out to stretch their legs, herding them back into the hut when a passing train stopped and a man got out, picked up some of the broken wires and reboarded the train, which continued north to Benalla. The man was Police Magistrate Alfred Wyatt, down for the licensing hearing. He had been on the train when the repairman had disembarked at Faithfull's Creek, and had noticed the broken wires. After the hearing, Wyatt hired a buggy and headed out to investigate the damage for himself. He soon decided it was too far and turned back to Euroa to catch the train instead. What he found made him believe the Kelly Gang might be in the vicinity, and he returned to Benalla to raise the alarm.

At 8.30 p.m., after treating their hostages to a display of trick riding, the Kelly Gang finally left Faithfull's Creek, riding through a night lit by a full moon – according to Ned's careful planning. By then Magistrate Wyatt had reached Benalla and was informing superintendents Nicolson and Sadleir that he thought the Kellys had struck at Euroa. Whereupon the two boarded the train and headed in the opposite direction. They'd been fed a rumour (probably by Joe Byrne's mate Aaron Sherritt) that the gang would head for the Murray River, and thus the police spent the night speeding away from the scene of the crime.

When the newspapers in Melbourne, Sydney and the north-eastern district of Victoria got hold of the story they had a field day. 'Disgrace', 'radically wrong', 'mismanagement' they chorused. Ned, meanwhile, was the embodiment of the 'gallant', 'brave', 'valiant' bush-ranger of the ballads he'd grown up on. Striking from his heartland, where the police seemed powerless to touch him, he'd virtually taken over an entire town. He didn't just use the bush to hide, he used it to outsmart and outmanoeuvre the police, challenging their control. While the Kelly mystique flourished, police morale sank.

Two days after the robbery Police Chief Commissioner Captain Charles Standish travelled to Euroa to see Nicolson, only to find him exhausted from chasing phantoms up to the Murray and back to Faithfull's Creek. Standish replaced him with Superintendent Frank Hare, and increased the police contingent in the district by fifty-eight men to 217. Professional soldiers were also deployed to protect the local banks. The reward for Ned's capture was increased to £1000.

The police began to arrest sympathisers. An accomplice of the Kelly Gang at Euroa, Ben Gould, plus six other sympathisers were identified and arrested for offences under the Outlawry Act. While the police had a good idea of who was involved, they lacked proof, and continually applied to the court for a week's remand while the cases were prepared. Twenty-one sympathisers were eventually arrested and held, without trial, for months. It became obvious after the Euroa robbery that many of the Kelly sympathisers were suddenly flush with money. Ned's largesse gave those aiding him plenty of incentive to continue their support. But for the Kelly Gang it was expensive.

On Saturday, 8 February 1879, in the south-western New South Wales plains town of Jerilderie, sixty kilometres north of the Murray River, Senior Constable George Devine and his wife (pregnant with their third child) were woken close to midnight. Someone outside was shouting something about a brawl in progress at Davidson's Hotel, three kilometres outside town. As Devine dressed hurriedly and headed out to the verandah of the station, Jerilderie's other policeman, Probationary Constable Henry Richards, emerged from the office to join him.

A man on horseback said that the fight was serious, as a lot of men were mad with drink. He asked if there were only two police to face the drunken mob, they answered yes.

The stranger pulled out a revolver and said, 'Move and I'll shoot you. I'm Kelly. Put up your hands.'

From both ends of the verandah Dan, Joe and Steve appeared. The policemen, unarmed and completely unprepared for the Kelly Gang to have crossed the border deep into New South Wales, had no choice but to surrender. Meanwhile the Victorian police, 250 kilometres away, were scouring the Murray upstream of Corryong, on a tip-off from an 'informant', Aaron Sherritt once again. They'd been told that the gang was planning to cross the river there and commit a robbery at far-distant Goulburn.

Mrs Devine was terrified her husband and the father of her children was in danger of being shot. Ned reassured her he'd be fine if he didn't try anything. The gang then enjoyed a supper prepared by Mrs Devine, before locking the two constables into a cell, along with a drunk who'd been brought in earlier that day.

While one gang member kept watch through the night, the others slept until morning. Ned and Dan dressed themselves in police uniforms and invited the genuine police to breakfast with the bushrangers. It being a Sunday, Mrs Devine pointed out that she had to arrange the flowers in the church. Rather than have anything appear amiss, Dan went with her. When the butcher came by with the meat for the Sunday roast, Mrs Devine greeted him at the door, watched closely by Ned.

During the afternoon, Joe and Steve took Probationary Constable Henry Richards with them while they reconnoitred the town. Richards was told to explain to anyone who inquired that they'd just been newly assigned. Joe and Steve took a particular interest in the Bank of New South Wales, housed in part of the Royal Mail Hotel's building, and the telegraph office.

Back at the police station the afternoon passed uneventfully. In the evening Ned read to Mrs Devine from a letter he and Joe had been composing, which he hoped to get the Jerilderie newspaper's editor to publish. At 7500 words (the equivalent of twenty-seven pages of this volume) it was an expanded version of the unpublished Euroa letter. Parts of the Jerilderie Letter might have helped Mrs Devine appreciate that Ned and his family had been the victims of considerable police harassment, which had driven him into crime. However, the parts about disbanding the Victorian police force, deporting his enemies from Victoria and allowing him to range the lawless countryside unrestrained would have left her wondering if he'd lost his grip on reality. Up to that point the police had been little more than an inconvenience to the wide-ranging Kelly Gang, let alone a restraint.

On Monday, in police uniform, Joe and Dan revisited the telegraph office to assess the task of destroying the telegraph lines, and returned to the police station. Ned then put on Joe's uniform and with Constable Richards the gang walked or rode into town. Just after 10 a.m., Richards introduced the Royal Mail Hotel publican to Ned, who promptly took him hostage. Dan and Steve gathered the other hotel staff and herded them into the parlour, where Steve stood guard.

Next door at the bank Joe pretended to be a drunk and blundered in the back door. The bank's accountant turned to throw him out when Joe drew a revolver and said, 'I'm Kelly.' The teller, who was waiting out the front for the bank manager to arrive, was bailed up by Ned. From the safe the bushrangers seized £691, but the safe had an inner compartment that could only be opened by two keys – the accountant had one, and the absent manager had the other.

The accountant and teller were being herded next door when the manager, John Tarleton, came into the bank by the back door and, in a curious business practice, ran a bath. He was in it when the accountant stuck his head around the door to tell him they were being held up. He was incredulous until Steve Hart appeared as well, with a revolver, to confirm the story. Tarleton insisted on finishing his bath, and Steve let him.

The schoolmaster called into the bank to make a deposit. The money went straight into the coffers of Messrs Kelly and Co. Then Steve and Joe held a sack open so that Tarleton, who Ned had persuaded to get out of the bath, could add £1450 from the inner safe to their haul.

Over at the telegraph office, Joe was doing a good job with the telegraph line. He had the telegraphist dismantle his morse key and directed some of his hostages to set about chopping down telegraph poles. As he'd done at Euroa, Ned's strategy effectively isolated the little outback town. With its police force under lock and key, the Kelly Gang were free to take over.

In a small town like Jerilderie, the arrival of four new policemen could hardly go unnoticed for long, and newspaper editor Samuel Gill scented a story. He went to the police station to ask Senior Constable Devine about it, only to be met by his wife, who told him to run for his life. Instead, Gill went into town and told a storekeeper, who then told another storekeeper, who suggested that if bushrangers were about they should warn the bank.

The bank was empty, but Ned was in the bank residence. When the men knocked on the counter he called out that he'd be there in a minute, whereupon it dawned on the three gentlemen that they might have walked in on the hold-up. They fled, with Ned in hot pursuit. One storekeeper fell and was pounced upon by the armed Ned Kelly and taken into the Royal Mail Hotel. When Ned heard that one of the men who had escaped was the newspaper's editor, he flew into a rage and threatened to shoot the storekeeper he'd caught. The other prisoners begged for his life while Steve Hart shouted at Ned to 'put the bugger on his knees and I'll put a bullet into him'.

It was Ned's second attempt to get his side of the story into print, and his determination was reflected by him immediately setting off in search of Gill. He eventually found the second storekeeper but Gill didn't stop running from what would have been the story of his life until he reached Carrah homestead, ten kilometres away.

Back in town Gill's wife was in the newspaper office when Ned, Constable Richards and the accountant came in to inquire after her husband. Ned had fifty-six handwritten pages of the Jerilderie Letter that he wanted set up and printed off and he was prepared to pay a fair price. Mrs Gill said she didn't know where her husband was, but in any event it would have been a brave printer who told Ned that, if it was instant printing he was after, he'd do well to come back in about a century. Typesetting a 7500-word letter by hand (and in 1879 that was the only way it could be done) would have taken the newspaper's typesetter at least twenty hours non-stop. The accountant offered to look after the letter and get Gill to print it. Reluctantly, Ned handed it over.

Back at the Royal Mail Hotel, Ned made a speech that varied in the recollections of the thirty-odd listeners, some of whom were quite drunk. Afterwards Ned and his gang released their hostages and headed for the police station. Some of the released hostages milled about, while others set about riding to nearby towns for assistance.

The town's parson tried to organise a party to pursue the Kellys but couldn't get any takers. Most of the townsfolk didn't see the need to get involved with dangerous men who had, nevertheless, done them no harm. So he set off in the hot afternoon sun to confront the bushrangers alone, hoping to at least get back a small black racehorse that belonged to the daughter of the Albion Hotel's publican. On meeting Ned, he persuaded him to speak to the girl's father. Ned and Steve rode back into town, and along the way Steve stole the parson's watch.

At the Albion Hotel, Ned put one of his guns on the bar and said, 'Anyone here may take it and shoot me dead, but if I'm shot, Jerilderie will swim in its own blood.'

There were no takers.

When the parson told Ned that Steve had stolen his watch, Ned made his gang member return it. He then went back into the pub for a last drink while his gang assembled on the outskirts of town. Ned arrived at last, with the news that the bank manager and the accountant had ridden to the closest police station for help. They set off to catch them but soon gave it up and turned their horses towards the Murray. That night heavy rain washed out all signs of their tracks. Once again, thanks to Ned's careful planning, a full moon shone through breaks in the cloud to light their way.

As it turned out there wasn't even the possibility of a police pursuit until seven-thirty that night. Jerilderie's two police constables and the men from the telegraph office were locked in the cells. Constable Devine's wife had the key but in obeying Ned's instructions she ensured that her husband, whose life she'd begged the bushrangers to spare, couldn't get himself into any danger.

The news of the audacious hold-up caused a sensation. Despite an immense manhunt, the Kelly Gang appeared able to strike at will. And the manner of their crimes was nothing short of spectacular. They'd now struck in three locations, hundreds of kilometres apart. Police seemed incapable of doing anything to contain the fast-moving bushmen of the Kelly Gang. An entire region extending across the rugged north-east of Victoria into the rolling plains of southern New South Wales appeared to be at their mercy. In towns, farmhouses, the big homesteads and on every lonely bush road, law-abiding citizens were haunted by the spectre of Ned Kelly, the embodiment of bushranging – seemingly invincible in the wilderness he had made his domain.

As Jerilderie was in New South Wales, that state's government topped up the Victorian rewards, increasing the reward for the gang's capture to a staggering £8000 – £2000 for each member of the gang. This at a time when a police sergeant's annual income was £50. As for Ned, yet another of his elaborate plans had worked successfully, though it wasn't flawless. It had failed in its objective of getting the Jerilderie Letter published.

Security in banks in both states was stepped up. The Kelly Gang had stolen £2000 at Jerilderie, enough to support them in comfort for some time, or to fund a flight far beyond the reach of the Victorian police. They chose to return to the safety of their support base in north-eastern Victoria.

The Victorian government, in an attempt to regain control, accepted a Queensland offer of an elite squad of Aboriginal trackers, led by Sub-Inspector Stanhope O'Connor. The six young men were the best of the best, but the Victorian media promptly labelled them cannibals, hastening to add that O'Connor would not permit them to eat Ned and his gang. An equally dismissive Victorian Police Chief Commissioner Standish was forced by the Victorian government to use the trackers. Hare was also unimpressed and didn't deploy them effectively. Consequently, the trackers' potential threat to the Kellys was neutralised amid racism and politics.

The following month, Superintendent Hare was removed from the hunt for the Kelly Gang after injuring his back. Nicolson was reappointed. The Police Chief Commissioner used the opportunity to downgrade the expensive patrols that Hare had engaged. He reduced the number of police at Nicolson's disposal by thirty-one, and revised the military guard of banks downwards.

The situation between the police and the Kelly Gang had descended into a stalemate. The police patrols couldn't track down the gang in the remote and uninhabited mountain ranges, and the gang couldn't rob the well-guarded banks. With the proceeds of the Jerilderie job, however, they didn't need to, but neither did they carry out the threat that Ned had foreshadowed in the Jerilderie Letter when he wrote: 'I give fair warning to all those who has reason to fear me to sell out . . . and do not attempt to reside in Victoria. Neglect this and abide by the consequences.'

For more than a year after the Jerilderie hold-up the Kelly Gang was silent. As 1879 rolled into 1880 the story grew cold, until the autumn of 1880 when things started to happen. On 22 March it was reported that mouldboards and steel plates from ploughs were being stolen from farms in the immediate vicinity of Greta. Then came a rumour from police informers that armour was being made. Former Greta schoolteacher Daniel Kennedy, codenamed Denny and the Diseased Stock Agent (the Kelly Gang being the Diseased Stock), wrote to Superintendent Nicolson on 20 May advising him that 'Missing portions of cultivators described as jackets are now being worked and fit splendidly. Tested previous to using and proof [presumably against gunfire] at 10 yards [nine metres].' He also commented that 'a break out may be expected as feed is getting scarce'. With the hard months of winter approaching, the hot fires of revenge were being stoked by a cash-flow crisis.

Trouble was also brewing in the Woolshed Valley. Aaron Sherritt, the young friend of Joe Byrne, had been 'assisting' the police with their inquiries, although he'd actually been planting rumours that had sent the police on false trails. Detective Michael Ward uncovered Sherritt's duplicity and started playing him as bait. It isn't clear whether he succeeded in turning Aaron against the Kelly Gang, but Ward made out that his relationship with Aaron had become cosier, hoping to fan the gang's suspicions. Ned had already spelt out what he'd do to informers in the Jerilderie Letter:

> *Any person aiding or harbouring or assisting the Police in any way whatever, or employing any person whom they know to be a detective or cad or those who would be so deprived as to take blood-money will be Outlawed, And declared unfit to be allowed human buriel their property either consumed or confiscated And them theirs and all belonging to them exterminated off the face of the earth, the enemy I cannot catch I shall give a payable reward for.*

Bloodthirsty stuff from a man who insisted he wasn't a murderer. It also assumed a position of authority over the territory. The letter concludes, 'I am a widow's son outlawed and my orders must be obeyed.' Ned clearly saw himself as a leader, secure within his domain, police patrols notwithstanding. There's a story that Ned intended to declare north-eastern Victoria an independent republic, and that handbills were printed to that end. Unfortunately, if they existed none have been located in private or public hands. Yet the bush that Kelly ranged over had become known as Kelly Country, anyway.

By June, Ward had succeeded in driving a wedge between Aaron and the Kelly Gang, in particular his one-time friend, Joe Byrne. Aaron's bush shack outside Beechworth was being watched by four police officers at night, who then sheltered in the cramped hut during the day. Rumours were circulating that the Kelly Gang was about to make a move. On Friday, 25 June, the Diseased Stock Agent informed Superintendent Hare, who was back in charge of the Kelly hunt, that the Kellys had bullet-proof armour and were about to do something 'that would cause the ears of the Australian world to tingle'.

Hare promptly sacked Daniel Kennedy, contemptuously remarking that with informers like this it was no wonder he and Nicolson hadn't caught the Kellys. Yet Hare failed to notice that the report of imminent action happened to coincide with a night when the moon was full. It had been full when the Kelly Gang escaped from Euroa and Jerilderie, lighting their way as they fled into the trackless bush after their daring robberies.

At approximately six-thirty the following evening, one of Aaron

Sherritt's neighbours knocked at the door of Aaron's hut and called out that he was lost. Aaron unlocked and opened his door to tell him that his house was where it always was. He didn't notice that the man was handcuffed. Joe Byrne emerged from the darkness, levelling the shotgun taken from Sergeant Michael Kennedy at Stringybark Creek at his former best friend. He blasted a hole in his throat and another through his body.

Aaron died at the feet of his distraught young wife Ellen, and her mother. In the bedroom, the four police were fumbling with their guns. Joe fired into the flimsy partition and challenged the men to come out. When they didn't he sent Ellen in to make them come out. They refused. After a second attempt they kept Ellen with them, so Joe sent in the mother. She too was detained by the cowering constables. Joe, joined by Dan, threatened to burn the place down. Two hours later, after attempting to set the place alight, they rode off into the night.

Forty kilometres away, Ned Kelly and Steve Hart were preparing to ride into the town of Glenrowan. Wearing their body armour under their oilskin coats, they left four saddle horses and a pack-horse carrying a drum of explosives in the bush south of the town. After the 9 p.m. train puffed past on its way north to Wangaratta, they made their move.

Using tools they'd brought with them, they tried to lift the train lines on the Wangaratta side of the darkened railway station. They couldn't budge the fish plates that held the rails, so they went to the nearby workers' tents for help. Six of them got up, but their boss, Louis Piazzi, had a woman with him and only vacated the tent after a gunshot interrupted his coitus.

Piazzi and his men weren't railway workers, they were quarrymen who lacked the tools and knowledge to lift the rails. It was now past midnight, and Ned moved on to the Glenrowan Inn, seventy metres from the tents, to rouse the publican, Ann Jones. She, her daughter and four young sons were taken hostage. Ned then roused John Stanistreet, the stationmaster, and told him to show the quarrymen how to sabotage the railway line. Stanistreet didn't have a clue but suggested local platelayers James Reardon and Dennis Sullivan might be more help. Helpful or not, everyone Ned encountered was taken hostage, just as had happened at Euroa and Jerilderie. Most were bundled into Ned's HQ, the Glenrowan Inn.

Dan and Joe arrived fresh from the bloodshed at the Woolshed Valley. When Ned returned with the two platelayers he learned that phase one of his plan had, literally, been executed. Phase two, the derailing of the trainload of police that would rush to the scene when the news broke, was proving more difficult. When Reardon (accompanied by his wife, eight children and their lodger) got to the site of the planned derailment he 'remembered' that he needed a crowbar so Steve Hart went to fetch it. Eventually, despite the stalling of labourers, stationmaster and platelayers, the job was done. An operation of a few moments had taken half the night.

Most of the hostages were escorted to the Glenrowan Inn where fires were kindled in the predawn chill. Some of the women and children went to the stationmaster's house, guarded by Steve Hart. The gang then settled down to await the demise of the speeding train and the ensuing carnage among the hated police travelling on it.

Remarkably, Glenrowan's policeman was left unmolested.

Constable Bracken was in bed with gastric flu. The town's remaining three policemen, also ill as a consequence of watching the Kelly house during the cold weather, were absent. Glenrowan's other publican and his family from the rival McDonnell's Hotel, sympathisers of the Kellys, were escorted to the Glenrowan Inn, if only for appearances. Other sympathisers tended the horses while more joined the 'hostages'. Glenrowan was, after all, just ten kilometres from Greta – the very heart of Kelly Country. The larger centre of Benalla was twenty kilometres south, and Wangaratta a similar distance to the north.

As the morning wore on and there was still no train, the number of hostages grew. At 11 a.m. schoolteacher Thomas Curnow, his wife and baby, and his sister and brother-in-law were bailed up by Ned. The women went to the stationmaster's house, the men joined the people in the Glenrowan Inn. Thomas was twenty-five, the same age as Ned, and had lived in the town for four years, studiously avoiding taking sides when the Kelly Gang tested the loyalties of everyone in the district. On the verandah of the inn, where the drink was starting to flow freely, Thomas learned of the plan to sabotage the railway line. Dan and Joe bragged, 'We're going to send the train and its occupants to hell.'

However, there was no sign of a train. Aaron Sherritt had been dead eighteen hours, but the four policemen hadn't managed to report the killing. The police response perfectly illustrated why their efforts to apprehend the Kelly Gang had met with such abject failure. The four constables had been too afraid to venture out in Kelly Country until daylight, twelve hours after the cold-blooded murder of Aaron Sherritt. Then, rather than expose themselves to danger by going into Beechworth themselves, the police sent locals to raise the alarm, who were initially delayed by a Kelly sympathiser, Paddy Byrne.

Word of Aaron Sherritt's murder finally reached Detective Michael Ward at one o'clock. He tried to telegraph Superintendent Hare in Benalla, but the operator couldn't get through until two-thirty in the afternoon. Hare had a contingent of mounted police, two local Aboriginal trackers and a special police train at his disposal, ready to get rolling. Instead, he telegraphed Police Chief Commissioner Standish in Melbourne for instructions.

When Standish got Hare's message he asked Queensland Sub-Inspector O'Connor if he and his Queensland trackers, who'd been sacked and were about to take a ship back to Queensland, would rejoin the hunt. O'Connor sent a message to Queensland for permission. The answer was no. Pressed to send a second request, permission was eventually granted. Standish, who had regarded the Queensland trackers with contempt, had to wait patiently while the men he had no time for were made available.

Back at Glenrowan, the hours passed slowly. So, in the afternoon, Ned organised sporting competitions –including running races and jumping. As the sun began to dip towards the western horizon, more than sixty hostages waited in and around the inn and stationmaster's house. A bonfire was lit behind the inn's kitchen and there was dancing. An entire day had passed. Ned began releasing some of the prisoners he trusted. When he decided to take Constable Bracken prisoner, Thomas Curnow asked to be released, telling Ned he was with him heart and soul. After taking Bracken prisoner, Ned let the schoolteacher and his family go.

Thomas drove his wife and sister to his mother-in-law's. He told them he intended to warn the train, whenever it finally did arrive, but his wife would have none of it. She refused to stay at her mother's, so Thomas drove her home and put her to bed. When she finally went to sleep, just after 2 a.m., he rode out along the railway line to Benalla to raise the alarm. Almost immediately he heard the sound of a train approaching at speed.

The train had left Melbourne at 10 p.m. but was delayed and slightly damaged when it struck a railway gate, which had been closed because trains didn't normally run on Sundays. At Benalla, O'Connor, five trackers (one tracker had died while in the colder Victorian climate) and a media contingent were joined by Hare, seven troopers and a civilian volunteer. Hare's special train left Benalla at two o'clock on Monday morning, speeding north with the damaged locomotive from Melbourne travelling ahead as a pilot.

The pilot engine was two kilometres from Glenrowan when the driver saw what he thought was a burning log up ahead. A little closer, he saw someone was signalling and applied the brakes as he passed, calling out, 'What's the matter?'

Thomas Curnow shouted, 'The Kellys!'

The driver sounded three warning blasts on his whistle and stopped the train. Thomas explained to the guard that the line had been sabotaged on the other side of Glenrowan and the Kellys had taken over the town. The guard headed back down the line to warn the special train. Before he left, Thomas begged him not to reveal his informant, fearing reprisals against himself and his family.

Back at Glenrowan, where the wait for the train continued, a party was in full swing. The remaining people at the stationmaster's house, including women and children, had been brought to the inn. As they grew tired, some were allowed to go home, while others stayed at the pub drinking and singing well into the night. Finally, Ned decided to let almost all of his hostages go, after he'd given them a little talk.

It was in the midst of his discourse that Joe Byrne came running back to the inn and cried out, 'The train's coming.'

Rather than let the remaining forty or so hostages go, Ned ordered them to stay in the pub. The Kelly Gang went into the dining room to put on their armour, their oilskin coats going on over all. Ned and Joe were dressed first and walked outside. Ned could see the train halted in a cutting near the approach to town. In the clear moonlight, the pilot engine was now coupled to the special train, its lights doused.

Ned also ordered the inn's lights to be extinguished. Things were not going to his elaborate plan, and there didn't seem to be an alternative in case things went wrong. The hostages watched and hoped that the train, which was moving with much more caution than Ned's plan had anticipated, would continue on through the town. But it could only get a short way past the station before it would be stopped by the torn-up line. All the occupants of the Glenrowan Inn looked on as the train chugged slowly forward. It pulled into Glenrowan Station and stopped.

Superintendent Hare disembarked and turned to the only civilian present, reputedly saying, 'What had we better do?' The volunteer, Charles Rawlins, who knew the town well, suggested they visit the stationmaster. He and three constables met with a terrified Mrs Stanistreet who told them her husband was a prisoner of the Kellys at the Glenrowan Inn.

'How many are there?' Rawlins asked.

'Forty,' she answered.

At the inn, Constable Bracken quietly warned the hostages to get down as low as they possibly could. Outside, Ned was watching as the train sat puffing in the station, then the sound of horses being unloaded carried far in the cold night air. Bracken chose this moment to slip out of the hotel, running the short distance down a slight incline to the platform.

Hare assumed the Kellys would flee (the same error police had made at Stringybark Creek) and that he would pursue them on horseback, but his plan had to quickly change.

Bracken reached the station, gasping out, 'Over there. The Kellys, not five minutes ago, stuck us all up. The four of them, quick, quick!'

Hare and those who had weapons immediately to hand – about half of the fourteen-odd police and Aboriginal tracker contingent, plus *Argus* reporter Joe Melvin – abandoned the horses and started to run in the direction of the Glenrowan Inn. By then all four of the Kelly Gang were standing in the shadows of the verandah, watching the police running towards them in bright moonlight.

A turnstile allowed pedestrians to pass through the railway fence, one at a time, and onto the sloping ground that led up to the Glenrowan Inn. Hare charged through in the lead, wielding a shotgun, oblivious to the men on the verandah. Ned aimed a rifle and fired at Hare from a range of thirty metres, hitting him in the wrist.

The superintendent cried out, 'Good gracious! I am hit the very first shot.'

The rest of the gang unleashed a volley that sent the following police scattering for cover – which comprised a few trees and a ditch in the railway reserve. At first the police only managed a sporadic return of fire and Ned, emboldened, moved out into the moonlight. A constable fired two shots from his .45 Martini Henry rifle. One shot passed through Ned's bent left forearm, then through his upper arm. The other hit his right foot, the bullet shattering bone and tearing flesh from toe to heel.

A few moments later all the police started firing at the Glenrowan Inn, causing havoc for the hostages hiding inside, as the thin walls gave no protection from the hail of bullets and splintering wood. Despite lying on the ground Jack Jones, the young son of publican Ann Jones, was hit in the hip. The bullet sliced upwards, leaving the boy screaming in agony, blood running from his mouth. Another bullet grazed his sister Jane's forehead as she and her mother carried him towards the kitchen at the back of the inn, putting him near the brick chimney for what little protection it could give. Then a labourer, Neil McHugh (no relation to the author), realising the boy was going to die if he didn't get medical attention, carried him out past the police to the house of platelayer James Reardon.

One of the quarrymen died when a bullet hit him in the eye. A line repairer, Martin Cherry, who'd gone to the pub for a look when he heard the Kellys were there, was hit in the groin as he got up onto a bed in the kitchen, the bullet caused massive internal injuries. Those around him tried to do what they could to help as bullets, flying splinters of wood and broken glass tore through the air.

Despite Ned's injuries, the Kelly Gang returned almost as much gunfire as they took. Then, in the midst of the volleys, two rockets were fired into the sky from the vicinity of McDonnell's Hotel, on the other side of the railway line. Who had fired them, and to who or what they were signalling was a mystery to the police. It might have been a call to Kelly sympathisers to rise up and throw the police out of the Kelly Country, once and for all.

Finally, amid the hail of gunfire a voice cried out that there were women and children in the hotel and to stop shooting. There was a pause, during which all the women and children, led by the wounded Jane Jones, ran from the building. The Reardons and their eight children, including a baby, weren't quick enough. Trailing behind the other hostages they were challenged as they approached the police lines. When they said they were women and children, the police heard male voices and opened fire. Three of the children ran to safety, the rest ran back to the Glenrowan Inn.

The police were now deployed at the front (south) and left (west) of the inn, but they lacked the manpower to surround the building. While the women and children were escaping, one of the constables heard Ned and Joe talking. Ned had asked Joe to help him reload his weapon and Joe had said he thought his leg was broken.

Having reloaded, Ned emerged from the breezeway at the back of the hotel separating the main building from the kitchen. Still exchanging gunfire with the police, he made his way towards the back fence of the inn. Bleeding profusely from the wound to his arm, he tried to staunch it using a cap he'd been wearing under his helmet. He reached the back fence, where he had a horse saddled and waiting. Despite his injuries, he climbed up and rode out of Glenrowan. There are suggestions, based on the oral histories of descendants of those involved, that Ned, seeing his grand plan going awry, went to warn sympathisers converging on the scene not to get involved.

Shortly after, two policemen, constables Kelly and Arthur, found Ned's blood-soaked cap dropped on the ground, along with his rifle. Constable Kelly was now the officer in charge. The injured Hare, having extracted himself, was on his way to Benalla seeking medical attention, while his men continued the deadly gunfight with the Kelly Gang.

Constable Kelly was trying to create the impression that he had the place surrounded, but the cap and rifle suggested that the gang were slipping away to the safety of Kelly Country, though severely injured. Word of the siege was spreading. Superintendent Sadleir was already on his way from Benalla with thirteen reinforcements. In Wangaratta, Sergeant Arthur Steele had been alerted by telegram. When Constable Bracken arrived and told him the gang was still at Glenrowan, Steele set out on horseback with five constables. In approaching the inn they might have passed extremely close to Ned, lurking somewhere outside the police cordon. By dawn, some thirty-five police were deployed around the Glenrowan Inn. The remaining gang members were effectively surrounded, outnumbered and outgunned by twelve to one.

At least one of them, Joe, had received serious gunshot wounds. Ned, also badly wounded, had slipped through the police lines, but there was little hope of escape for the others, even if the gang's armour was able to protect them in a last desperate shootout. Ned could have left them to their fate, but it appears that he either returned to the vicinity of the inn or had remained there after escaping. As the first faint glimmer of dawn started to light the eastern horizon, Ned made a move. In full armour, including his roughly welded helmet, he struggled to his feet and walked slowly back towards his mates at the Glenrowan Inn.

Margaret Reardon tried once again to get herself and her remaining children clear. Dan let them go and when they got into the yard in front of the inn Margaret screamed at the police not to shoot. Sergeant Steele told them to put up their hands or he'd shoot them like dogs. She and her oldest son Michael did the best they could as Margaret was carrying a baby and Michael was leading a child by the hand. Despite this, Margaret maintained that Steele started shooting. Margaret kept going but Michael's courage failed him and he turned back. She managed to escape, perhaps because Constable Arthur told Steele that if he fired at her again he'd shoot Steele himself.

Steele reloaded and fired two shots at Michael Reardon, just as he reached the inn. One bullet deflected off his shoulder and lodged behind his breastbone. As he collapsed, his father, who hadn't dared try to leave, helped his son inside.

While this was happening, Ned reached the back of the inn, where he found Joe pouring himself a whisky in the bar.

Joe Byrne saluted his leader with a toast, 'Many more years in the bush for the Kelly Gang.'

Just then another volley of police bullets tore through the building. Joe paid dearly for not keeping low, for, despite his armour, a bullet tore through his groin. With blood pouring from the wound, he collapsed, and moments later died.

Ned went out onto the verandah and challenged the police. They made no reply, so he turned back indoors to gather his remaining men. In the murky building, strewn with the dead, the dying and those trapped but still alive, he couldn't see his brother and Steve Hart. He assumed they'd made a break for it and decided to break through the police line once more. He walked out the back again, where there were seven or eight police on his left flank. None fired as he made his way up the paddock to the horses until a constable, thinking Ned was trying to escape, called out to the police on the other side of the inn, risking being caught in the crossfire, to stop him. One of the horses broke through a sliprail and galloped away, the rest were shot in the yard.

Seeing Dan and Steve's horses, Ned might have realised that the pair were still inside the Glenrowan Inn. Oral histories suggest sympathisers might have told him they hadn't escaped. In any case, Ned Kelly turned once more, injured and wearing body armour that at fifty kilograms was half his own bodyweight, and staggered towards the police lines.

As dawn broke, the figure that emerged from the mists and gunsmoke would never be forgotten by those who saw it – police, journalists and sketch artist Thomas Carrington. In full armour, a cloak thrown over his shoulders, a helmet accentuating his height so he seemed larger than any ordinary man, Ned Kelly moved slowly down the slope to the north of the Glenrowan Inn. The police lines were being threatened by a figure some likened to the headless ghost of Hamlet's father.

Constable Arthur thought it was a prankster until Ned raised his right arm from within the folds of his cloak and, using his left hand to support it, aimed a revolver. Arthur fired, hitting the helmet at close range. The armour stopped the bullet but the force caused

Ned to lurch to one side. He then raised his revolver again and fired, but his arm was crippled and the bullet hit the ground a metre in front of Arthur. Arthur fired again, hitting Ned but only causing him to lurch once more. The other police nearby started firing, too, with little effect. One heard Ned say, 'Fire away, you buggers. You cannot hurt me.' From ten metres away, constables Healy and Mountiford fired at Ned with shotguns. He laughed. The police continued shooting, as Ned slowly advanced.

At first Sergeant Steele couldn't see what the police were firing at, then he saw a tall black man wrapped in some kind of rug. He called on his men to cease firing at the stranger, a surprising move since he'd had no qualms about shooting women and children earlier. Ned called to Steve and Dan, who ran from the inn and out the back, firing at the tree Steele was using for shelter.

Ned moved forward, the way ahead of him opening as police fled. But they closed in behind, on the left and right, firing constantly and causing Ned to stagger first one way, then another. To the artist Thomas Carrington, the figure was moving as if drunk. In a clump of three small trees, 100 metres from the northern side of the inn, Ned rested for a moment in the crossfire. At that moment, amid all the shooting, Joe Byrne's mare Music approached him, possibly sensing his distress. While the police feared he might mount and ride off, such athleticism was beyond Ned. As Music moved away, she was shot, though not fatally, by the police.

Ned's revolver was out of ammunition. He drew a second, which was promptly shot from his hand, the bullet ripping through flesh and bone. Nevertheless, he drew a third revolver, his last weapon.

Sergeant Steele was at risk of being caught between Ned, and Dan and Steve, who were firing from the breezeway at the back of the inn. Hoping Ned was trying to reload, Steele charged the trees where Ned had sunk to his knees. Ned fired. Steele dived low, dirt from the shot spraying into his eye. Other police gave their sergeant covering fire, Constable Healy again hitting Ned's hand, severing a finger. Ned rose and staggered on, veering towards a large fallen tree that lay in the direction of the train station.

Behind the tree, the railway guard from the special train, Jesse Dowsett, saw the monstrous apparition heading straight for him. He aimed his railway-issue Colt revolver and fired half a dozen shots. The figure kept coming.

Ned made it to the tree and slumped against it, exhausted. Dowsett suggested he surrender, but Ned would have none of it. So Dowsett shot him in the head. Thanks to the armour, the bullet bounced off.

'How do you like that, old man?' Dowsett asked.

'How do you like this?' Ned replied, and fired back, narrowly missing the railway man.

Behind Ned, Sergeant Steele had closed in. He realised that the armour only extended to Ned's thighs, and was about to take a shot that would bring him down when the mare Music charged back into the midst of the action, turning Ned's attention towards Steele. To no avail. The policeman fired, and the shot hit Ned in the right knee. Ned fought to stay on his feet as Steele charged him and fired again, the shot tearing through his hip, thigh and groin. Finally, Ned fell forward, crying, 'I'm done. I'm done.'

He was still gripping his revolver when Steele leapt on him.

Blood spurting from his wounded hand, Ned tried to bring the gun over his shoulder to fire. Guard Dowsett and Constable Kelly dived on Ned as well, bodies flailing as Ned fought to the last. Dowsett grabbed Ned's wrist, trying to tear the gun away. A shot rang out, barely missing Steele's face. Finally, he was disarmed, and they were able to pull away the helmet to discover which member of the Kelly Gang they had caught. It was Ned. He was alive, but only just.

As Ned lay on the ground, pale and near death, others converged on the scene, trigger happy and fired by the bloodlust of capturing the gang's leader. For a few moments it seemed the police, who'd been terrorised by Ned Kelly for over two years and at last had him at their mercy, would shoot him where he lay. Then railwayman Dowsett shouted, 'Take him alive!'

Constable Hugh Bracken stood over Ned with a shotgun, threatening, 'I'll shoot any bloody man that dares touch him.'

Only 100 metres from the inn, the police tried to bear Ned away as Dan and Steve kept a constant fire trained upon them. They seemed determined that none of the gang would be taken alive. Police returned fire, especially at Dan, who had ventured outside the building. He was hit in the leg before being forced to retreat. Ned was taken to the stationmaster's house, where he gave newspaper reporters the first of several versions of his intended plan at Glenrowan. After wrecking the train, the gang planned to ride to Benalla, blow up the railway line from Melbourne and, with the town thus isolated, plunder the Bank of New South Wales.

There was a stand-off at the inn until ten o'clock, when Superintendent Sadleir (he had arrived on one of the many trains filled with more police, and the plain curious who had raced to the scene as news of the siege spread) negotiated the release of the thirty remaining prisoners. There was a rush for safety, made more terrifying by some police threatening to shoot those who were trying to flee the building. Some, like Michael Reardon, received medical attention in time to save their lives. Others were beyond help. Martin Cherry, still bleeding from the wound to his groin, couldn't be carried from the inn and remained inside, near the kitchen, with the only others left alive – Dan Kelly and Steve Hart.

There was some talk with Ned about ordering his men to surrender, but he doubted his ability to sway them. A priest suggested a man of the cloth might be trusted, but Ned thought the priest would be suspected of being a policeman in disguise and shot. As the afternoon wore on, the stalemate continued. The police had noted the presence of Kelly sympathisers around the town and gathered in McDonnell's Hotel, on the other side of the railway tracks. Emotions were running high, but it would have been an extraordinary step if the Kelly sympathisers, more used to raising crops, cattle and kids, raised hell with the cops instead.

Sadleir, meanwhile, had requested an artillery piece be sent from Melbourne, a drastic approach to resolving the situation. Then Senior Constable Charles Johnston suggested setting the Glenrowan Inn ablaze. Sadleir agreed, and at 3 p.m. police fired volleys into the building to cover Johnston as he approached with straw and kerosene. By then over a thousand people were involved in or watching the unfolding drama, among them the Kelly sisters Maggie, Kate and Grace. Police tried to persuade them to call on their brother and Steve Hart to surrender, as the preparations for burning the boys out were being finalised. Maggie refused, but

Kate agreed. The building may have already been alight when she approached. There is a photo of the scene that shows a woman outside the building as smoke billows from its eaves.

As the building burned more fiercely, the priest, Dean Gibney, ignored police warnings and approached. He was joined by Superintendent Sadleir on the verandah, where they were confronted by a wall of fire. Gibney walked into the burning building and found Joe Byrne's body. He then leapt through a burning doorway to find Dan and Steve's bodies in one of the bedrooms. He took one of their hands and formed the opinion they'd been dead for some time. The siege was over.

Police managed to carry Joe's body from the scene before the flames engulfed it. The fire all but incinerated Dan and Steve. Martin Cherry was found, still alive, near the kitchen, but he died of his wounds shortly after. Police, media and sightseers swarmed over the scene, some of them scavenging for souvenirs. Any fires of rebellion were quenched in the scenes of mourning at the station, where the bodies were taken, and at the stationmaster's house, where Ned remained alive despite nearly thirty bullet and shotgun wounds.

Amid the tumult of emotion surrounding Dan and Steve, the police capitulated and allowed the Kelly sympathisers to remove their bodies. Later attempts to recover them for an inquest met with such threats and intimidation that they were eventually buried by their families and friends without a full examination. Joe's body was taken to Benalla. On the following day it became a macabre freak show, tied to a door of the gaol for a photo opportunity.

The media reports initially celebrated the capture of the Kelly

Gang, but, as the smoke around the ruins of the Glenrowan Inn cleared, they started counting the cost, focusing on the police action in firing with reckless disregard for life at a building full of innocent people. Three hostages had died and a number of others had suffered serious gunshot wounds. The post-mortem then considered the failings of the police throughout the hunt for the gang – their unseemly manoeuvring for credit (and for the significant reward money that was about to be distributed), and the widely differing accounts of innocent people being fired at, such as Michael Reardon, were raised.

Ned, meanwhile, had been rushed by train to Melbourne, ostensibly for urgent medical attention, but conveniently getting him far away from the heartland of his support base, from where it was feared a rescue attempt might be launched. For the Kelly Gang was made up of more than just four men; their network of relatives, sympathisers and friends was extensive. Ned Kelly and the others might have been captured or killed but Kelly Country remained undefeated.

Ned was taken to Melbourne Gaol, where his captors took the task of healing him particularly seriously. They had to keep him alive long enough to stand trial, and should he be found guilty, to hang. As it happened, his mother was interred in the woman's section of the same prison, and, while he was recovering, she was permitted to see him.

In the lead up to Ned's trial, Kelly supporters remained a matter of concern for the authorities, as the government actively prevented the land of sympathisers being mortgaged to pay for Ned's defence. Kelly nevertheless enlisted fiery MP William Zincke to represent him at his committal hearing in Beechworth. However, when he added Zincke's political rival David Gaunson to his team, on the night before the hearing, Zincke walked out, leaving Gaunson to pick up the pieces. Ned was committed to trial on the single charge of the murder of Constable Lonigan. The trial was initially set down for Beechworth, but fears for the safety of the jury saw the case moved to Melbourne.

The problems for Ned's defence continued. The cost of a barrister was quite simply beyond him and his hard-pressed sympathis- ers – £50 for the first two days and £10 a day after that. The man David Gaunson recommended for the job, Hickman Molesworth, suggested a delaying tactic while the Kellys raised the cash. His junior, Henry Bindon, would appear and admit that he was com- pletely ignorant of the case (which was true). He would then ask for an adjournment until he was sufficiently briefed to properly conduct the defence, which would open the door for Molesworth to conduct the case. Before Judge Redmond Barry in the Central Criminal Court on Monday, 18 October 1880, Bindon had the trial postponed until the 28th.

The increasingly desperate defence sought help from the Crown. It provided £7. Further efforts to raise money were an abject failure, and, on the 28th, the woefully inexperienced Bindon was flung before the court to defend Ned Kelly, having been handed the case only two days earlier. To the charge of the murder of Thomas Lonigan Ned pleaded not guilty.

The court, with Judge Barry presiding, heard evidence for two days, during which the prosecution sought to have a copy of the Jerilderie Letter tendered. It was a curious action. In modern times,

Kelly supporters regard the document as a testament to his inno-cence. Neither the prosecution nor Ned's own lawyer Bindon saw it that way. Bindon objected to the letter being admitted on the grounds that it wasn't written in Ned's hand. The author, and therefore the only person who could reliably be said to hold the letter's opinions, was the deceased Joe Byrne. It seems both the prosecution and defence in Ned's trial looked upon the letter as incriminating.

The evidence was concluded on the afternoon of the second day of the trial, the defence having made little headway against the flimsy recollections of Constable McIntyre in particular (it was only thirty-three years later that Superintendent John Sadleir admitted in his book *Recollections of a Victorian Police Officer* that McIntyre's initial statement, given three days after Stringybark Creek, largely substantiated Ned Kelly's version of the shooting of Lonigan). In his summing up, Judge Barry dismissed Ned's defence that he'd shot Lonigan in self-defence. Barry contended that no one had a right to challenge police when they were acting to maintain the peace. However, the real question was whether they were upholding the law or were acting as an execution squad.

The jury retired at 5.10 p.m. on 19 October and took just thirty minutes to arrive at a verdict. The foreman, a dairyman named Samuel Lazarus, rose to his feet and when asked for his verdict replied, 'Guilty.'

Ned was then given an opportunity to speak.

'Nobody knows about this case except myself,' he said. 'And I almost wish now that I had spoken – and I wish I had insisted on being allowed to examine the witnesses myself. I am confident I would have thrown a different light on the case.'

As he prepared to deliver sentence, Judge Barry felt compelled to disagree.

'No circumstances that I can conceive could have altered the result of your trial,' he said.

'Perhaps if you had heard me examine the witnesses, you might understand. I could do it. It is quite possible for me to clear myself of this charge if I liked to do so. If I desired to do it, I could have done so in spite of anything attempted against me,' Ned replied.

'The facts against you are so numerous and so conclusive,' said Barry, 'not only as regards the offence which you are now charged with, but also for a long series of criminal acts which you have committed during the last eighteen months, that I do not think any rational person could have arrived at any other conclusion. The verdict of the jury is irresistible.'

He was right, of course, up to a point. Had Ned been tried on every charge that could have been brought against him, even his own belief that he was fighting for liberty and justice might have crumbled. Did he expect anyone to believe he had pursued Sergeant Michael Kennedy for two kilometres through the bush in order to shoot him in self-defence? Was there a point during the killing of constables Thomas Lonigan and Michael Scanlan, robbing two banks, taking dozens of hostages and robbing many of them at gunpoint, executing Aaron Sherritt, attempting to kill a trainload of police and using dozens of hostages as human shields, resulting in the deaths of thirteen-year-old Jack Jones, George Metcalf and Martin Cherry (plus fellow gang members Steve Hart, Joe Byrne and his brother Dan), when his claim of police provocation was no longer justified?

Ned wanted the justice system to look at everything from his perspective and declare him innocent. It was never going to happen. Judge Barry sentenced Ned to death and the Victorian government acted with almost unseemly haste in setting the date of his execution for 11 November 1880. Thousands rallied to plead for clemency and a petition collected over 30 000 signatures.

Despite the pressure that was brought to bear, the Victorian government refused to commute the sentence. Far from the eucalypt-scented air of his mountain haunts, Ned was hung within the dank confines of Melbourne Gaol. Just a few metres away in the women's section, his mother was excused work detail. As with so many aspects of Ned's life, there are several versions of his last words, the most famous being, 'Such is life.' A death mask was made, then the body was decapitated and the brain removed for study by the now discredited science of phrenology. The body was then made available for dissection by medical students – a modern interpretation of quartering. What remained was buried in an unmarked grave in the prison grounds. Ned Kelly was just twenty-five years old.

The justice system had not let Ned walk free; however, shortly after his death, it did take a long hard look at his case. A Royal Commission was announced to examine police conduct throughout the period that Ned and his gang were at large. Not surprisingly, it found serious deficiencies in aspects of police conduct and in a number of officers.

After his death, the image of the armoured Ned Kelly seized the imagination of a nation. The apparition of the iron-helmeted man that loomed out of the morning mists of 27 June 1880 differentiated Kelly from every other bushranger. His brief but defiant reign as an outlaw in the bush ensured he would hold a unique place in Australian history. Ned was admired for his refusal to bow to injustice, and for his independence, initiative and skill in outwitting a corrupt system. The combination of Ned's politics and Australia's imminent nationhood, when the nation broke free of the English yoke at last, transformed him into an enduring folk hero. But in giving the Australian bush its most recognisable image, the Kelly mask, his embodiment of the faceless stranger also ensured no one would feel entirely safe in the outback again.

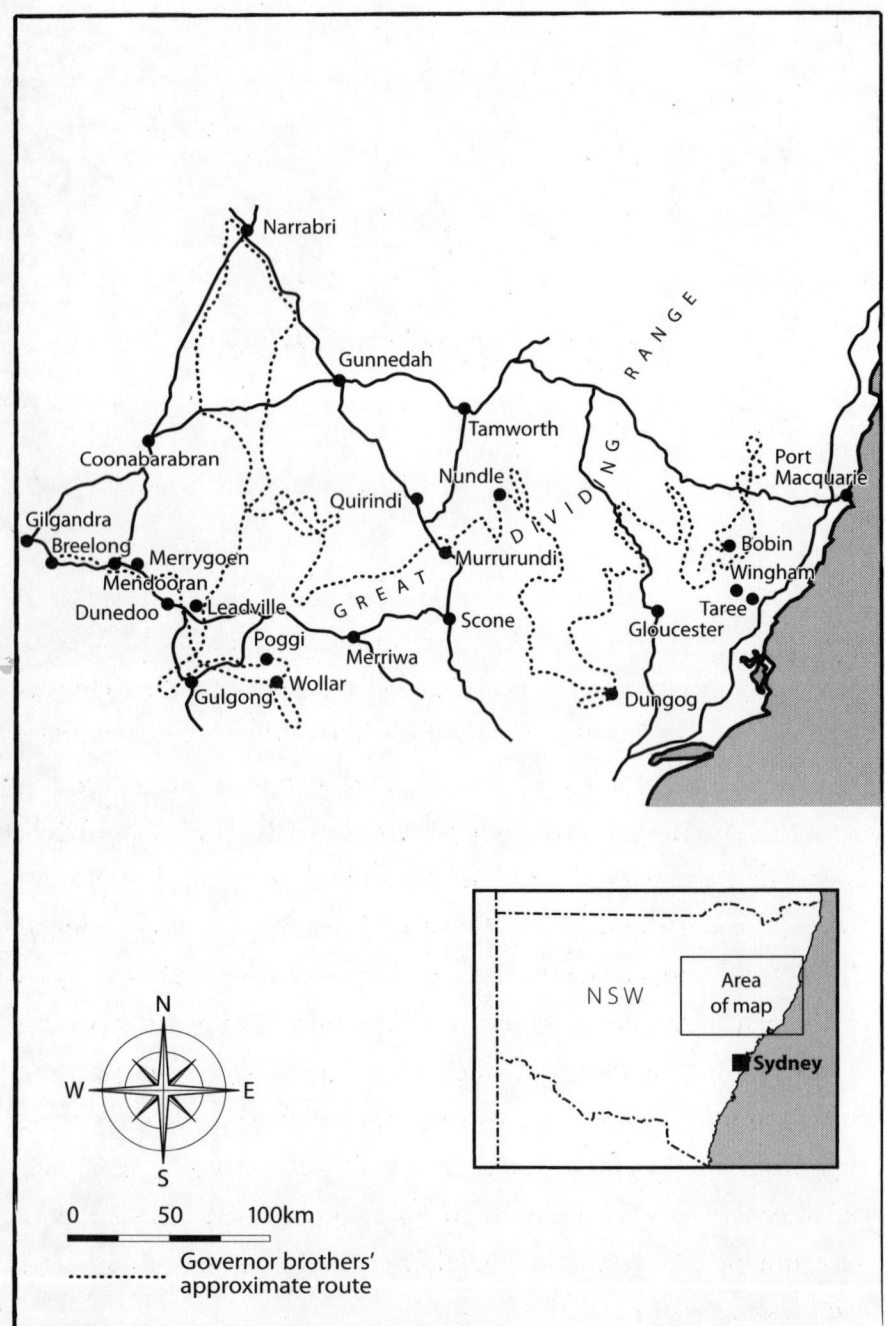

Narrabri

Gunnedah

Tamworth

Coonabarabran

Nundle

Quirindi

RANGE

Port
Macquarie

Gilgandra
Breelong

Murrurundi

Merrygoen

Bobin
Wingham

Mendooran

GREAT

DIVIDING

Taree

Dunedoo Leadville

Scone

Gloucester

Poggi

Merriwa

Dungog

Gulgong Wollar

N

W E

S

NSW

Area
of map

Sydney

0   50   100km

········· Governor brothers'
          approximate route

4

BLACK AND WHITE

Jimmy Governor may have been slow to anger, but the fury had been growing within him for nearly all of his twenty-five years. He was born around 1875, although exactly when and where isn't known because at the time it wasn't considered necessary to record the details of Aboriginal births. He was the son of a full-blood, while on his mother's side he had an Aboriginal grandmother and an Irish stockman grandfather. His father, an itinerant worker, ranged across the Mudgee region in central-western New South Wales all the way to the coast, looking for whatever employment was on offer – mining, stock work, tree-felling – but as an Aboriginal he was often paid in rations rather than money. The lack of cash made supporting a family of eight children, a constant struggle. However, the alternative, settlement on an Aboriginal reserve subsisting on government rations in an atmosphere of violence and despair, was even less appealing.

Jimmy and his siblings learned the meaning of prejudice early in life at the hands of Europeans who rarely missed a chance to express the belief that Aboriginal people were inferior. They learned, too, that the indignities didn't end when you were dead. Jimmy's father passed away in May 1900, amid suspicions he'd been murdered by Aboriginal men from the police reserve at Wollar, forty kilometres north-east of Mudgee. His grave was desecrated by a Chinese hawker named Gee Li who didn't like having Aboriginal neighbours.

Jimmy was working by then, and like his father was often paid in food rather than money. Hoping for a better deal, he joined the police force, working as a tracker. There, however, his hard work and application amounted to nothing, as his white bosses had no qualms about taking the credit for his achievements. He soon realised his chances of advancement were non-existent and quit, returning to working on stations around the Mudgee district, where he had a reputation for hard work and diligence.

Discrimination reoccurred when he showed an interest in a young white girl on a property near Ulan. The station owner threatened to whip him. Then he caught the eye of sixteen-year-old Ethel Page, who was living and working in Mudgee, the daughter of a poor, struggling gold fossicker in the Gulgong district, thirty kilometres north of Mudgee. She became pregnant to the handsome, dashing Jimmy, and he did the right thing by marrying her. Ethel's parents promptly moved from Gulgong to Dubbo in an attempt to escape the disgrace of their daughter's marriage to an Aboriginal. Incensed townsfolk publicly insulted the Governors.

After their child was born, Jimmy found fencing work on

Breelong Station, near Gilgandra in central-western New South Wales, hoping to escape the taunts and insults he experienced in town. Unfortunately, it wasn't to be. The station owner's wife, Sarah Mawbey, her daughter Grace and the local schoolteacher, 21-year-old Ellen Kerz, made no attempt to hide their disgust for him and his family. Jimmy, his wife and baby (and other members of his family who had come to help with the work) were forced to camp in the open through the bitter winter of 1900, barely earning enough from fencing land that, little more than a generation before, had been home to his forebears. John Mawbey refused to pay full price for some of the fenceposts Jimmy cut, but he used them anyway. His wife inflated the price on the rations Jimmy bought from her. Ethel Governor worked for the Mawbey women for no pay while being subjected to their daily abuse. Jimmy ended up owing the Mawbeys money, and he and his family went hungry. He'd had enough.

On the evening of Friday, 20 July 1900, he went to see John Mawbey at the Breelong Inn to ask for rations. Mawbey and the station's menfolk spent their nights at the inn due to overcrowding at the homestead, a kilometre away. Mawbey was already in bed when Jimmy, his brother Joe, close friend Jack Underwood and Jimmy's wife Ethel called. Mawbey got up to talk to them and agreed to send flour and sugar to Jimmy's camp the following morning. All seemed well.

Then Jimmy and the others (exactly who was present isn't clear, but it was probably the four who had seen Mawbey; Jimmy's eleven-year-old brother Peter and eighty-year-old Jack Porter remained at the camp) continued to the homestead to speak to Sarah Mawbey and Ellen Kerz. When Jimmy asked them to apologise for their treatment of his wife and child, they laughed sneeringly.

'Pooh! You black rubbish,' Ellen said. 'You ought to be shot for marrying a white woman.'

The insult struck deep. No sooner was it out of her mouth than Jimmy punched Ellen in the jaw so hard she fell to the ground. Then the attack started in earnest.

Ten women and children were in the house. In the sittingroom Sarah Mawbey was struck repeatedly about the head, neck and arm, according to Jimmy, with a nulla-nulla, an Aboriginal club. One blow almost severed her spinal cord, another broke open her skull.

Ellen Kerz and Grace Mawbey ran into the front bedroom, off the sittingroom, where eleven-year-old Hilda Mawbey and her aunt Elsie Clarke were in bed. Ellen and Grace shut the door just as Sarah's son Percy rushed into the sittingroom from the verandah and tried to defend his mother. His cousin George heard a sound like tomahawks clashing. Percy's younger brother, Albert, looked through the front door and saw an Aboriginal man standing over Percy, clubbing him. Percy's skull was fractured and his head nearly severed. Albert turned away from the onslaught and hid with George under a bed on the verandah. When the Governors and Jack Underwood turned their attention to the door of the front bedroom, Albert bolted from under the bed and ran for his father at the Breelong Inn.

The door to the bedroom was smashed into splinters by the frenzied attack. Ellen Kerz, Grace and Hilda Mawbey escaped out of the window and ran down the road with Jimmy, at least, in pursuit.

The fact that none of the three made it to the inn suggests they may have had more than one assailant. The attack on Ellen Kerz was perhaps the most violent. Her head was described as 'smashed to a pulp'. She fell on the left side of the track to the inn, Grace Mawbey fell on the right side, clubbed and hacked repeatedly.

Hilda got 200 metres from the house before Jimmy caught her near the creek that ran through the property. She fell down the bank and there Jimmy struck her five times with the nulla-nulla. On his way back along the road, Jimmy noticed that both the women on the track were still breathing. He struck at least one of them again before continuing to the homestead. Elsie Clarke had been attacked in the bedroom with a tomahawk. The blows were concentrated on her face and head, and went so deep that her tongue was split in two.

John Mawbey reached the homestead less than ten minutes after the attack began. With his son Reggie and brother-in-law Fred Clarke, they found Hilda, Percy and Ellen Kerz dead. Despite their horrific injuries, Sarah and Grace Mawbey, and Elsie Clarke were still alive. Grace died the following morning, Sarah died on the 23rd, haunted by the scenes she'd witnessed. Her delirious testimony was inadmissible in court, yet it suggested that Ethel Governor had been present during the attack. Elsie Clarke managed to survive, but her injuries left her permanently deaf. Out in the kitchen, which was separated from the main building by a breezeway, two of the younger Mawbey children, Cecil and Garnett, aged seven and four, slept through the murders undisturbed.

Word of the atrocity spread rapidly and locals headed to the Governor's camp. It was deserted. All the crockery in the camp had been smashed, suggesting the Governors were symbolically breaking with their past. They travelled south-east through much of the night, only pausing before dawn. Jimmy, reputedly in a state of high excitement, made plans. He told Ethel to leave with the baby and head to her parents at Dubbo, as she couldn't keep up, and if she was caught with him she would be accused as well. Jack Underwood later testified that Jimmy had wanted to settle a family grudge with members of the Aboriginal community at Wollar, then go bush and find a vantage point from which to kill every police-man he saw.

One of the parties that had joined the hunt found Ethel on the road to Dubbo. She was briefly held at Breelong Inn before being taken to the Dubbo lock-up where she was kept, mainly for her own protection. In her first hours in custody she made many wild claims about Jimmy's intentions to hunt down and kill those who had wronged him and his family.

The following day, Sunday, old Jack Porter and young Peter Governor separated from the group. A party of four searchers spotted the remaining three men on the Dunedoo–Mendooran Road and fired on them. One of the men was separated, the other two escaped into the scrub. The two then stole a horse, which they rode together. For a while they were tracked, heading south-east, but then they doubled back, perhaps to avoid their pursuers. It was Jack Underwood who had been separated from the Governor brothers, Jimmy and Joe.

The Governors continued on their way after darkness fell until they reached the home of Charlie Wade, an old gold prospector, and his wife. Wade had always treated the Governors well and that night was no exception. It was to be the only help they got.

Jimmy and Joe moved on again in the early hours of the morning, heading south-east past Gulgong. Not only were they moving deeper into their traditional country (despite having an Irish stockman as a grandfather, Jimmy retained his tribal connection with the land through the goanna totem), they were also moving closer to the wild and rugged western flanks of the Great Dividing Range. It had been the haunt of many a bushranger of the preceding 100 years. It was isolated, uninhabited country where, if you had the skills, you could disappear and never be found. Heading east from Gulgong the terrain was steeper, wilder and more heavily forested. It was also closer to the people with whom they sought to settle old scores. Ethel Governor, still in custody, named fifteen people who might have cause to fear Jimmy.

Monday was also the day that Sarah Mawbey succumbed to her injuries, becoming the fifth fatality of the Breelong attack, and old Jack and young Peter were found twenty kilometres east of Breelong.

Meanwhile, the Governor brothers were heading east, towards the Aboriginal reserve at Wollar. Along the way, outside the township of Ulan, was the farm of one of the people who had been on Ethel Governor's list. Seventy-year-old Alexander McKay was the man who had once threatened Jimmy with a whip for showing an interest in a young white girl in his care. Alexander McKay now faced him, not having heard the news of the killings at Breelong, even though the countryside was overrun with almost a hundred police and many more volunteers. Jimmy aimed an unloaded rifle at the man. Alexander never saw Joe coming from behind with a tomahawk.

The pair then approached the house, where Alexander's wife Mary and her niece Louisa Johnson were sitting on the verandah. The women fled indoors, but Mary wasn't quite quick enough. Joe caught her with the tomahawk, gashing her face, just before she got inside and bolted the door. The Governor brothers broke the windows, then started smashing the door with an axe. Jimmy told the terrified women he wouldn't hurt them if they didn't run away. Fearing she was about to die no matter what she did, Mary McKay opened up.

Jimmy, however, was true to his word. The women were unharmed as the two brothers set about robbing the place. They were searching for weapons and ammunition but came up empty-handed. Eventually, they made do with the money from Alexander McKay's pockets, a small supply of stores and McKay's horse.

After they were gone, Mary and her niece found Alexander out in the fields, still alive. They brought him into the house but he died two hours later, never regaining consciousness. As word of the latest attack spread, fear in the community around Gulgong grew. Many people examined their memories, if not their consciences, and found ample cause to be afraid of the vengeance now stalking the countryside. Soon people were converging on the town from the outlying properties, seeking safety in numbers. For those who had long regarded the Australian landscape as alien and dangerous, the elusive Governors became their worst fears made flesh.

Together on McKay's horse the Governors headed into the foothills of the Great Dividing Range that rise a short distance south-east of Ulan (now the Goulburn River National Park). They met two hawkers who they asked to get them some ammunition

and hide it near Wollar. The brothers told them they were heading towards the home of one of Jimmy's former employers, Henry
Neville, to kill him. Insead, they stole another horse and detoured
to the home of Bert Byers. What the Governors had against Byers
isn't known, but fortunately for him he had left to join the hunt as
a volunteer, and his family weren't home either.

The Governors continued on to Henry Neville's place. Well
aware that he hadn't been a good boss, Neville had already vacated
his property on the Goulburn River. The Governors took advantage
of his flight and grabbed themselves a saddle, clothing and a gun.
The hawkers, meanwhile, had put the police onto the Governors'
trail. However, they arrived too late at Neville's place. All they found
was the remains of a hearty breakfast.

The Governors continued east to the remote property of Michael
O'Brien at Poggi, twenty-five kilometres north-east of Wollar, by
cutting through what is now the Goulburn River National Park.
O'Brien had humiliated Jimmy when he was just a kid by throwing
him in a river, and Ethel had named him as a target for Jimmy's
revenge. Michael was away from the house collecting firewood
when the Governors approached. Unfortunately, Michael's heavily
pregnant wife Lizzie and district nurse Catherine Bennett were in
the kitchen with Lizzie's fifteen-month-old son James.

When Jimmy appeared outside Lizzie went to talk to him, only
to find him armed and threatening. He told her to surrender or he'd
shoot her. Lizzie ran. She got as far as the kitchen, where Jimmy
and Joe attacked both women – Jimmy with the rifle, Joe with his
tomahawk. Then Jimmy turned on the toddler and used the butt
of the rifle to club him to death.

The brothers then ransacked the house, taking the time to write a note to Michael O'Brien (You dog, I shoot you also). The appallingly injured Catherine Bennett climbed through the kitchen window. Some distance away, Michael was approaching with a cartload of wood. She managed to reach him, turning him away to get help.

There was in fact, a large contingent of police just a kilometre away. They'd been tracking the Governors from Henry Neville's place and had found their horses. Ignorant of the tragedy unfolding nearby, the police were waiting in ambush for the Governors to return. The Governors didn't reappear. Circling around, to return to their mounts from behind, they'd picked up the tracks of the police and promptly left the scene on foot. Meanwhile, the police continued to wait. Lizzie and her unborn child and young James O'Brien were already dead, but Catherine Bennett lay in the open for the next six hours, fighting for life until the help that would save her finally arrived.

In the wake of the O'Brien killings, terror gripped the district. Most of the homesteads and bush shacks outside the towns were abandoned. The countryside was deserted but for the armed patrols hunting the Governors. A reward of £200 was offered for the capture of the Governors and a team of bloodhounds was sent from Mudgee. Yet the initiative seemed to be with Jimmy and Joe. Their bush skills and knowledge of the country gave them a distinct advantage over almost everyone who was chasing them. They were at ease with the remote landscape, using it to avoid their pursuers. Rather than behaving like fugitives they were moving through the country, working through their hit list. The hunted were more like the hunters.

Despite the thousand or more volunteers and over a hundred

police surrounding the Poggi area, Jimmy and Joe slipped through. Travelling on foot, they reappeared two days later at the home of Thomas Hughes, about fifteen kilometres south of Poggi. Hughes had cleared out quickly, leaving a Winchester rifle and plenty of ammunition for the Governors to take.

Rearmed, their next stop was the home of Keiran Fitzpatrick (a former employer Jimmy suspected of poisoning his dogs), north of Wollar. Seventy-four-year-old Fitzpatrick and his 23-year-old nephew Bernard were moving about the property, armed. The Governors waited until Bernard left at around ten in the morning, then the brothers approached the property, calling for Keiran. He appeared at the door of his cottage, rifle in hand. Joe shot him, then Jimmy grabbed an axe left lying nearby and finished off the old man with two blows.

Bernard Fitzpatrick heard the shot and returned to find his uncle slain and the Governors ransacking the property. They had two Winchester repeating rifles; nevertheless, Bernard fired at them before fleeing to get help. When it came, in the form of a posse of volunteers, the trampling of men and horses destroyed all trace of the Governors' tracks.

On Saturday, 28 July, Jack Underwood turned up at a farm of a man named William Shaw and asked for food. While he was eating, Shaw's wife got help from her neighbours, who seized Jack and led him away to the police at nearby Leadville. Underwood added more names to the list of those who Jimmy was intent on visiting, including Ethel's father at Dubbo. He believed Jimmy would head to Digilah, a property just north of Dunedoo. Underwood said his intention was to murder everyone there.

In fact the brothers were heading west, returning to their friend Charlie Wade north of Gulgong, who again took the desperate men in. They stayed the Saturday night and then went to pay their old neighbour, hawker Gee Li, a visit. Like many who believed themselves to be a target of the Governors' wrath, Gee Li had sought safety in town. He returned on the Monday to find his hut ransacked. The following day the Governors were sighted west of Gulgong and, evading search parties converging from Gulgong and from the west, they slipped away again. One party got to within 350 metres of them, but went for reinforcements rather than give chase.

During the following week the pair moved west, then north and back to the east, easily avoiding the patrols searching for them. By Friday, 3 August, they were just north of Charlie Wade's place, at the home of Joe Davis. Jimmy later said that his wife Ethel thought Davis and his wife were bad people and that he should shoot them. Davis wasn't there.

The Governors now set off north at a cracking pace. The police didn't so much track them as follow their route from robbed property to robbed property. The police had been told of several potential targets, but rather than stake-out these properties they chose to cast their net over the entire district. The tactics of the police officer in charge of the hunt, Superintendent Thomas Garvin, were soon the subject of criticism by the newspapers in the districts affected.

Under the circumstances it was little wonder the Governors grew contemptuous of the police efforts. They would read about their exploits in newspapers they picked up along the way. On Wednesday, 8 August, near Tambar Springs east of Coonabarabran,

they brazenly bailed up a man and gave him two written messages for the police that, using vulgarities and insults, decried the
prejudice they'd been subjected to. The messages declared: 'Now
I bushranger', and warned that 'If I get a shot at J. Dowland he not
only crack shot he sees first get to hell.'

The Queensland government offered the New South Wales
police the assistance of its highly skilled trackers. Just before they
arrived on 17 August the pursuit almost caught up with Jimmy
and Joe. The fugitives had continued north from Tambar Springs,
moving quickly across the open rolling plains towards Narrabri,
where a former employer of Joe's, Andrew Doyle, had a property.
Doyle had given Joe a beating for kicking a cow. The police following their tracks caught sight of them near the Namoi River, twenty
kilometres south of Narrabri. A constable called out and they fled,
the policeman firing as they went. A civilian tried to fire as well,
but only managed to load his rifle with the wrong cartridge, causing it to jam.

The trail of robberies and hold-ups turned back south, to what
is now known as Governor Knob, east of Coonabarabran. The
brothers were seen by a police search party who started climbing
the Knob to get a better view. As they did so, a single shot rang out
followed by some colourful opinions about the police and their
abilities. The search party scoured the bush finding nothing, but
when they returned to their horses they were shot at six more times
and sent packing. The police were supposed to be ambushing the
Governors. Instead, the Governors were ambushing them.

The crime spree continued south-east then east to the locality
of Bundella in the Liverpool Range. On the night of Wednesday,

22 August, a month after the Governors started their crimes at Breelong, the police were waiting in ambush at the house of another of their targets, in the Liverpool Range. Unnoticed by the police, the Governors had crept up to the house and fired six shots into it. The police started shooting at the muzzle flash, alerting the Governors to their presence. Jimmy and Joe stole away into the night.

The police guessed correctly that the next home in danger was that of nearby Ambrose Rawlinson. A police search party went there and warned Rawlinson to leave, which he did. Then, quite bizarrely, the police moved ten kilometres away to a place where they could get hot food and comfortable beds. That night, Jimmy and Joe burned Rawlinson's house to the ground.

The crimes continued in the area the next day, the New South Wales police showing the same reluctance to pursue the Governors as the Victorian police had done with the Kellys. Many officers faced armed and dangerous criminals almost daily in the course of their duty, but away from their desks their superiors were reluctant to confront the brothers, especially at night. Thus unhindered the pair continued south until they reached the Krui River, north-west of Merriwa, then they followed it north-east towards Oxley's Peak. Towards the end of August they moved through the mountainous country between Murrurundi and Quirindi, arousing suspicions that they might be heading for the coast. Along the way they robbed the home of Henry Hall, brother of the bushranger Ben Hall.

On 2 September, the chase should have ended when four civilians came upon the brothers without being noticed. Armed with only one weapon they crept closer and called on the Governors to surrender. Instead, Jimmy and Joe grabbed their rifles and returned fire as they fled.

Jimmy continued writing letters to the police. They were addressed 'From the Breelong Murderers'. In one letter he promised to turn himself in if his wife Ethel was released and allowed to come alone to meet him. The offer wasn't taken up, even though it was probably the best chance the police had of catching him. Throughout September the pair remained at large, causing a large area of rural New South Wales – from the coast north of Newcastle to Dubbo – to be depopulated. It was simply too dangerous to stay on the land, as the Governors moved freely and struck somewhere nearly every day. The Europeans fled to the towns, surrendering the bush to the Governors.

The feelings of fear and hatred towards the Governors spilt over and affected attitudes towards all Aboriginal people. The consequences for them throughout the rural districts were drastic. Many were taken into police custody without charge. A group of Aboriginal men from Wollar, including Jimmy and Joe's brother Jack Governor, were first held in the police cells then taken to the prison at Mudgee, where they were held indefinitely on charges of vagrancy. This despite the fact that some of them had been threatened by Jimmy, which he never acted on.

The atmosphere throughout the countryside was tense. Livestock, wallabies and kangaroos moving around properties at night were shot by accident. Police who camped unannounced in a hut might wake the next morning to find themselves surrounded by armed locals. One night, a policeman moving about in the dead of night was set upon by his colleagues; when a black tracker got up to see what the commotion was about, he was nearly shot.

The scale of the Governor hunt continued to grow. By mid-September there were 2000 volunteers and 200 police involved. The Governors themselves had committed an estimated eighty crimes – more than one a day. They'd killed nine people (ten counting Elizabeth O'Brien's unborn child) and injured three others, robbed and burned down houses, held up numerous travellers, property owners and workers, and exchanged gunfire with several police and civilians. They'd cost the government of New South Wales thousands of pounds and the local economy even more in lost production.

On Saturday, 22 September, Jimmy added a new and shocking crime to his list. In a lonely location at Cobark Creek, he raped fifteen-year-old Isabella Maud Burley. The same night police almost caught the Governors at a nearby hut. As they approached there was a gunshot. The police rushed the place but the Governors had once again melted into the bush. The rape of Isabella Burley spurred the New South Wales government to further action. The reward for the capture of the Governors was increased to £1000 each; a decree was also issued calling on the Governors to surrender themselves at Maitland Jail. If they didn't do so by 16 October, they would be outlawed, meaning they could be shot on sight.

None of it made any difference. If anything it made the Governors bolder. They continued on a meandering route (possibly with a notion of heading up the coast to Queensland), passing Wingham and Taree and on 10 October holding up a house on the Doyle River in the Hastings Valley. An old man was boarding the windows against the Governors when he felt a tap on his shoulder. It was Jimmy, who proceeded to make off with all the food he could carry.

Two days later police staked out a hut on the Hastings River west of Port Macquarie, having finally realised that waiting in ambush was their best chance of catching men who could outpace and outsmart even the Queensland trackers. Inside were Constable Richard Harris and tracker Jimmy Landsborough. Other police were stationed outside. None, however, were keeping watch. Harris was reading a newspaper and heard a noise; as he got up to investigate he was shot in the hip by Jimmy. He and Joe had pulled a couple of slabs off the back of the hut and crept inside. Both men then fled, Harris firing at them from the door despite his wound, Landsborough firing from outside the hut having jumped from a window. The Governors returned fire as they retreated from the scene.

The Governors got a reality check the next day. Police were waiting in ambush at a property twenty-five kilometres north of Port Macquarie on the Forbes River. Three civilians – Bert Byers (as previously mentioned, a Governor target who'd already joined the hunt when Jimmy had called at his home), Robert Woods and a man named Scrivener – keeping watch from one of the houses on the property saw the Governors approach. When they were 250 metres away Byers thought he could hit one of them but Woods said they should wait. Over a period of four hours the wary Governors edged closer, always keeping to cover wherever possible. Then, suddenly alarmed, they fled. At a range of 100 metres, though, Jimmy turned. Through cracks in the wall of the building, Byers and Woods fired. Byers' shot hit Jimmy in the face, slicing through his cheek and knocking out five teeth. Woods hit Jimmy in the buttocks. The men in the hut didn't give a moment's thought to waiting until 16 October, when they could legally shoot the Governors on sight.

Jimmy went down and all three men rushed out to pursue. Joe started to fire at them, and they fired back. Joe was shouting to Jimmy to move. Finally he got up and, though he fell twice, kept running. Scrivener, Woods and Byers followed for half a kilometre until it got dark and they could no longer see the trail.

Next morning a huge contingent of police, trackers and volunteers arrived; not even they could obliterate the trail of blood that led from the scene. It was thought Jimmy would soon be captured as the amount of blood suggested he couldn't get far. Two kilometres from the shooting they found a waterhole stained with blood where Jimmy had washed. Also found were a quart and a pint pot, dropped by Jimmy as he tended his wounds.

Two days later, 16 October, the deadline for the Governors to surrender or be made outlaws came and went. A change in policy alone could not tame the outlaws. It was no surprise that the Governors were nowhere to be seen at Maitland. Instead, they were on the Forbes River again, sixteen kilometres downstream from where Byers and Woods had shot Jimmy. On another property they took nineteen-year-old William Coombes prisoner, right from under the noses of an ambush party. They took him to his uncle's house and made him promise to bring them back some food. Inside the house William was met by a police constable and a group of volunteers. He wasn't permitted to leave. By then it was dark but the constable, to his credit, ventured out to look for the Governors. He found nothing.

The young Coombes reported that the gunshot to Jimmy's mouth had torn his bottom lip and tongue. He was extremely weak, but had bandaged his wounds as best he could with rags torn from his shirt. The observant young man also noted that while both men had Winchester rifles, they appeared to have little or no ammunition.

The next day on the Hastings River a few kilometres away, George Branston spotted the brothers by the river. They called him over and told him that if he gave them rations they'd leave the district for good. Branston agreed and went up to his house where a policeman and a tracker had been assigned. The policeman slipped out and ran two kilometres to alert a police contingent, while Mrs Branston made up a food package and put it on the verandah for the Governors.

Yet again, timorousness informed the police response. They refused to go to the Branston house. Undaunted, the policeman and a tracker returned just as the brothers were crossing the river. At a range of ninety metres the policeman opened fire. Joe had already made it to the bank, but Jimmy was still in the water when a shot kicked up the water in front of him and he beat a hasty retreat. The Hastings River now lay between the two brothers, with a policeman and tracker hot on their heels. Forced to escape separately, they never saw each other again.

Jimmy's situation was all but hopeless. Seriously wounded, barely able to eat, he made his way a short distance south to the area around Bobin. Beehives there were found disturbed. Then, on 19 October, John Wallace and William Cant were working in Wallace's paddocks when they knocked off for a morning smoko only to discover their food, a billy can and a coat had been stolen. They noted one set of footprints and blood.

The same day Joe was spotted not far from Bobin scrounging in a campsite at dusk. Three days later he was seen well to the south, near Gloucester, heading back towards the ranges around Gulgong, the country he knew best.

For the next week, Jimmy stayed in the vicinity of Bobin, too weak to travel far, living on fruit and honey that was probably all he could get past his mutilated teeth and tongue. He returned to John Wallace's property where he managed to get hold of Wallace's food once again. At 3 p.m., when Wallace noticed his dinner had been stolen, he got on his horse and galloped for home.

Or so it appeared. In fact, Wallace returned to his camp just across the creek and hid, hoping to catch a glimpse of who was stealing his food. Near dusk he saw a single Aboriginal approach one of two fires Wallace had made in the paddock near his beehives. Whoever it was looked like he intended to camp there so Wallace slipped away to round up some mates. By 1 a.m. eight men, all civilians, had assembled at the property of Thomas Moore – his relatives Fred, Old Thomas and William, Wallace and locals Tom Green, Alex Cameron and John McPherson, plus Thomas himself. They sketched the site, planned where they would gather, worked out how to avoid crossfire if shooting broke out, then set off into the night.

The paddock lay on the south side of Bobin Creek, with a fence running down its eastern side just over 100 metres from the bee-hives and the larger of the two fires. Bill Moore, Alex Cameron and John McPherson positioned themselves along the fence line; Thomas and Fred Moore positioned themselves to the south of the tree; and Old Thomas and Tom Green to the west. John Wallace took up a position on the north side of Bobin Creek. Whoever was in the paddock, they had him surrounded.

Close to dawn the figure stood up, not more than twenty metres from where Tom Green lay in hiding. He was right at the edge of the group that had attempted to surround him. Green shouted to the figure to surrender. Instead, Jimmy grabbed his rifle and fled past Green, angling towards the creek. Green fired, then from the other side of the creek Wallace opened fire as well. The figure kept going, passing between both men. He dashed across the creek bed and scrambled up the steep bank into the thick ferns growing on that side, all the time being fired upon by an increasing number of men. Tom Green was sure that one blast from his shotgun struck the man at fifty metres.

The men crossed the creek in hot pursuit. Fighting his way through the thick scrub Jimmy struggled to stay ahead, then after just fifty metres he dropped, exhausted. His pursuers were upon him; the chase was over. In the faint light the men had to light matches to see that they had caught Jimmy Governor.

Three months and six days had passed since the killings at Breelong. Jimmy had covered over 3000 kilometres in a remarkable display of bushmanship, which might have been admirable if it hadn't been punctuated by violent and merciless crimes along the way.

Four days later Joe Governor's luck also ran out. Grazier John Wilkinson was returning to his property at Carrow Brook, north of Singleton, when he noticed a fire burning in one of his paddocks. Thinking it odd he continued on to his house where he found his brother George. The Wilkinsons, with only one rifle between them, made their way to a nearby hilltop from where they could see the fire. When they saw it flare they became more certain that someone must be stoking it.

In the hours before dawn on 31 October they closed in on the fire until they were just fifty metres away. Joe Governor was so deep in sleep that he noticed nothing until he was called upon to surrender. According to the Wilkinsons, he tried to reach for his rifle. John fired, the bullet passing close enough to Joe's head that it stunned him. A second shot misfired, so John tried to use his weapon as a club. Joe avoided the blow and tried to make a run for it without his weapon. Wilkinson reloaded and with brother George, who now had Joe's Winchester, they gave chase, firing as they went. Then from a range of 280 metres John Wilkinson fired a shot that hit Joe in the back of the head, exiting above his right eye. The range may have grown in the telling but it has also been suggested it was a complete fabrication, and that Joe was fatally shot at close range, either as he slept or shortly after waking.

The trial of Jimmy Governor began in Sydney on 19 November 1900. Jack Underwood had already been found guilty for his part in the killings at Breelong and had been sentenced to hang. Jimmy's wife Ethel had been released, as had old Jack Porter and young Peter Governor. At Jimmy's trial the racism he had endured from Sarah Mawbey and Ellen Kerz, Alexander McKay and Michael O'Brien – in particular, the words of Ellen Kerz – was put forward as the motive for his actions. According to Jimmy's barrister, F. S. Boyce: ' . . . They were the Turning point. When those words were spoken to him the sudden passion rose and that was the last of self control.' John Mawbey maintained that it was all news to him. Shortly after the Breelong killings Mawbey had said he thought there might have been tensions between Jimmy and his brother over Ethel, and that Jimmy had long talked about becoming a bushranger and perhaps had decided to act out the heroic lifestyles he'd read about when working as a tracker for the police. However, that scenario fell well short of explaining the frenzied attack.

The idea of a black man wanting to be treated as an equal was almost impossible to grasp in a country that had embraced a white Australia policy. However, the murderous rampage and three-month manhunt for the Governors gave impetus to a shift in government policy – for the worse. Herding Aboriginal people onto reserves continued, in a process that came to be known as 'softening the dying pillow'. The idea was that Aboriginal people were a dying race but that a humane society should make the process of extinction less painful while keeping the wider community safe from those who dared resist. Full-blood Aboriginals were considered savages beyond redemption but many part-Aboriginal children were taken from their parents so they could be 'raised white'. The social havoc caused by the creation of what became known as the stolen generations subsequently spanned the twentieth century and the consequences continue into the twenty-first. Trying to raise children 'white' wasn't enough, as the Governor brothers had discovered. Many people couldn't see past the colour of their skin.

When Jimmy was found guilty, like Jack Underwood, he was sentenced to hang. Both sentences were delayed until after the celebrations marking the Federation of the Commonwealth of Australia on 1 January 1901. Jack was executed on 14 January, asking naively as he went to the scaffold if he would be in heaven in time for dinner. Jimmy Governor met his date with the hangman on 18 January 1901.

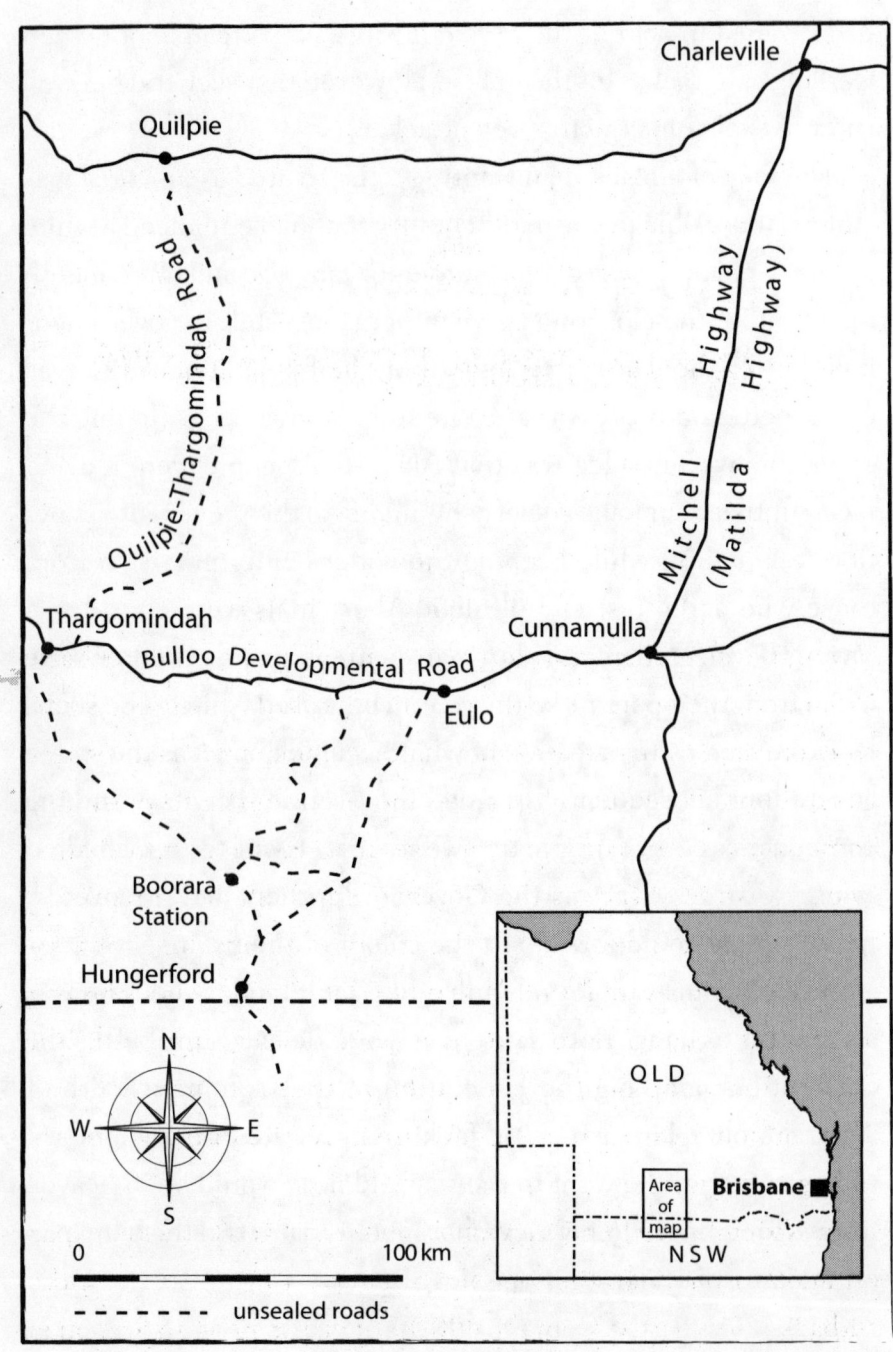

Charleville

Quilpie

Quilpie-Thargomindah Road

Mitchell Highway (Matilda Highway)

Thargomindah

Bulloo Developmental Road

Cunnamulla

Eulo

Boorara
Station

Hungerford

N
W — E
S

0   100 km

- - - - - - unsealed roads

QLD

Area
of
map

Brisbane

N S W

5

BURY ME DEEP DOWN BELOW

Throughout history, people have disappeared in the outback without trace, never to be seen again. Explorers staggered into oblivion; station hands got lost or injured and perished; prospectors discovered treasures, lost them and then vanished themselves. Sometimes the explanation for a disappearance is mundane – stockmen tired of the rough, hot and dusty work, long to quench their thirst in the nearest pub, which may be hundreds of kilometres away. They might walk off without telling anyone, popping up months or even years later as if nothing had happened. But until they do, the doubts remain. Have they met with an accident, or something worse? Unfortunately, the outback guards such secrets well.

In November 1940, 65-year-old labourer William Groves became yet another name on the long list of people to go missing in the outback – in his case, from the 400 000-hectare Boorara Station in the far south-west of Queensland. He was a likeable bloke known as Old Bill, but he may have had good cause to leave.

He'd been drilling water bores around the property for some years in sparsely treed, stony 'gibber country', enduring shadeless heat, constant dust and relentless flies in remote locations far from the comforts of the homestead (such as they were). He and his boss, sixty-year-old drilling contractor James Callaghan, spent weeks at a time with only each other for company in their isolated and often desolate camps. They slept under canvas, cooked on open fires fuelled by branches of the hardy mulga scrub, went to bed when the sun went down and rose with first light. In between they worked at the drilling or did maintenance on the equipment. The only break in the monotony was when they returned to the homestead for supplies every couple of weeks or headed for the nearest flyspeck outback towns, Hungerford (fifty kilometres south) or Eulo (120 kilometres to the north-east), to savour the pleasures of a pub – a shady verandah and cold beer.

Neither was married (though Callaghan had been through a messy divorce some years before) and they had no one to speak of in the way of family. Old Bill had worked for Callaghan for three years, but lately their relationship had begun to sour.

Callaghan had been drilling for close to forty years, in New South Wales and Queensland. Considering his business, he should have been doing well, since the pay went a long way towards compensating for the harsh conditions. However, the only thing deeper than the water bores Old Bill and James Callaghan were drilling around the sprawling outback station was the financial hole Callaghan was in. It just kept getting bigger. Callaghan owed Boorara Station money, as well as businesses in Cunnamulla and Charleville. From the comfort of Brisbane, 900 kilometres away, the source of most of his troubles, his former wife, was suing him for maintenance, having long since left him to the hot, rough and lonely outback life. Beset by financial worries, Callaghan was growing increasingly temperamental.

Callaghan also owed his employee money. Old Bill may have been a kind-hearted type but he eventually had no choice but to call in his Australian Worker's Union representative for help in getting his wages. By early November 1940, Callaghan owed him two years' pay. Old Bill met with union rep Tom Holloway at Boorara Homestead to discuss the details of his complaint. Calling in the union rep didn't go down well with Callaghan. Holloway was present the next morning when Callaghan confronted his employee. Old Bill was fit and strong for his years but, as Callaghan advanced snarling, he was clearly intimidated by his bigger, stronger and heavier boss. According to Holloway, '[Old Bill] became very agitated and went pale . . . Groves' face indicated that he was afraid of Callaghan.'

Afterwards, Holloway asked Old Bill if he was returning to work with Callaghan on the Glencoe Bore, their current drilling location in one of the remote corners of the station many kilometres from the homestead.

'No, the old bastard is mad,' Old Bill replied. 'He's always trying to quarrel with me. I wouldn't trust him. He might do you in.'

Nevertheless, that's just what Old Bill did. All he'd got from Callaghan was promises rather than wages, but on 7 November they loaded up their truck and drove back to their lonely campsite. After Old Bill got there, though, it appeared he'd had a change of heart. A few days later, Boorara's overseer, Jim Cotter, was in the area checking on stock when he dropped in at the borehead and noticed Old Bill wasn't there.

'He went off to Charleville [400 kilometres north-east] in a truck with a couple of blokes he knew,' Callaghan explained to Cotter. 'I don't expect him back until after Christmas.'

Cotter wasn't entirely surprised. Why do such back-breaking work for nothing, especially as the furious heat of summer was growing every day? And James Callaghan's reputation as a difficult man to get along with made Old Bill's decision even more understandable.

While Old Bill may have been a crusty old bachelor with no family, he was well known and liked around Boorara, and well versed in the courtesies people paid each other in the outback. Cotter thought that he might well have told Callaghan where he could shove his job, but he wasn't the kind of bloke who'd leave without saying goodbye to his mates. Over the ensuing days, as the sun baked the wide open plains of Boorara Station, there was no word from Old Bill or sign of him anywhere. After a week, the only thing that filled the void left by his disappearance was a growing concern for the missing man's safety.

By 21 November, Boorara's manager, Arthur Seale, the man responsible for the property's employees, was sufficiently worried that he spoke to Constable Doyle at Eulo, north-east of Boorara.

'Old Bill has never wandered off before,' Seale explained.

Doyle was happy to lay any fears to rest. He contacted Constable Lewis at Charleville and asked him to check around Old Bill's haunts. Lewis also called Constable Weller at Hungerford, a town on the Queensland/New South Wales border that was closest to the Glencoe Bore (which in outback terms meant it was only fifty kilometres away). While Lewis checked around Charleville for any sign of Old Bill, Weller drove out on the rough, dusty station tracks to try to see if he could get any more information from James Callaghan.

Callaghan might have been surprised to get a visit from a policeman at such an isolated location, but he did everything he could to assist Constable Weller with his inquiries. Once again, Callaghan said Old Bill had left with two men in a utility truck two weeks before, adding that he'd managed to scrape together the money he owed him, £160 in backpay. That explained why Old Bill might have taken the opportunity to be rid of an employer who he didn't get along with. It also presented the possibility that his companions might have been tempted by all that cash on the long drive to Charleville. Fortunately, Callaghan was able to give Weller a detailed description of the two men – one named Jack Gordon, the other just named Tom – including their mannerisms and style of speech. He was just as detailed when it came to their truck.

The information should have been enough to track down Old Bill, or the other men, even in the wide open spaces of the outback. Constables Lewis in Charleville, Doyle in Eulo and Weller in Hungerford made extensive inquiries throughout south-western Queensland but came up with a complete blank. It was as if Old Bill had disappeared from the face of the earth.

Constable Weller went back to see the last person known to have seen Old Bill alive: Callaghan. This time he searched the campsite. He found some of Old Bill's belongings, among them the kinds of things one wouldn't normally abandon. There was a diamond ring with five stones in it and a wrist watch. Old Bill had even left his glasses behind. Weller also took possession of Callaghan's rifle, which looked like it had been thoroughly cleaned quite recently. When he returned to Hungerford he wrote up his report and forwarded it to the Brisbane headquarters of the Queensland Police Department, with a request for assistance from the Criminal Investigation Branch in the search of Old Bill Groves.

Four CIB officers were despatched from Brisbane to carry out the investigation – Sub Inspector Smith, Detective Sergeant Frank Bischof, Detective Constable Jack Mahoney and Constable Krieger. Just getting to Boorara involved three long hard days of travel. They covered some of the distance on passenger and goods trains, but for the last 400 kilometres they were driven by local police on bone-jarring rough dirt tracks. By the time they arrived at Boorara, on 30 November, they had an appreciation of the daunting logistics that would be involved in any search for Old Bill. The next morning Bischof and Mahoney went to see James Callaghan out at the Glencoe Bore.

'I've told the police all I know about it,' Callaghan said, 'and all I can tell you is that Groves left with those two men going to Charleville.'

He repeated the story he'd told Constable Weller, adding, 'I liked Old Bill, he didn't disappear to get on the booze like other men. He only decided to leave because he was suffering stomach pains.'

Did Callaghan know the men he'd left with?

'Jack Gordon and a bloke I only knew as Tom.'

What about the money Callaghan owed Old Bill?

'Before he left we talked about wages. I worked it out at £160 and gave it to him.'

Where did Callaghan get the money?

'I sold a boring plant.'

Who to?

'A man named Bill Gordon. After paying Old Bill, I've got about a pound to my name and another boring plant that isn't worth much.'

What about the union rep's story about Old Bill being afraid of him?

'Those union bastards would tell you anything to get a man hanged.'

Callaghan may have sounded sure of his story when he'd first told it to the local police, but it was clear that the two detectives were anything but convinced. Without a scrap of hard evidence to accuse him with, only their suspicions, they might have secretly thought that the case was a likely dead-ender – lots of hard work for no result. However, Bischof was one of the CIB's rising young stars and Mahoney was on his way to becoming a top investigator, and they weren't going to let the outback defeat them without a fight. Instead, they contemplated the 400 000 sun-scorched hectares of Boorara (and the millions more that lay between the station and Charleville), knowing that, if their suspicions were justified, the answer was out there somewhere.

'Mr Callaghan,' Bischof said, 'we intend to conduct a thorough search of Boorara Station.'

Callaghan only shrugged and stuck to his story. 'I know you fellows think I've done something to Old Bill, but you'll find him either in Charleville or Cunnamulla.'

The police search of Booràra was just one of several leads they pursued with equal vigour. To verify Callaghan's story they needed to track down Jack Gordon, 'Tom' and the newly mentioned Bill Gordon. Any one of them could shed further light on Callaghan's version of events and perhaps provide a lead on the whereabouts of Old Bill. But despite Callaghan's information and the best efforts of the police, their inquiries came up as empty as their quest for Old Bill. The more the police searched, the more probable it became that the three men didn't exist. Consequently, the suspicions about Callaghan continued to grow.

Nevertheless, if he had done anything to Old Bill, the outback was on Callaghan's side. There was absolutely no chance of any eyewitnesses, and his body could have been concealed in any one of a million locations so that the chances of finding it were practically nil.

All the attention must have been novel for the boring contractor. He rarely saw another human being but was now surrounded by a small tent city, set up for the police search parties led by detectives Bischof and Mahoney. Day after day, on horseback and on foot, the police scoured the immense property, examining where fires had been lit and any ground that appeared to have been disturbed. They endured temperatures that rose to forty-six degrees Celsius in the shade. It hadn't rained at Boorara for two years but that didn't bother the flies that pursued the police relentlessly. Whirlwinds uprooted the tents. Everything was covered in dust. If it turned out that Old Bill had just upped and left, they certainly wouldn't have blamed him.

Yet their efforts yielded nothing. The only consolation was that the longer the search went on, the more nervous James Callaghan became. Everyone was sweating from the heat, but Callaghan was sweating most of all.

On 3 December, Callaghan sought out Bischof and Mahoney at their tent.

'I'm fucked if I know what to do about this,' he said. 'I can see now that my story has more holes in it than a sieve, and I'm trying to think of a way out. It's a serious business. The first barrel misfired and the second has got to be word perfect.'

It was a strange thing to say, but the detectives didn't interrupt. They let the boring contractor keep digging himself deeper into a hole.

'You fellows are only wasting your time riding and walking about. You won't find Old Bill. I know you fellows think I killed Old Bill. I have thought out about three or four stories which I thought might be all right. I even put myself in the witness box and cross-examined myself and fucked myself every time.'

It may not have been a confession but it wasn't far from it. Bischof's response was to tell Callaghan he was a suspect in the disappearance of Old Bill and to inform him of his rights.

'You need not be frightened of me running away,' Callaghan replied. 'That would only make the thing worse.'

He was right there. Not only would it be an admission of guilt, but – in the wide open spaces of Boorara – there was virtually nowhere he could run to.

Investigation into 'the thing' continued for the next two days without finding anything. Yet the police remained convinced that Callaghan had something (or someone) to hide. The search parties went back and checked every potential site again. Rather than simply rake through the coals of old fires, they started sieving the ashes.

That's when they found a button. It was in an old fire just thirty metres from James Callaghan's tent. He'd really meant it when he told Bischof and Mahoney they were 'wasting their time riding and walking about'. They should have been concentrating on Callaghan's camp.

Bischof and his men continued sieving and turned up several more buttons, as well as other burnt items of clothing and a flat piece of steel. Their discoveries shrank the search area considerably – it was no longer the whole of the outback, it was just the immediate vicinity of the Glencoe Bore. They scoured the campsite but couldn't find a single remnant of Old Bill himself. Whatever had happened, James Callaghan certainly wasn't telling, so there was still a chance that, if they didn't find Old Bill, he could walk free. No body. No crime. Callaghan had to hope the outback could keep his secret.

Then it occurred to Bischof that there was one place they hadn't looked.

'I want to use your sand pump to bring up whatever might be at the bottom of the Glencoe Bore,' Bischof said.

Callaghan was shocked. 'You don't think I'd put him in my drinking water and the water that you fellows have been using?' he protested.

It was a sickening prospect but Bischof suspected he might be onto something when Callaghan started making excuses.

'You've no chance of starting the engine,' he said. 'It hasn't been going for weeks. It's out of order.'

'If you won't work the pump, we'll get someone else out here who will,' Bischof replied.

Callaghan reluctantly agreed. However, before the pump could be used, the boring tools had to be lifted from the shaft. Callaghan started lifting them, then let them drop. When he did it a second time, potentially pulverising what lay below, Bischof challenged him.

Chastened, Callaghan lifted the boring tools properly. Then the sand pump was lowered. In the process, it became obvious that the bore was nothing like the 275-metre depth it was supposed to be – for which Callaghan had been paid thirty shillings a metre. It was more like 135 metres.

'I backfilled the bore for about 100 metres after striking an obstruction I couldn't get through,' Callaghan explained. 'I then drilled past it from higher up.'

The Glencoe Bore held more water than that story, and Bischof knew it.

'All right,' Callaghan eventually admitted. 'I falsified my returns to get more money.'

As it happened, he'd merely confirmed suspicions that Boorara's management had held for some time. In fact they'd asked Old Bill about it, but he'd been too afraid of Callaghan. Old Bill had replied, 'I would sooner not discuss it with you. If old Jim knows I told you anything about the bore he'll kill me.'

For Callaghan, every turn of the boring equipment was another turn of the screw. As the sand pump sank deeper into the shaft he continued to mishandle the equipment. When he didn't lower the pump quickly enough for it to open at the bottom of the shaft,

Bischof warned him again. Finally, he lowered the pump correctly and the first load of sand was brought up.

After days spent searching for Old Bill, Bischof couldn't wait to see what the sieves revealed. As the sand pump was emptying he reached into the flow and caught a handful of debris, peering closely at what was buried at the bottom of the Glencoe Bore. There, among the sand and chips of broken rock, he saw tiny fragments of bone.

James Callaghan had had the entire outback at his disposal when it came to getting rid of the body of Old Bill. Instead, he'd set some kind of record by burying him 135 metres down in the Glencoe Bore. In dumping the remains in his own water supply, he'd engaged in a somewhat diluted form of cannibalism. If he'd chosen another bore, far from his own camp, he might have got away with it, but the long arm of the law (135 metres long in this case) had caught up with him at last.

As the police sieved the sand, turning up more bone and pieces of charcoal, Callaghan walked away from the boring equipment. Bischof followed.

'Well, that's the end of it,' Callaghan said. 'Those are Old Bill's bones in the bore hole. I killed him, but I'm no murderer.'

Callaghan might have spent the previous couple of days concocting a new version of Old Bill's death that he'd hoped would cast things in a better light. As reported from his trial in the *Courier-Mail* of 8 January 1941, he admitted to Bischof that:

Old Bill and I got back here about three o'clock on the afternoon of November 7. Next day Bill put water into the truck's tank

Alexander Pearce was the sole survivor out of eight escapees from Tasmania's Macquarie Harbour penal settlement. This drawing was made by Thomas Bock after Pearce's execution in 1824 for cannibalism. *(Image: courtesy of Dixson Galleries, State Library of New South Wales)*

Henry Redford, ringleader of the duffing of 1000 head of cattle from Bowen Downs Station in Queensland in 1870. In the process he pioneered a new stock route to South Australia. *(Photo: courtesy of John Oxley Library, State Library of Queensland)*

Following Ned Kelly's capture at Glenrowan, he was rushed to Melbourne Gaol. This photo was taken the day before his execution in 1880. *(Photo: reproduced with the permission of the Keeper of Public Records, Public Record Office of Victoria)*

Joe Byrne, a member of the Kelly Gang, died at the siege at Glenrowan in Victoria in June 1880. Police put his body on public display by suspending it from a door of Benalla Gaol. *(Photo: courtesy of National Archives of Australia)*

The Kelly legend inspired numerous books, films and artworks. Sidney Nolan painted a famous series based on the Kelly story; this painting was simply titled *Kelly*. *(Image: Kelly by Sidney Nolan, 1946, enamel on board, 635 x 761 mm; collection: Nolan Gallery, Cultural Facilities Corporation, Canberra; photo: Rob Little)*

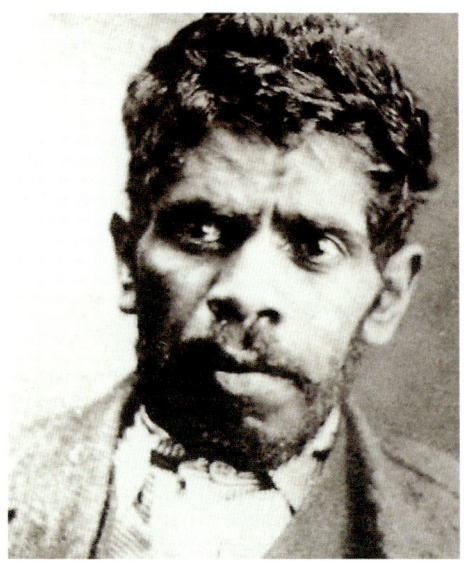

Jimmy Governor outsmarted and eluded the police for four months. He was eventually captured in October 1900 and executed in January 1901 for the Breelong massacre and other brutal crimes. *(Photo: courtesy of Shirley Trethowan)*

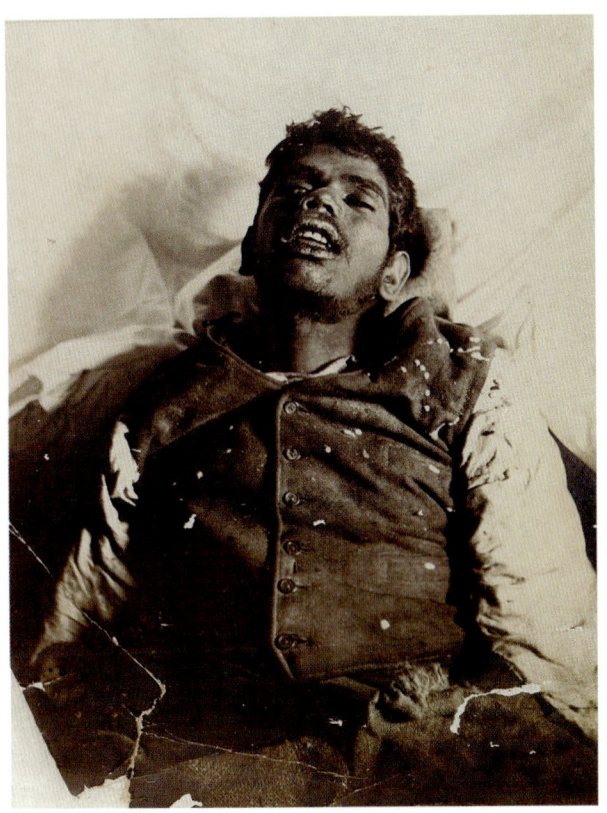

Joe Governor, separated from his brother Jimmy in their final days on the run from police, was shot dead near Singleton, New South Wales, in October 1900. *(Photo: courtesy of Dixson Library, State Library of New South Wales)*

Sarah and John Mawbey employed Jimmy Governor and his wife Ethel on Breelong Station. They were unaware of the dire consequences that their mistreatment of Jimmy was about to unleash. *(Photo: courtesy of Shirley Trethowan)*

The Breelong homestead, scene of the massacre of six women and children, which signalled the beginning of the Governor brothers' rampage throughout central New South Wales. *(Photo: courtesy of Shirley Trethowan)*

Schoolteacher Ellen Kerz worked at Breelong Station. Her racist taunts triggered the brutal attack at Breelong on 20 July 1900. *(Photo: courtesy of Shirley Trethowan)*

Itinerant worker 'Old Bill' Groves's disappearance in 1940 triggered a search that covered much of south-west Queensland. *(Photo: courtesy of John Oxley Library, State Library of Queensland)*

Outback boring contractor Jim Callaghan employed Bill Groves on Boorara Station. He became the number one suspect following Bill's disappearance. *(Photo: courtesy of John Oxley Library, State Library of Queensland)*

A bore in the harsh and isolated gibber country of Boorara Station circa 1935, similar to the one that Jim Callaghan and Old Bill were drilling in 1940. *(Photo: courtesy of Museum Victoria)*

This car was blown up outside the Angel Hostel in Kalgoorlie–Boulder in 1939. The bombing, one of several blasts in the twin towns around the same time, wasn't linked to miner Pero Raecivich, but it highlighted the potential danger resulting from the ready availability of gelignite. *(Photo: Peter Radanovich, courtesy of J. S. Battye Library of Western Australian History)*

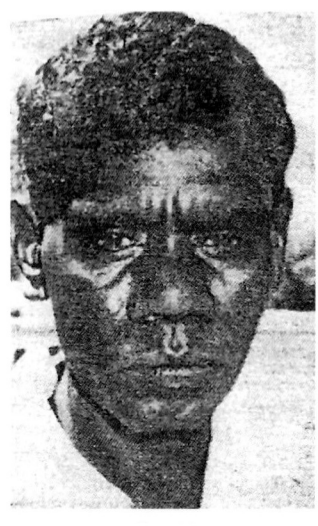

Larry Boy's murder of his wife instigated a manhunt in the Northern Territory that lasted forty days. It required helicopters and scores of police on foot, on horseback, on motorbike and in 4WDs to track him down. *(Photo: courtesy of Northern Territory News/ Newspix)*

Tracker Tony Mullagully (left) and Constable Bluey Harvey, whose extraordinary bush skills eventually cornered the elusive fugitive Larry Boy. *(Photo: courtesy of Northern Territory Police Museum and Historical Society)*

Stockman David Munroe (also referred to as Dave Hanson) and tracker Joey McDonald intended to patrol the roads around the Jungle in search of Larry Boy but, shortly after this photo was taken, McDonald's spurs destroyed the bike's rear wheel. *(Photo: courtesy of Northern Territory News/Newspix)*

Trackers in the open forest country in the ranges north of Elsey homestead following the trail, despite the long grass, left by the fallen leaves from a branch that Larry Boy was using to brush out his tracks. *(Photo: courtesy of Northern Territory Police Museum and Historical Society)*

Lindy Chamberlain with her baby daughter Azaria at Uluru in 1980. That night Azaria disappeared from her tent, sparking one of the most controversial cases in Australian criminal history. *(Photo: courtesy of Michael Chamberlain)*

The Chamberlain family's Torana parked beside the tent from which Azaria was taken by a dingo. The barbeque area where the family prepared the evening meal on the night of her disappearance is just twenty metres beyond the vehicle. *(Photo: courtesy of Michael Chamberlain)*

Soon after Azaria's disappearance, the Chamberlain family returned to Mount Isa, where Michael Chamberlain was a Seventh Day Adventist pastor. From left: Reagan, Lindy, Aidan and Michael. *(Photo: courtesy of Newspix)*

Throughout the three inquests, one trial, two appeals and a Royal Commission, the media's appetite for the Chamberlains was insatiable. *(Photo: courtesy of Newspix)*

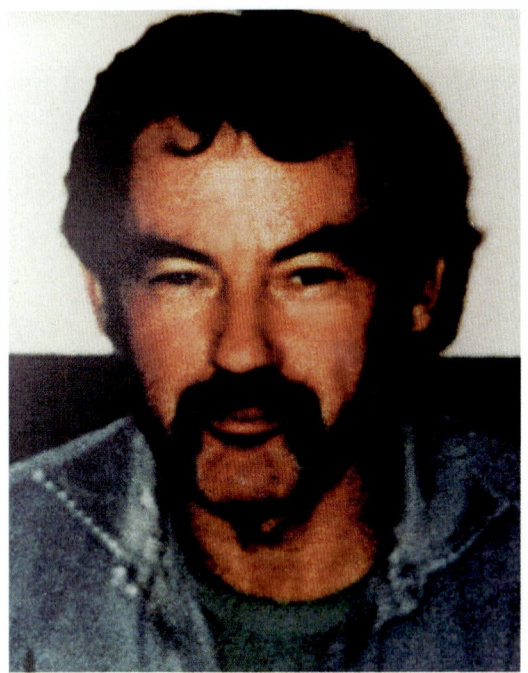

The face of evil. In 1996 Ivan Milat was convicted for the murders of seven young backpackers whom he'd picked up hitchhiking on the Hume Highway south of Sydney between 1989 and 1992. *(Photo: courtesy of Newspix)*

The isolated, dirt road leading into the Belanglo State Forest where the murders of the backpackers took place between 1989 and 1992. *(Photo: courtesy of Michelle Havenstein)*

Hundreds of police and volunteers searched the entire 22-square kilometres of the Belanglo State Forest, at times crawling through the scrub on hands and knees. *(Photo: courtesy of Newspix)*

THIS PLAQUE COMMEMORATES THE MEMORY OF THE FOLLOWING PERSONS
WHOSE REMAINS WERE FOUND IN THE BELANGLO FOREST DURING 1992 AND 1993

CAROLINE JANE CLARKE	UNITED KINGDOM
DEBORAH PHYLLIS EVERIST	AUSTRALIA
JAMES HAROLD GIBSON	AUSTRALIA
ANJA HABSCHIED	GERMANY
GABOR KURT NEUGEBAUER	GERMANY
SIMONE LORETTA SCHMIDL	GERMANY
JOANNE LESLEY WALTERS	UNITED KINGDOM

ACKNOWLEDGEMENT IS MADE OF THE EFFORTS OF MEMBERS OF THE NEW
SOUTH WALES POLICE SERVICE AND STATE EMERGENCY SERVICE IN EXTENSIVE
INVESTIGATIONS AND IN SEARCHES UNDERTAKEN IN THE ADJACENT AREAS

"NOTHING CAN SEPARATE US FROM THE LOVE OF GOD IN CHRIST JESUS OUR LORD"
Romans 8:39

UNVEILED BY
THE HONOURABLE JOHN FAHEY, M.P.
PREMIER OF NEW SOUTH WALES
AND MEMBER FOR SOUTHERN HIGHLANDS

5TH FEBRUARY, 1994

In the Belanglo State Forest a plaque commemorates the seven backpackers murdered and the police and state emergency service staff who searched the forest for their bodies. *(Photo: courtesy of Michelle Havenstein)*

Joanne Lees and Peter Falconio in their Kombi van before setting out from Sydney in 2001 on what should have been the road-trip of a lifetime. *(Photo: courtesy of Newspix)*

A lonely stretch of the Stuart Highway – south of the Devil's Marbles in the Northern Territory – where the attack on Joanne Lees and Peter Falconio took place. *(Photo: courtesy of Newspix)*

The 4WD vehicle thought to have been driven by the attacker of Joanne Lees and Peter Falconio was captured on video at a Shell Truckstop on the northern side of Alice Springs. The driver of that vehicle was also videoed at the Shell Truckstop. *(Photos: courtesy of Newspix)*

On one of the few occasions Joanne Lees gave a press conference, she provoked further negative press by wearing a singlet with Cheeky Monkey written across it.
(Photo: courtesy of Newspix)

Bradley John Murdoch is led from a South Australian court after being found not guilty in a rape case. He was immediately extradited to the Northern Territory to face trial for the murder of Peter Falconio. *(Photo: courtesy of Newspix)*

instead of benzine, and the truck would not go. After I found out what the trouble was we packed the tucker box and set out for Boodeheree Bore. After crossing the creek he let the clutch in suddenly and chewed off a key in the drive shaft. We came home and I started to make a new key on the bench near the camp. I told Bill that he could not drive a wheel barrow, and he made a hit at me with his left fist, and I hit him with my left fist. His head bumped the anvil above his left ear and he became unconscious. He lived for about twenty minutes.

I got panicky so I decided to get rid of his body. I built a fire at the back of the cooking galley and I burnt him. I put Old Bill on a heap of mulga about three or four feet [one metre] high. I started the fire about ten o'clock that night and at three o'clock next morning he was burnt practically to nothing. There is a hell of a heat in mulga and the bones were well and truly burnt. I cracked some by walking on them with my boots. I dumped some water on the coals and collected the bones at sunrise, and dropped them down the bore hole. I poured kerosene on the coals and what was left of some of the burnt bones and let them burn to powder. A severe dust storm blew everything away.

After that I burnt charcoal on two occasions where the fire was. Bill was wearing a pair of overalls and old slippers when I burnt him. I raked the buttons and other things from the fire, and put them in another fire. I was still panicky when I told the first story to police. There isn't any Bill Gordon. I have not seen Jack Gordon for years. There is no such person as Tom, no £160 paid to Old Bill, and no sale of any boring plant to Bill Gordon.

Most station hands in the outback spend their spare time mending equipment or yarning round the fire. Instead, as Callaghan spent night after night brooding over his situation in the remote campsite, it seems he'd concluded that he could solve at least some of his problems. He'd watched Old Bill going about his work and contemplated that, if you disappear in the emptiness of the remotest parts of Australia, people might not even realise that you're dead.

Detectives Bischof and Mahoney subsequently checked the anvil. They found no traces of blood or hair that might corroborate Callaghan's story that Old Bill had struck his head. The ground around the anvil was smooth, with no suggestion of a struggle or anything that Old Bill could have tripped on.

Pieces of bone recovered from Glencoe Bore and the fire where Old Bill had been burnt were sent for examination to the director of the laboratory at the State Health Department. He found that they were human and glued some of them together to make a human femur. He later testified that whoever the leg belonged to could only be alive if the leg had been removed by a surgeon. This statement might have been an attempt to head off a defence that Old Bill might still be alive, based on the famous Shark Arm Case of 1935, where defendant Patrick Brady got off because an arm, with a distinctive tattoo, vomited up by a newly caught shark at Sydney's Coogee Aquarium was insufficient evidence that its owner, criminal underworld figure James Smith, was actually dead. However, part of a tooth, part of a skull and many other fragments found at Boorara suggested that Old Bill had suffered far more severe injuries than losing an arm to a shark.

When the case went to trial, it was the biggest thing the

south-west Queensland town of Cunnamulla had seen. The small courthouse was filled to overflowing in the first week of January 1941. So were the streets for that matter, as floods swept through much of far-west and central Queensland, preventing some of the witnesses from reaching court on the day of the trial.

The debt-ridden Callaghan appeared without representation. Throughout the evidence he asked no questions. His explanation that the death was an accident was contradicted by the strong motive of avoiding paying Old Bill his two years' wages and stopping him from telling what the true depth of the Glencore Bore was. He'd done such a good job of destroying Old Bill's remains that the exact cause of death couldn't be determined, and therefore couldn't confirm his story about Old Bill hitting his head on the anvil. It was just as likely Callaghan had taken advantage of their isolated location to shoot Old Bill in cold blood. There was no one to hear the shot, no one to see Old Bill die and no one to see Callaghan go about the ghastly business of trying to erase every vestige of Old Bill's existence.

Jim Callaghan had felt sure nobody would take much notice when an unremarkable, casual labourer went missing. Instead, the reality was the complete opposite. The people who live in the outback appreciate that it's an isolated and dangerous place, so they tend to look out for each other. There are so few people out there to begin with that when someone they know does go missing it's noticed almost immediately. That's not always the case, but it certainly was for Old Bill. Even then the chances of finding him were as remote as the crime scene itself. However, Old Bill's fate was one secret the outback didn't get to keep.

James Callaghan was found guilty of the murder of William 'Old Bill' Groves and sentenced to life imprisonment. In delivering sentence, the judge noted: 'The whole police force deserves the congratulations of the community for the work they did in this case.' In fact, the Bore Hole Murder was remembered for years as 'one of the great investigation classics of the Queensland Police Force'.

Callaghan served twelve years of his sentence before being hospitalised with a heart ailment. He died on 17 June 1953, aged seventy-two. Bischof went on to become Queensland Police Commissioner before being forced from office in 1969 amid corruption allegations relating to prostitution and SP betting. The Fitzgerald Inquiry into police corruption in the late 1980s noted that 'in some respects police corruption had acquired a quaint quasi-legitimacy by the Bischof era'. It was an ignominious end to the career of a man who'd taken a major police investigation to the furthest corners of the outback and built a reputation as one of Queensland's dogged finest.

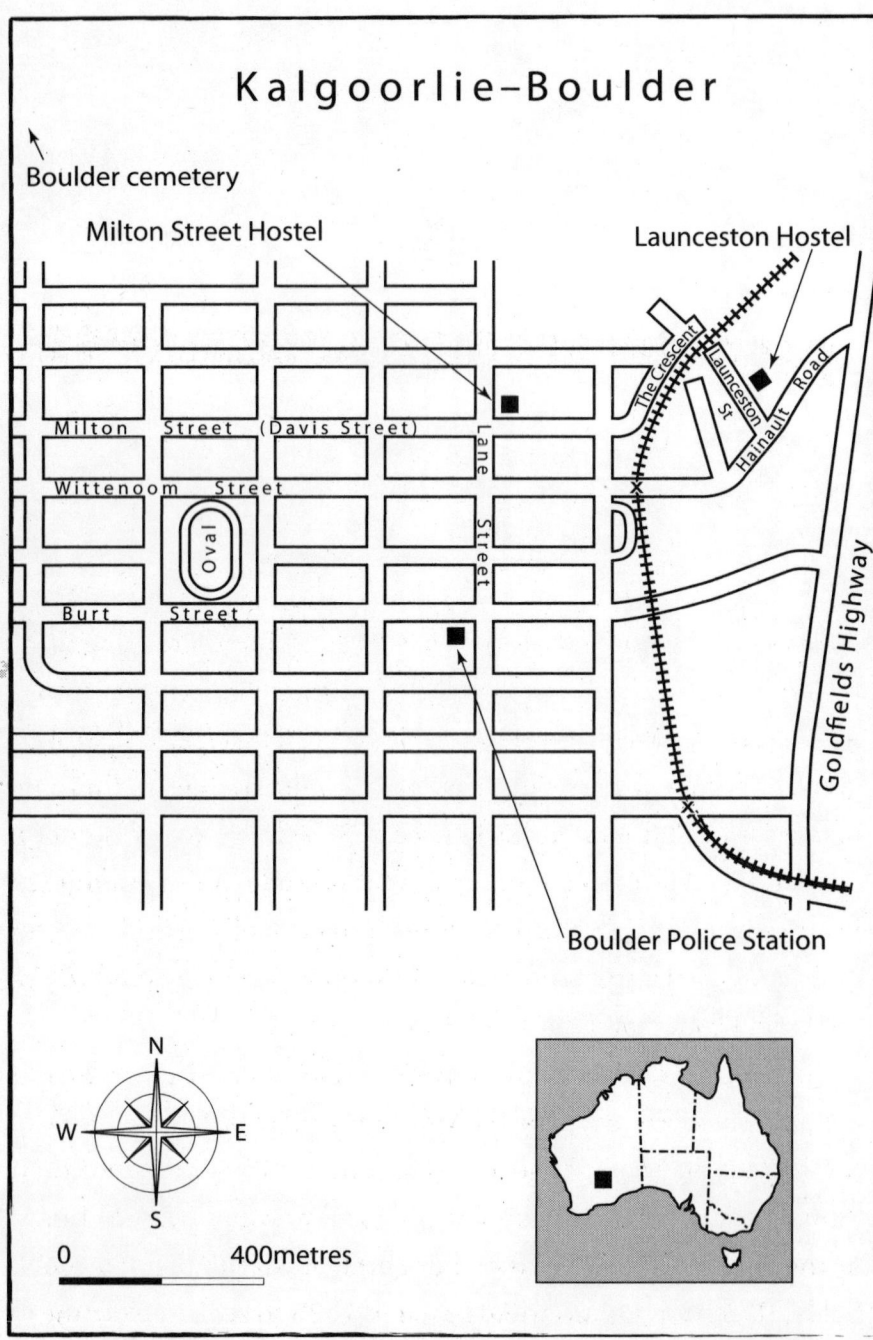

Kalgoorlie–Boulder

Boulder cemetery

Milton Street Hostel

Launceston Hostel

The Crescent

Launceston St

Hainault Road

Milton   Street   (Davis Street)

Lane Street

Wittenoom   Street

Oval

Burt   Street

Goldfields Highway

Boulder Police Station

N
W   E
S

0   400metres

6

PERO RAECIVICH'S APOCALYPSE

It may be one of the emptiest places on earth but there's one thing the outback is full of – hard-luck stories. You don't have to look far in an outback town to find fractured bodies, lost hopes and broken dreams. Lonely figures prop against bars, nursing beers they can barely afford. Others mask their pain in a dry sense of humour, or wrap themselves in an impenetrable solitude. A few become so lost in the failure of their lives that despair finally gets the better of them. Usually the immediate consequences are limited to the individual concerned, but not always.

In the case of outback miner Pero Raecivich, it devastated a community. Born in Bulkovik, Montenegro, in 1897, like many of his generation he left Yugoslavia for a better life away from their ethnically divided and economically backward homeland. Lured by the chance to make good money in the Western Australian gold-fields, Raecivich moved to Australia in 1928 to seek his fortune in the diggings that dotted the parched and barren landscape around the twin towns of Kalgoorlie–Boulder. Men – and in the 1930s they were almost all men – were drawn from around the world to try their luck. Those who enjoyed success sent money home or brought their wives or loved ones out to join them and start a family in what could be a land of opportunity. Yet the relentless searing heat, the harsh life of the mining camps and the dangerous work could also break a man. In few places was survival of the fittest more starkly defined.

Raecivich was doing well until the middle of 1937; on 8 June he had a healthy bank balance of £290. After that date he never worked again. He stopped making deposits and for the next five years he lived off his dwindling savings. According to Sam Perazich, who knew Raecivich for seven years and lived in the same mining camp, Raecivich ended up needing regular medical attention. It's possible Raecivich had injured his back, which would explain his inability to work in the mines or, indeed, do any kind of manual labour to earn a living.

For four years Raecivich continued to live in shanty-like conditions or under canvas in the mining camp, where comforts like running water, heating and electric light were rare. Eventually, the rough lifestyle told on the ailing unemployed miner, and as the winter of 1941 approached he moved into a room at the Launceston Hostel in Launceston Street, Boulder. With his shrinking finances it was a move he couldn't afford. The accommodation and regular meals provided by hostels like the Launceston were luxuries that only successful working men could pay for, not unemployed miners down on their luck.

Around the same time, there was an incident involving Raecivich and other members of Boulder's Yugoslav community. He and four or five others had gone to another hostel, at 16 Milton Street, Boulder, to play cards. The Milton Street Hostel tolerated illegal gambling among its guests and visitors, in return for a small fee. Raecivich and the others were playing when one of them got into a dispute with Marin Kunjunzich, the hostel's proprietor, about 'the box' – the contribution (placed in a money box) that covered the cost of lighting and using the hostel's rooms to gamble. To keep the peace Marin said he didn't want any money but one of the men grabbed him by the throat.

'You'll pay for this,' the man snarled.

It was probably an empty threat but it was later remembered as the first incident involving Raecivich. To add to Pero Raecivich's despair, the outbreak of World War II had brought nothing but bad news from his homeland. Yugoslavia had dared oppose the Nazis and had been crushed without mercy, in particular its Serbian community. The Balkan states that aligned with the Nazis – Croatia, Hungary, Bulgaria and Albania – became part of the occupying forces, and reports filtered out that some of these countries' troops were inflicting terrible atrocities on sections of the civilian population.

In the months following the incident at Milton Street, Raecivich wasn't noticed much among the gamblers, but during December he became a regular visitor. In January 1942 he called at Milton Street every day to play cards. By then, he had less than £20 out of the £290 he'd started with in 1937. Perhaps he hoped his luck would turn, a big win probably being his only hope. Instead, the gamblers soon took most of the pitifully small savings Raecivich had left.

The gambling may have been the forlorn man's only real human contact. The rest of the time he wandered the streets of Kalgoorlie–Boulder, a lonely figure who often passed people he knew without speaking. Boselko Pavlovich, who ran the Launceston Hostel, lived in the same building but hadn't spoken to Raecivich for two months. The *Kalgoorlie Miner* later reported: 'The man, it is stated, was of a morose, sullen disposition, with no special companions.'

Raecivich's crisis mirrored world events. At the beginning of 1942 Australia was fighting for its existence. In Europe the German war machine had engulfed the continent from Russia to the English Channel. It was as if everything was going up in flames.

Pero Raecivich said as much while playing rummy at Milton Street. He was losing.

'It would be better to blow all this up,' he remarked.

The men he was with dismissed the comment as merely bitterness because he'd just lost seven or eight shillings. Yet in a mining town, where gelignite was readily available, it was the kind of threat that was too easily carried out. Indeed, the previous year a car belonging to a member of the Yugoslav community, Mark Tamburovich, had been blown apart outside the Angel Hostel. In November two bombs were detonated at the home of Kalgoorlie Police Court Magistrate Les Stotter. He sustained only slight injuries, although the windows and doors in the house were blown out. Stotter was targeted again on 12 January 1942. In the early hours of that morning he heard his front gate close and went to investigate. Shining a torch into the front yard, he saw a man putting something under the house. The man ran, jumped over the front gate and leapt on a bicycle, pedalling away into the night. In his haste he lost a shoe and dropped a bag. Inside were twenty-seven sticks of gelignite, a detonator and nearly a metre of fuse. It was more than enough to completely destroy Stotter's house and kill everyone in it.

By the end of January, Pero Raecivich had just £1 9s 4d in one savings account, 2s 3d in another, and seven one-pound notes in his pocket. The recent news of the war in Europe was also weighing heavily on his mind.

On the night of 31 January there was another incident at the Milton Street Hostel. Late in the evening, one of the men who'd been present when Raecivich had made his previous threat to 'blow all this up' was warned away from the place by a visitor, Vido Durasevich.

'Go away,' Durasevich said. 'Anything might happen.'

'What do you mean by that?' the other man asked.

Durasevich didn't answer. He just turned and walked away. It was strange and cryptic behaviour, but it was remembered clearly in the light of subsequent events. It's possible Durasevich had heard Raecivich make more specific threats, or that he'd supplied him with the materials to carry them out.

By then, Pero Raecivich was compiling a list of people he felt had wronged him in one way or another. It probably included, among others, the proprietor of the Milton Street Hostel, Marin Kunjunzich, and his wife Maria; the proprietor of the Launceston Hostel, Boselko Pavlovich; fireman Kristo Kosich; and miner Peter Bokan. Raecivich had also begun writing two letters explaining what he was about to do.

There was nothing out of the ordinary in Pero Raecivich's behaviour on Sunday morning, 1 February 1942. He went through his normal ablutions in the Launceston Hostel's bathroom. He was seen walking the streets of Boulder, as usual, not speaking to anyone. At around midday he had a meal at the Milton Street Hostel and spoke to Maria Kunjunzich. Back in his room, however, Pero Raecivich had gathered together sticks of gelignite, mining fuses, metal tins, scrap metal, binder twine and containers of kerosene.

Night had fallen when Pero Raecivich started moving about the town again. At around 7 o'clock he went to the home of Peter and Janica Bokan on the outskirts of Boulder.

'Is Peter home?' he asked, when Janica answered the door.

'No,' Janica told him. 'He might be at his brother's.'

Raecivich went to look for Peter at his brother's mining camp, outside town. When he had no success there, he returned to the Bokan home.

'Is Peter here?'

'He's gone to town,' Janica now told him.

Pero nodded, then asked, 'Can I have an Aspro?'

'Sorry,' Janica replied. 'I don't have any.'

'Okay. I'll go to town to get some.'

There was a pause, then Raecivich asked again, 'Where's Peter?'

He left without explaining why he was looking for Janica's husband.

Four hours later, he found him. Peter Bokan was one of about thirty men gathered in the dining room at Milton Street, playing cards and games of dice. Raecivich watched the gambling but, unlike other nights, didn't play. He chatted to miner Nick Boban, whom Raecivich had known since childhood. They came from the same town in Montenegro.

Raecivich drew Nick's attention to a man who had won a pool of £55.

'If he had any sense he'd go home while he was ahead,' Raecivich said. 'If I had £6000 I'd give £100 to everyone here so they could have a good game and play to their satisfaction.'

'If I had that much money,' Nick replied, 'I wouldn't be giving it away.'

Nick Boban might have thought Raecivich's remarks unrealistic but he had no way of knowing that, for Raecivich, his money worries were about to be over. Boban had just heard the last words Pero Raecivich would ever speak. Not long after, Raecivich left the hostel and Boban didn't see him again.

Just after midnight, a man standing outside the Milton Street Hostel noticed a figure in the shadow of the verandah. He lit what looked like a mining fuse before throwing something into the building. It happened so fast there was no chance to stop him or to alert the occupants. Inside, the place was packed.

A master tailor named Chris Dimson was watching the men playing dice when he saw sparks shooting up in the centre of the room. Before he realised the sparks were from a burning fuse, a huge explosion ripped the building apart.

The blast blew men's legs off; clothing and skin were torn from bodies. Others suffered terrible burns or were deeply lacerated by flying fragments of metal. Parts of the roof collapsed on dead and dying men. What remained of the dining room was full of smoke, debris and the cries of the injured. The floor was awash with blood.

Nick Boban had been leaning against a window when the force of the explosion hit him in the chest and threw him onto the verandah. Dazed and deafened, he staggered away.

Maria Kunjunzich was thrown out of bed by the explosion but was unharmed. When she opened her bedroom door she came face to face with a seriously injured man who was crying in agony. She didn't understand what had happened but her first thought was to wrap her two children in a rug and get them to safety. She then went back to find her husband. Marin Kunjunzich had been lucky, only suffering a broken foot and lacerations. His wife helped him from the wrecked building.

Those who were relatively unscathed started pulling bodies out of the wreckage. The dead were laid out in a line on the floor. With men dying all around what was really needed was a doctor. One of the survivors rode off on a bicycle to get one.

Kristo Kosich, despite severe leg injuries, had managed to escape the building. He was heading back to his lodgings at the nearby Launceston Hostel when he found Nick Boban, collapsed, about ten or fifteen metres from the back gate of the Launceston Hostel. He was crying out, 'Somebody come to me or I will die on the road.'

Men at the Launceston Hostel who'd been woken by the explosion just a block away went to their aid. Kristo was helped into the kitchen while someone went to get Boselko Pavlovich, Kristo's cousin. At the sight of his injured legs awash with blood, Boselko went to wake her still sleeping husband, Remo.

'Get up,' she cried. 'Kris Kosich has come.'

Outside, another Launceston resident was helping Nick Boban when he saw Pero Raecivich enter the yard, holding two bombs. One was slightly larger than a jam tin, the other was about the size of a beer bottle. Both had burning fuses. Raecivich ran towards the Launceston Hostel.

Boselko Pavlovich, following her husband back to the kitchen, saw Pero Raecivich coming through the yard and onto the back verandah. Kristo Kosich saw Raecivich at the back door, staring into the kitchen for a moment. Then Pero opened the door and threw something burning into the room.

'Look out,' Kosich shouted. 'We'll be killed again.'

The bomb landed about three metres from him, near the stove. Remo Pavlovich, facing away from the door, didn't see the bomb thrown. However, when it landed on the floor, he recognised what it was immediately – 'all the same, like fuse in mine' – and dived away. The badly injured Kosich was nowhere near as fast. Raecivich, in fact, had thrown one bomb onto the verandah, and the second into the kitchen.

Boselko Pavlovich had started running back to her bedroom when the first explosion knocked her to the ground. Fearing for her husband, Boselko got up, only to be thrown to the ground again by the second, larger explosion. This time she had hurt her leg but she still went to rescue her nineteen-month-old son. Her calls to her husband went unanswered.

After the second explosion, Remo Pavlovich was badly injured but still alive. Kristo Kosich took the worst of the blast. All he could remember was a flash, then scrambling desperately into the yard through a hole in the kitchen wall made by the explosion. Then he realised he was on fire. Despite severe lacerations and spinal injuries, he started tearing off his clothing.

Raecivich had stayed in the yard, surveying his handiwork. But when he saw someone helping Nick Boban, he ran straight at the man and tried to strike him. As the man struggled to break free, a 35-centimetre carving knife fell from Raecivich's hand, and Raecivich ran off.

Another hostel resident, Ante Yukich, woken by the two explosions, thought the house had been struck by lightning. Then he noticed that the window had been blown in and the floor of his room was covered in glass. Outside his room, in the eerie darkness, he bumped into Boselko Pavlovich, who was carrying her closely bundled child out of the smoke-filled building. Down the hall Ante noticed a faint flickering light coming from the room of Pero Raecivich. There was a strong smell of gas or kerosene. Gingerly approaching, Yukich saw that the bedding and mattress had been set alight. He grabbed a bucket of water and tried to douse the flames, but the bedding continued to burn. While he went to get more water, another man dragged the mattress outside.

The police and a doctor named Hogan were on their way to Milton Street when they heard the second and third explosions, just seconds apart. Constable Mick Leeder was the first to arrive at Milton Street. He found the building in darkness and the nearby street lights blown out. In his torch beam he saw several injured men lying in the front garden, and from inside the building he heard cries for help. Some survivors were still struggling to get free.

Dr Hogan immediately began to deal with the horrific injuries, and was soon joined by another doctor and then ambulances from Kalgoorlie, Boulder and the larger mines close by. Transportation was arranged to Kalgoorlie District and St John of God hospitals in any vehicle available, including trucks and private cars. The arrival of over twenty seriously injured people overwhelmed the resources of the two hospitals, yet staff worked desperately, trying to save lives. At Milton Street, seven men were already dead. As it turned out, if Vido Durasevich had some foreknowledge of what was about to happen it didn't help him. He was among the dead and would take whatever secret he might have had to his grave.

The *Kalgoorlie Miner* headlined with 'Terrible Scenes of Slaughter' and reported that: 'In a fine drizzling rain, and in the eerie light of torches and the spotlight of a motor car, the police officials, ambulance men and other helpers worked on their gruesome task of removing the bodies, some of which, frightfully mutilated, lay huddled in heaps in various directions, amid twisted sheets of iron and shattered boards.'

Kalgoorlie CIB Detective Sergeant Lewis got the call to attend the scenes of the bombings at 12.30 a.m. After making some preliminary inquiries, he went to the Launceston Hostel and examined Pero Raecivich's room. The odour of kerosene was still in the air and he found two empty kerosene bottles. Lewis had the room locked and guarded while he started a search for Raecivich. He returned later and went through all of Raecivich's possession. Among them were Raecivich's hit list and two blasting caps with fuses attached. In the vacant lot beside the hostel he found a bundle of fuse-lighters.

At around 2 a.m. a fourth explosion shook the town of Boulder, reigniting fears that the terror was not yet over. The blast seemed to have come from some distance away and initial police efforts to locate the source proved fruitless. When no reports of another attack came in they continued tending the injured, identifying the dead and conducting an investigation into what was emerging as the worst multiple murder in Western Australian history.

By midday the source of the fourth explosion had been located – three kilometres from the bomb sites at Milton Street and the Launceston Hostel, in the Boulder Cemetery. Sexton Albert Armstrong and the Reverend Forbes saw what they initially thought were horribly mutilated pieces of a woman's body lying beside the main drive. Looking closer, however, they realised they'd found the legs and lower body of a man. The feet were bare, the shoes having been blasted a dozen metres away. Ten metres from the legs, near the base of a tree, was a small crater. And lodged in the branches of the tree were pieces of the upper body and items of clothing. Body parts were strewn nearly 100 metres in every direction.

The Reverend Forbes called Constable Leeder; Leeder called Detective Sergeant Lewis and they headed to the scene. As the *Kalgoorlie Miner* reported: 'The task of recovering the remains for removal to the morgue was gruesome in the extreme, as it was necessary to dislodge some from the tops of adjacent trees. Apparently the man . . . placed the charge under his chest on the ground and ignited the fuse.' One thing that couldn't be found was the victim's head.

However, in the bomb crater there was a sovereign, compressed into the ground and bent slightly by the explosion. People who knew Pero Raecivich recalled that he had kept a similar sovereign as a lucky token. Binder twine similar to the twine found in Raecivich's room was also found at the cemetery.

At the morgue, Lewis removed the trousers from the legs. Inside the left pocket was a handkerchief and seven one-pound notes. In the other pocket were two envelopes containing letters written in Croatian. Despite the evidence pointing to the body being that of Pero Raecivich, Lewis refused to confirm the identity of the man. The tailor Chris Dimson, who'd been at Milton Street when it was bombed, was called to assist the police with their inquiries. He'd made two suits for Pero Raecivich and recognised the material of the trousers. He pointed out that, in accordance with tailoring practice, Raecivich's name should have been marked on one of the trousers' pockets. It identified the owner of each suit while it was in the shop. Detective Sergeant Lewis used infrared photography to make out the name on the trousers found in Boulder Cemetery. They belonged to Pero Raecivich.

By the end of the day, the death toll had risen to thirteen, including the man in the cemetery. Urgent calls for blood were made to the public, and extra men were needed to dig graves at the cemetery. The following day two more men lost their fight for life – Peter Bokan and Mate Gregich. Many others remained on the danger list, some having had legs amputated.

That same day, Sexton Armstrong made another grisly discovery: a part of a head, an ear, and a strip of skin from the shoulder with a distinctive black wart. Detective Sergeant Lewis called on an acquaintance of Raecivich, miner Sam Perazich, to help identify the remains. Perazich recognised the wart as being Raecivich's. Lewis was finally able to confirm the identity of the remains in the cemetery.

The inquest got under way on 18 March 1942, before Coroner Ansell. Nearly everything relating to Pero Raecivich's state of mind was suppressed, possibly because it related to the sensitive ethnic tensions between sections of the Yugoslav community. Nor were the names on Pero Raecivich's list disclosed, but several witnesses were asked by the Coroner if they'd heard Raecivich threaten them or anyone else, suggesting they may have been targets of his brief but terrible revenge. In giving evidence, Kristo Kosich stated that he'd known Raecivich for nearly seven years but had never argued with him. Boselko Pavlovich testified that there was certainly no quarrel between them, and Maria Kunjunzich also said she'd had no arguments with Raecivich.

The contents of the two letters found with his remains were also suppressed. However, the Coroner's reference to them, albeit in vague terms, indicated they explained what might have tipped Raecivich towards his appalling acts of violence. According to Coroner Ansell:

Each envelope contained writings in a foreign language and one also contained a cutting from a newspaper of recent date. A note in English had been made on the newspaper cutting by Raecivich. The letters were translated into English by two interpreters. In Raecivich's room at the Launceston was found a sheet of paper on which words in English appear. In all these writings reference is made to a certain subject which had preyed on Raecivich's mind and I am drawn to the conclusion that they explain the reason for the bombing of the Milton Street House and the deaths of the fourteen people.

While the Coroner was circumspect, the local newspaper had already revealed on 5 February some of the contents of the letters gleaned from police investigators. The *Kalgoorlie Miner* had reported that:

> *Among the effects found by the detectives in Raecivich's trousers were two letters, written in Slav, which indicated that he had been worried, for some time past, by the suffering of his countrymen in Europe and greatly disturbed by the fact that he was not able to be with them.*

Raecivich's state of health might have added to his frustrations. He had been too ill to join the army, which would have solved his financial problems and given him an opportunity to fight the common enemy of both his adopted country and his homeland.

Yet it was noted at the time that the nationalities of many of his victims shouldn't have made them targets. The *Kalgoorlie Miner* had reported: 'With the exception of one, all of those killed in the explosions were Jugoslavs, seven being from Dalmatia, four from Montenegro (Raecivich's own countrymen) and two from Herzegovina. The exception was a Macedonian.'

In his closing remarks at the inquest, on 23 March, Coroner Ansell arrived at the self-evident conclusion that in carrying out the bombings: 'Raecivich was at the time of unsound mind. The writings referred to show also an intention to take his life, and I come to the conclusion that this is a case of suicide, and, as I have already said, while of unsound mind.'

However, Pero Raecivich was also a sick man about to end up

on the street, begging for food. In attempting to solve his problems by gambling, he merely accelerated his road to ruin. He had reached the end, alone and friendless, his dreams shattered in an alien land, while the places he called home were going up in flames. In his despair, the only way out had been to 'blow all this up'.

After the death of Pero Raecivich, the attacks on Police Magistrate Stotter ceased. The *Kalgoorlie Miner* speculated that all the incidents might have been Raecivich's work, but police were unable to link him with the previous crimes. They suspected another Kalgoorlie resident was responsible but there was insufficient evidence to lay charges.

The events of 1942 soon faded from memory, despite the fact that they constituted a mass murder on an unprecedented scale. The public was more focused on the events of World War II. In February Singapore fell to the Japanese and Australia was threatened as never before. Eastern states' newspapers only carried initial reports of the incident within their pages, while their front pages were dominated by war news.

There are almost no historical references to the event. Far more attention has been given to the race riots in Kalgoorlie that occurred a decade earlier. It's pure speculation that this prior experience may have left many unwilling to dwell on the actions of Pero Raecivich in case it stirred up further ethnic unrest. In a country fascinated by crime and criminals, it's remarkable that fourteen people were murdered but very few people have heard of the incident. It's almost as though one of the darkest days in outback history never happened at all.

Postscript

In outback mining towns, gelignite has quite a history as a weapon of choice when it comes to settling disputes. There were more bomb blasts in the Kalgoorlie region in 2000 after the shooting of a member of the Gypsy Joker bikie gang at the historic Ora Banda mining town, sixty kilometres north-east of Kalgoorlie. Former Senior Detective Don Hancock had bought the pub and in October 2000 a group of bikies went there to drink. During the evening they became abusive towards other patrons and the barmaid, Hancock's daughter, until Hancock closed the pub. That night one of the bikies, Billie Grierson, was shot dead at the bikies' nearby campsite in a sniper-style attack.

Grierson's killer was never found although Hancock was closely investigated. Meanwhile, his pub and home became the target of attacks and both were blown up in the following months. Hancock decided it was prudent to leave Ora Banda and relocate to Perth. However, in March 2001, the peace in suburban Lathlain was shattered by a massive explosion. Hancock and a racing identity, Lou Lewis, were killed when a bomb, placed on their vehicle, was remotely detonated.

Five members of the Gypsy Jokers were charged in relation to the murder of Hancock and Lewis after one of the gang gave evidence to police. However, most were found not guilty of the charges. Gypsy Joker master-at-arms Graeme Slater was charged with two counts of murder but was eventually found guilty of arson.

Kalgoorlie's most recent bombing was in January 2005. Two men stole explosives from the nickel smelter and used them to blow up television transmitters, blacking out two commercial tele-vision stations for several hours. An ABC broadcast facility was also found to be wired with explosives, but they didn't go off. The police, however, put the attack down to high spirits. According to Detective Senior Sergeant Bernie Hett the men involved were just having 'what they thought was a bit of fun'.

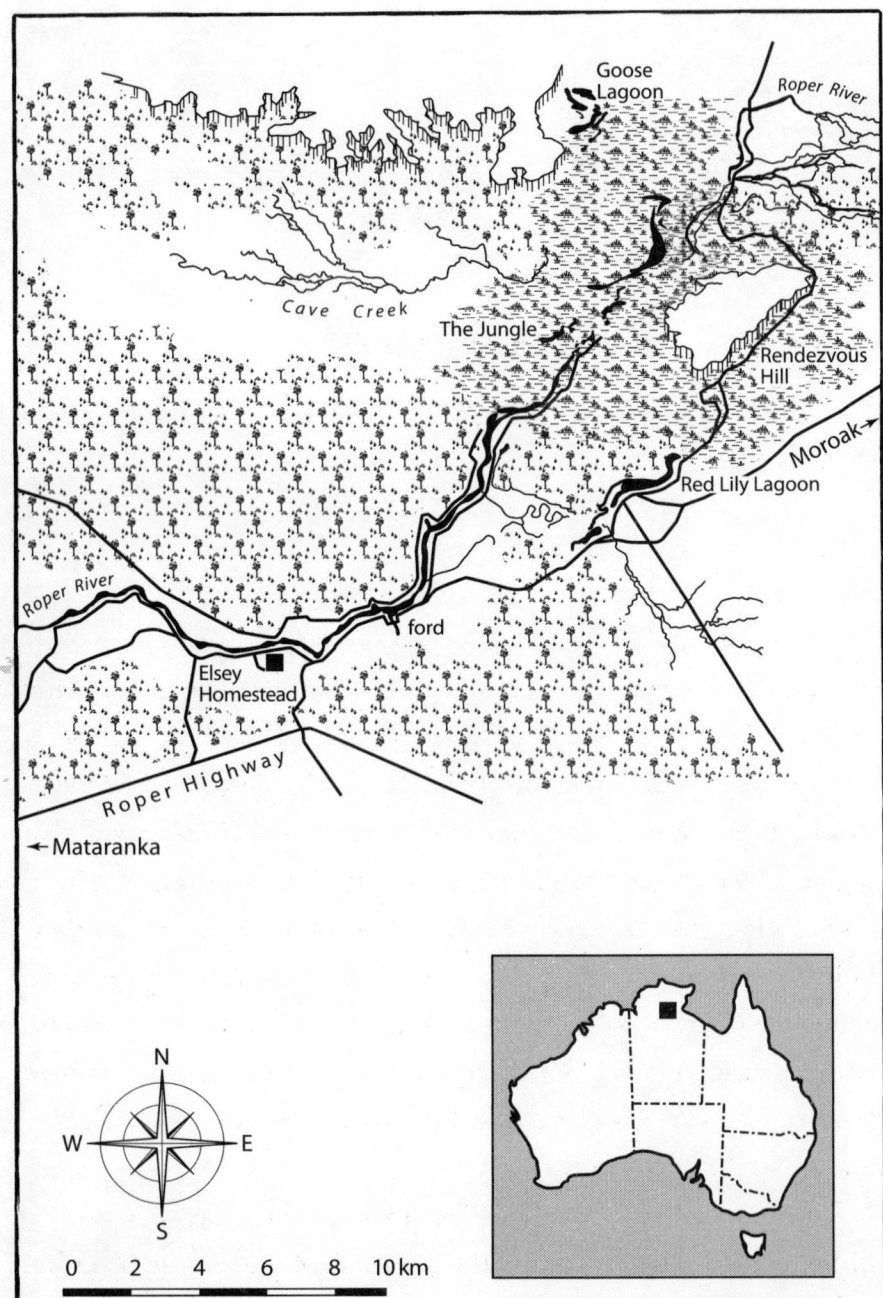

Goose
Lagoon

Roper River

Cave Creek

The Jungle

Rendezvous
Hill

Moroak

Red Lily Lagoon

Roper River

ford

Elsey
Homestead

Roper Highway

← Mataranka

N
W   E
S

0   2   4   6   8   10 km

7

MANHUNT

From the earliest days of European settlement, the tracking skills of Australia's indigenous inhabitants have been regarded by many as bordering on the supernatural. The use of trackers has been described in previous chapters of this volume, notably in the hunt for the Kelly Gang and the Governor brothers. Those cases also highlight the broad range of opinion as to their usefulness – from unrealistic expectations of what was possible, to contempt for their skills that approached racism. Extraordinary claims have been made about the trackers' skill, in circumstances where the truth can no longer be ascertained. But there *is* a case that illustrates just how good trackers can be, and just how hard it would be to track a tracker who didn't want to be found.

The hunt for Larry Boy Janba began on the morning of Saturday, 21 September 1968, following the discovery of the body of his tribal wife, an eighteen-year-old known only as Marjorie, outside the servants' quarters on Elsey Station in the Northern Territory, 400 kilometres south-east of Darwin. Marjorie had died from an axe blow to the head and multiple stab wounds to the face and throat. Lucky to be alive was a young white jackaroo who'd been sleeping with her after a Friday night party at the station. He'd never seen his attacker coming. His only memory was of regaining consciousness in the servants' quarters covered in his own blood, with his cheekbone collapsed by the power of a blow from a tomahawk.

The motive was jealousy, pure and simple. After Marjorie had left him, Larry Boy started threatening her, causing her to move closer to the homestead on Elsey Station until she sought refuge in the servants' quarters. But when she took up with the jackaroo (who'd met Larry Boy and thought him 'quite a nice bloke') his behaviour turned violent.

Station manager Peter McCracken rang Police Constable Roy 'Bluey' Harvey at the nearby township of Mataranka at 3 a.m. and told him he had a murder on his hands. Harvey called fellow officer Gary Burgdorf at Larrimah, eighty kilometres south, for assistance, then notified his superiors in Darwin before heading out to Elsey. There in the blood on the concrete floor of the servants' quarters were the prints of someone in bare feet. With the assistance of an Aboriginal police tracker and Elsey Station's Aboriginal workers, the footprints were identified as belonging to Larry Boy Janba. They recognised the distinctive shape of the right big toe. The tracks led to the body of Marjorie.

While senior police from Darwin and an ambulance from Katherine made their way to the station, Harvey and the newly arrived Burgdorf started mustering men and equipment for the search. They had learned that Larry, who though 'educated' was living off the land in the wild swamp country on the Elsey property, had visited one of his older relatives on the station and borrowed a tomahawk and a .22 rifle saying he was going bush. Now Marjorie was dead and many of the other Aboriginal station workers were fearful of what else Larry Boy might do. In the complex kinship relationships and responsibilities of traditional Aboriginal life, they feared he might exact revenge against anyone who he suspected had come between him and his wife.

As soon as there was enough daylight to see, attempts to follow Larry Boy's tracks began, but even the best trackers couldn't find any sign of him leaving the station. The search continued as more police arrived, including Sergeant Bob Jackson from Darwin to take command.

The next day search parties, comprising more than a dozen police, trackers and station hands, set out in 4WDs. Some headed thirty kilometres west through rocky escarpment country and open bush land to Mataranka Station (where Larry Boy's mother and other relatives lived). Another group drove fifty kilometres east, in the low-lying swamps and thick jungle on both sides of the Roper River, towards Moroak Station, as well as concentrating on the area in the immediate vicinity of Elsey Station. But it was one of the Aboriginal women working at Elsey who first found Larry Boy's tracks down at the Roper River. They were heading towards an area of dense scrub known as the Elsey Jungle, a 100-square-kilometre area thick with venomous snakes, mosquitoes and pandanus. There were crocodiles, mostly the smaller and relatively harmless fresh-water species, but encounters with wild buffalo or pigs were other potentially fatal hazards. However, Larry had been knocking around the Jungle since childhood and knew it intimately.

Once police contemplated this possibility, they started thinking it might take longer to find the fugitive than initially believed. So they were surprised when, late in the afternoon, the tracks led them to Larry's camp in the Jungle. It was a simple bark shelter with small fires at both ends so that the drifting smoke kept the ubiquitous mosquitoes at bay. The trackers pointed out that Larry still had the rifle with him – they could see the impression the butt had left on the ground when he'd leaned it against a tree.

It was impossible to travel quietly in the thick scrub and Larry had heard the searchers coming, giving him plenty of opportunity to escape. Nevertheless, the discovery meant police could concentrate their search, recalling the parties that were further afield. A camp was set up at Goose Lagoon, on the northern side of the Jungle at the foot of a rocky escarpment. The next day at dawn dozens of police, trackers and station hands assembled on foot, horseback and in 4WDs to search Larry's favourite haunt, drawing the net tight around him.

Larry Boy, however, had other ideas. There was no sign of him, as he wasn't leaving any tracks. Eventually they realised he must be wearing thongs, the same as the rubber sandals worn by many of the trackers and volunteers, making his tracks indistinguishable from those left by the search parties. Sergeant Jackson decided that further searching was futile until sandshoes were found for all the thong wearers. Out in the jungle, Larry Boy wouldn't be able to get a pair.

As well as sandshoes, a helicopter was hired by the Northern

Territory police. Early on Tuesday, 24 September, it was used to rapidly deploy sandshoe-wearing trackers at key creek crossings and lookout points in the Jungle. The chopper then flew low over the swamps, flattening the reeds in the hope that Larry Boy would be forced into the open. Other searchers scoured the perimeter of the Jungle in case the fugitive tried to flee. Bluey Harvey and tracker Tony Mullagully (who had once been a 'suitor' of Marjorie's) scoured the limestone ridges and escarpments near Elsey Station, checking caves that could be used as a hideout.

The following day, some of the search party patrolled the Roper River by boat but no tracks were found – barefoot, thonged or otherwise. However, searchers did discover, in the Jungle, tunnels cut through the otherwise impenetrable undergrowth.

On Thursday, the hire of the helicopter ran out and Sergeant Jackson had to reorganise his search. He again spread his resources between Mataranka and the Jungle, suspecting that Larry Boy might still try to reach his relatives, but also hoping that a less-concentrated search would encourage him to move about more. This strategy, however, posed a problem for the poorly equipped Northern Territory police (funded and administered by the Commonwealth Government in Canberra) as they had no portable radios with which to coordinate their movements. So parties searching in the same vicinity planned to rendezvous over lunch to compare notes, and a mobile police patrol in a 4WD bush-bashed the thirty-five kilometres from place to place trying to keep in contact with all parties.

On Friday afternoon, a partially butchered wallaby was found by Bluey Harvey, Tony Mullagully and another tracker, named Jacob.

It appeared to have been killed that morning using a spear; Larry Boy was too cautious to risk firing a shot that would have brought search parties swarming around him. The trackers noticed that Larry Boy's big right toe – having worn through the thong – was again putting in an appearance. They were now looking for a thong print with a distinctive toe mark.

They also saw dog prints. Larry Boy had his dog with him, carrying it sometimes to hide its track. Occasionally he abandoned the animal and it would make its way back to the homestead, then disappear again. Unfortunately, the police couldn't get the dog to lead them to its elusive master.

The searchers regrouped in the vicinity of Goose Lagoon. The scrub was so thick here that it couldn't be reached on horseback, only on foot. The horses were borrowed, as were the bridles and saddles.

On Saturday, 28 September, a week after the attack, twenty police, trackers and volunteers formed four parties that converged on the Jungle from all sides. Battling through the swamp on foot, one party found Larry Boy's tracks and believed they were hot on his trail. Sure enough, the tracks led to another camp and another partially eaten wallaby. This camp consisted of bark stacked in the shallow water until it was high enough to form a dry platform. Once again, Larry Boy had been warned of the approaching party by their inevitable splashing through 200 metres of water to reach his camp. Bluey Harvey later reported in the *Northern Territory Police News* that they'd got close enough to see the ripples in the water left as he'd fled.

None of the other three parties had sighted Larry Boy so they knew he must have gone to ground in the immediate vicinity. They were right on top of him but couldn't penetrate the scrub to uncover him. Little did they know that, at times, they were so close that Larry Boy could have reached out and touched them.

After repeatedly criss-crossing the area, the searchers eventually had to admit defeat and made their way forlornly back to camp at Goose Lagoon. The men were exhausted from hunting a dangerous man in a particularly hostile environment. Despite low morale, there was a camaraderie growing between the police, station hands, trackers and volunteers. Station manager Peter McCracken was also working tirelessly, and visitors to the station were well looked after by his wife, Mary, no matter what time they turned up.

Sunday, 29 September, was a day of rest for the searchers. Many hadn't seen their families for a week. Some patrols had ventured more than 200 kilometres from Elsey homestead following possible trails. A piece of good news was received that day. Sergeant Jackson learned that the RAAF was able to make available a helicopter. In fact, the chopper was returning to Australia from a tour of duty in the Vietnam War, when it was offloaded and diverted to the search.

The next day, with the help of the chopper, the search patrols located another camp in the swamps and thick scrub of the Jungle. There was evidence that Larry Boy was eating cabbage palms, suggesting he dared not risk hunting wallaby. Again, they must have been very close. The RAAF helicopter pilot, who had also returned from duty, commented that the terrain surrounding Elsey Station closely resembled Vietnam. There the countryside concealed the entire North Vietnamese Army; here the searchers were trying to find just one man.

The chopper was used for two days before returning to Darwin. Its presence had been a morale boost, and it made deploying the twenty-five searchers faster and easier. Yet, even with this advantage, they had still come up empty-handed, although the trackers on the ground noticed that at one point Larry Boy's footprints had done a U-turn. He'd been walking along a track when he realised, just in time, that a search party was coming towards him. He'd almost walked into their arms. After the chopper left, the police hired forty additional horses from contract musterer Bill Fordham for $50 a day, which also covered the cost of tucker for Fordham (who was part-Aboriginal) and six of his men. The *Northern Territory News* imbued him with extraordinary qualities when it wrote: 'Bill Fordham has the quiet manner of most bushmen and an uncanny knack of looking neat, tidy and fresh under the most torrid and trying conditions outback. Horses, cattle and bushmen are all he has known in his twenty-eight years to date.'

There was one major drawback with hiring horses: most of the police couldn't ride. The days of mounted police had largely passed with the coming of the motor car. So Bob Jackson drove back to Darwin to dragoon anyone who could hold a rein and was prepared to admit it.

Back at Elsey on Thursday, 3 October, Bluey Harvey, Tony Mullagully, Bill Fordham and tracker Billy Fulton were learning another of Larry Boy's tricks. They were heading to one of their camps at Red Lily Lagoon on the south-west side of the Jungle when they spotted his tracks heading up into the limestone hills that curved around that side. The tracks were on a cattle pad, a path the cattle used as they came down to the Jungle every evening for water. Their hooves would usually have churned up the ground and erased his tracks. Today, though, either he was too early or the cattle were late, for his tracks were still visible.

With night approaching there wasn't time to follow the tracks, but back at camp Bluey Harvey and the others decided to shift their patrols to the surrounding hills, the cattle pads in and out of the Jungle and the places where it was easiest to cross the Roper River, which cut between the two areas. Sure enough, up in the hills, away from the marauding mosquitoes, they found another of Larry Boy's camps. There were ration tins discarded by the RAAF crew when they'd landed to have their lunch. Larry Boy had actually watched them land, eat and take off again, and then wandered over and enjoyed a meal of half a tin of meat, half a tin of Spam and some condensed milk.

Now that Larry Boy was out of the Jungle it was feared that he might go anywhere in the Top End and never be found. In the rocky limestone country he leapt from rock to rock, making his tracks more difficult to follow. This new development meant the trackers had to try to anticipate what Larry Boy would do. It was possible he might go north into what's known as the Stone Country, where he could hide among the rocks and caves. Tony Mullagully thought otherwise. He believed Larry Boy would double back to the country he knew could feed and hide him best.

Bob Jackson returned from Darwin on Friday. He seemed to have plundered a museum, underlining the Northern Territory police's woeful preparation for a prolonged search in a rugged, inaccessible area. The irony was that this described most of the Territory. The saddles he had brought with him were so old they were too dangerous to use and the .303 rifles were antiques. He also had pills to be taken in the event of snake bite. The searchers felt a lot better for having them, though, later, a doctor from Katherine saw Bluey Harvey's bottle and laughed out loud – the pills were Phenergan, which simply slowed down blood flow. If they were taken quickly enough they would probably give a snake-bite victim perhaps an additional thirty seconds of life.

The search fanned out between the Jungle and Mataranka but found no trace. A cache of food was found near Mataranka Station, where Larry Boy's relatives lived, but a watch placed on it turned up nothing. Tony Mullagully and Billy Fulton were still convinced that Larry would stay near the Jungle. They were soon proved right. On Sunday, 6 October, Fulton and Peter McCracken found a freshly cut cabbage palm on the banks of the Roper River near the Jungle. It was back to the swamps for the search parties.

The next day, after slogging through the muck in the heavy tropical humidity, the police at Goose Lagoon were far from happy campers. Morale hit rock bottom. Bluey Harvey noticed that even close friends were testy with each other. Then word came that the head of the CIB, Sergeant Roger Textor, would be arriving the next day to discuss the future of the search, which was costing a small fortune. They'd got very close but in seventeen days no one had actually seen Larry Boy.

On Tuesday, 8 October, Bob Jackson went to pick up Textor. That day, *Northern Territory News* editor Jim Bowditch and a photographer asked if they could accompany Bluey Harvey and Tony Mullagully on patrol. Bluey agreed but doubted they'd last long. After half a day, despite finding Larry Boy's tracks on the perimeter of the Jungle, the newsmen passed up the possibility of being on the spot for his capture. With a new-found appreciation of what the searchers were enduring, they returned to camp with another tracker and Mullagully's horse, which had broken a shoe. Bluey Harvey and Tony Mullagully continued on, but once again the search proved fruitless. Jim Bowditch turned in particularly early that night.

Harvey and the other police sat up into the night discussing the hunt with Sergeant Textor. An experienced bushman, Textor had first-hand knowledge of the problems the parties were facing. The next day he had the patrols cover both the Jungle and the surrounding hills but there was no sign of Larry Boy – not a single track or indication of his presence. Textor left for Darwin warning that unless some clear sign of the fugitive was found, the search would be cut back.

This news didn't go down well with the McCrackens at Elsey Station. Their workers were gripped by fear and work on the station had ground to a halt. There was no mustering and the domestics were locking themselves into their accommodation at night. There was no point telling them they had nothing to fear from Larry Boy. His ability to outwit and outmanoeuvre his pursuers only added to his stature. Until they brought him in, the area wasn't safe and no work would be done. Nevertheless, the news came back from Darwin the following day that the search would be cut back severely. It would comprise Bluey Harvey, assisted by Detective Barry Frew who was to be dispatched from Darwin. Officers Dave Swift from Daly Waters, Gary Burgdorf from Larrimah, Colin Eckert from Maranboy, Bob Jackson from Darwin, John Francis from Borroloola and Vic Hoy from Roper Bar would return to policing their own districts. Half the Top End had been without any law enforcement for nearly three weeks and it was time they got back to their normal duties.

The media backlash was swift. The *Northern Territory News* criticised the lack of training, equipment and support that had hampered the police effort, which had gone far beyond the call of duty. Peter McCracken attacked the claim made by Textor's boss, Northern Territory Police Commissioner McLaren, that he had withdrawn the men in order to give them a rest.

'The policeman who has done most and spent more time on the job, Constable Bluey Harvey, has been left on the job,' McCracken said. He also pointed out that Bill Fordham and he weren't giving up. They would continue the search, paying for the men and horses out of their own pockets.

On 11 October, Bluey Harvey and Elsey Station's head Aboriginal stockman, Leo, mounted on the station's horses, patrolled the route between Elsey and Mataranka, in the hope of finding Larry Boy's tracks. At Mataranka they questioned his mother for the first time. She denied having seen him since the murder. By the time they'd returned to Elsey to meet Barry Frew, they'd ridden just under 100 kilometres.

The next day Harvey was out again with Tony Mullagully and Jacob, but again found nothing. Several members of the search party were sick. Peter McCracken had been forced to bed with a flu-like virus and seven Aboriginal men had been taken to Katherine Hospital. Harvey was starting to suspect that Larry Boy might be sick as well. Some of the Aboriginal art that abounds in this area includes images of evil spirits, and Aboriginal guides at Manyallaluk, in the Stone Country to the north, have explained to this author that some of the drawings indicate taboo areas – places that will make people sick.

Continuing the search around Red Lily Lagoon on the south-east side of the Jungle, Harvey, Mullagully and Jacob managed to give a crocodile poacher and his girlfriend a real scare (the hunting of freshwater *Crocodylus johnstoni* and saltwater *Crocodylus porosus* was outlawed in 1964 and 1971, respectively). However, they had higher priorities and pressed on into the jungle on foot. Not long after, they heard the sound of chopping. Moving as quietly as possible, they crept towards the noise, but Larry Boy had heard them first. When they arrived at the scene he'd already gone, leaving behind a mystery for the trackers to unravel.

He'd been chopping a small cabbage palm to eat, but there were no tracks. Then Mullagully noticed smudges on the ground. He suggested that Larry Boy had wrapped his feet in wallaby skin to hide his tracks. To confirm this theory, he wrapped his shirt around his feet and, sure enough, reproduced the smudges. Now they definitely knew that Larry Boy was still at large in the Jungle, and the wallaby-skin trick explained why no tracks had been seen for days.

Harvey rang Darwin to break the news about the fresh sightings. The search was immediately reinforced with police from all over the Top End, and Bill Fordham, his horses and men were rehired. Sickness was still taking its toll, but, nevertheless, those who were able to set off next morning. Soon after, policeman Dave Swift, a tracker and two stockmen heard the sound of chopping again. They ran towards the sounds, almost catching Larry Boy, but he'd heard them and fled just in time. In his haste he'd abandoned the wallaby hides and the party easily tracked him to another camp in the Jungle. There he and his tracks disappeared, but the near miss did mean that the police could concentrate their efforts once more.

That night, seven police, twenty-two volunteers, five vehicles, forty horses, a motorbike and a police boat were assembled for the search. Peter McCracken, still unwell, arrived at Red Lily Lagoon and said he would hire a helicopter out of his own pocket.

The helicopter carried parties to their designated search areas in the Jungle; others set out on horseback to patrol to the north and west. The motorbike traversed the dirt road (now the Roper Highway) that ran to the south; however, it didn't get far. Tracker Joey McDonald had been assigned to a horse patrol but at the last moment was switched to ride pillion on the bike with Roper Valley Station's David Munroe. Unfortunately, Joey was still wearing his spurs. On the first bump they hit, the spurs went into the spokes of the back wheel, destroying it. He and Munroe patrolled the road on horseback instead.

Effectively surrounded, Larry Boy had nowhere to go – or so it would seem – but the intense scrutiny by foot patrols, horse patrols, vehicles and a helicopter still failed to uncover this uncannily elusive fugitive. That evening, as the parties straggled back to their camps, defeated once again, Tony Mullagully discovered a tin of tobacco, papers and matches, carefully placed beside a track. Not only that, Larry Boy's tracks were on top of those of the search party. According to Mullagully, the tracks were only twenty minutes old, indicating he was shadowing the searchers and keeping to places where they'd already looked.

In the camp that night, the realisation that someone in the search party was helping Larry Boy added to the gloom of another day of failure. The presence of a sympathiser did go some way to explaining Larry Boy's miraculous escapes.

Next morning the exhausted searchers set out once more, despite some of them being ill from the virus that had depleted the number of people available for duty, especially among the trackers. The chopper hire lasted just long enough to drop men in the Jungle, then it flew off leaving the searchers to slog through the hot, wet, humid, buzzing, snake-infested, barely navigable terrain. And that day there was no sign of Larry Boy.

Fearing he may have left the Jungle, on 17 October the search went back to a perimeter patrol with checks around Elsey Station. Bob Jackson tried to do a surreptitious check around Mataranka Station that night under cover of darkness. He had been warned that the property's peacocks and dogs would sound the alarm long before he got anywhere near the place. Nevertheless, around midnight he and Bluey Harvey approached on foot. They were still twenty minutes away when they heard the birds, then the dogs. Persisting, they approached one of the huts that the station's Aboriginal workers had locked themselves into. A voice whispered, 'Is that you, Larry Boy?' They were asked the same question at other huts, suggesting the workers knew far more than they were admitting.

The following day, there came further confirmation that Larry Boy was getting help. Tracker Billy Fulton noticed sandshoe tracks on the side of the Roper River, five kilometres from Elsey Station.

They weren't Larry Boy's but they led to a cache of cooked meat, bread and condensed milk. That night the cache was staked out. Larry Boy didn't show.

Over the next few days the Aboriginal people at Elsey grew restless and lingered closer to the homestead. Tracks made by Larry Boy in the limestone hills between the homestead and the Jungle were found and lost among the rocky terrain. On 19 October the *Northern Territory News* reported that Larry Boy's dog, a small blue heeler, had wandered into the Elsey homestead. It was starving. The police took it as a sign that the pressure they were putting on Larry Boy by their constant patrols was taking its toll. If the dog had abandoned its master, maybe Larry Boy was starving too.

Jackson decided to move his operations to Mataranka and concentrate his patrols there, hoping that Larry Boy would try to get help from his family. On 21 October, eight kilometres from Mataranka, tracks were found at the junction of Salt Creek and Roper River that led to a camp where wrappers for bread and cold meats, and empty tins of beans were found. A check at the local store revealed they'd been bought by Larry Boy's mother two days before. The trackers could tell from the impressions on the earth where Larry Boy had slept and that he was naked except for a *naga*, or loincloth.

The searchers continued to comb the area that day and the next. The following day, 23 October, Police Commissioner Bill McLaren and Inspector Tim Tisdell drove the 480 rough kilometres from Darwin to meet with Peter McCracken, Sergeant Bob Jackson and Constable Bluey Harvey. It was intended to show the media that, as the search entered its thirty-second day, they still took the matter seriously. The visit led to a headline on page one of the *Northern*

Territory News: 'Police send a message to Larry Boy: "come in"'. In the article Inspector Tim Tisdell was quoted as saying, 'We want him to know that he will not come to harm by coming in to talk with us and we have conveyed this information to people we hope can get it to him.'

Down at Mataranka, the police on the toughest job in the Territory were amused by the suggestion put to them by the top brass that they 'try to make contact'. As Bluey Harvey said: 'What did they think we'd been doing for the last thirty-three [sic] days?' They'd have been less amused if they'd realised that the inspector's comment to the press would be used at Larry Boy's trial to have his record of interview ruled inadmissible. Tisdell's words compromised the required warning that anything Larry Boy said could be used in evidence against him.

The search continued throughout the next week without finding any tracks. Larry Boy wasn't wrapping his feet in wallaby hide or wearing thongs but he'd come up with new ways to confound the trackers. On 30 October, Tisdell informed Bluey Harvey, who'd been on the search for all of its thirty-nine days, that he'd finally be relieved by Gary Burgdorf from Larrimah. When Inspector Tisdell told Bluey that the 'handover of gear' would take place at Elsey Station, Harvey simply replied, 'What gear?'

The very same night there was a robbery at Elsey Station. Bread, meat and sandshoes were taken, the latter clearly another attempt to confuse Larry Boy's tracks with those of his trackers. In the early hours of the morning Peter McCracken got through to Bluey Harvey at the police station, telling him of the find and that he'd have horses ready to go as soon as Bluey got there.

Harvey and Tony Mullagully rode out at first light, picking up Larry Boy's barefoot tracks near the school house. However, they were few and far between. Then Mullagully dismounted and picked up a leaf. He said it was from a tree that only grew in the Jungle. Once again he'd uncovered the explanation for the lack of tracks over the previous few days: Larry Boy had been erasing them with branches of leaves as he went. The two men slowly followed the trail.

When they reached the road to the homestead things got interesting. Throughout the search the road was being graded every night so that if Larry Boy crossed it his tracks would stand out. Sure enough, in the middle of the road there was a single distinctive toe mark, and on the side of the road there was a small branch from the tree that only grew in the Jungle. In the rocky open country on the other side of the road from the homestead, Larry Boy could hop from rock to rock and brush out any footprints, leaving absolutely no track to follow. However, the branch he was using kept dropping leaves. Despite the millions of leaves on the ground there were enough of the kind that Larry Boy was dropping, and they were sufficiently distinctive, for Tony Mullagully to track him. Even so, it was like following a trail of needles in a series of haystacks. For forty days Larry Boy had been extraordinarily skilful in concealing his tracks and confusing his trackers, but on the morning of 31 October he had finally met his match in Tony Mullagully.

Curiously, the trail didn't head towards his relatives at Mataranka as expected. Instead it entered the limestone caves area that had been checked many times with no result. Outside the entrance to one of the caves they found the branch that Larry Boy had been using to brush out his tracks. This cave had been inspected many times and its entrance had always been blocked by thick cobwebs. Even now, they appeared intact, but as Harvey and Mullagully looked closer they saw that the cobwebs had been split down one side. The split was just wide enough for a man to slip inside.

Tony Mullagully voiced what both men were thinking: 'We got him, Bluey.'

It was then that Bluey Harvey realised he was unarmed. Back at Elsey Station, when he'd been about to mount an unfamiliar horse, he'd taken off his revolver in case the animal threw him and it went off when he hit the ground. Now he was facing a cornered fugitive, who was possibly armed. Fortunately, Mullagully had a .22 rifle that put the pair on relatively equal terms with Larry Boy. From the entrance to the cave Harvey called on Larry Boy to surrender. He got no reply. Plagued as always by a lack of equipment, Harvey didn't have a portable radio to call for backup. Instead, he had to hope the other patrols would realise he and Mullagully were missing and come to investigate, but that would take some time.

One thing they weren't going to do was give Larry Boy a chance to escape, so he and Mullagully peeled back the spiderwebs from the entrance to the cave and went in after a potentially armed and dangerous man.

A short distance from the entrance the cave split into two small passages. At the opening to one of the passages was a bucket that had been stolen from the school that morning. Harvey tried to crawl into the passage but he soon found the air unbreathable and was forced to crawl back out. There was no sign of Larry Boy in the other passage, which could only mean he was in the first one. It was hard to believe because the air was so foul. Yet he had to be there.

Harvey realised he and Mullagully were taking a terrible risk trying to get Larry Boy out on their own, so he guarded the entrance to the passage with the rifle while Mullagully went back to Elsey to raise the alert. He returned with Peter McCracken and Jacob, then Constable Colin Eckert and, some time after, Bill Fordham and one of his men, Joey McDonald. Several attempts were made to get into the passage but they all failed, either because the tunnel was so narrow or the air so stifling. Then Joey McDonald, who was related to Larry Boy, had a go. He managed to crawl in further than anyone. He crawled further, the tunnel narrowing, until finally, in the furthest recess of the tunnel, he caught sight of something. For the first time, in one of the most extensive searches in Northern Territory police history, he laid eyes on the fugitive. It was Larry Boy. The hunt was finally over.

After weeks of using every trick in the book to avoid capture, Larry Boy wasn't going to give up easily. In the incredibly confined space that he'd retreated to, the only way they were going to get him out was if he did so voluntarily. McDonald tried to impress upon him the reality of the situation – there was no hope of escape. Sooner or later, he'd have to leave his refuge. Initially, Larry Boy refused, but after considerable coaxing McDonald convinced him that he should come out.

In the end, Larry Boy surrendered without bloodshed after a search that had lasted forty days. Larry was completely naked and it turned out he'd been using his *naga* as a carry bag. He was taken to Mataranka where he was finger-printed and foot-printed. A search

of the cave revealed the .22 rifle with thirty-nine rounds of ammunition, and a small axe that was found by forensic examiner Pat
Salter to perfectly fit the hole in Marjorie's skull.

Larry Boy Janba was committed to trial and found guilty of
the murder of Marjorie and assault on the jackaroo. His record
of interview was struck out because the judge, Justice Blackburn,
found the guarantees reported in the *Northern Territory News* and
the caution police had given Larry Boy in explaining his rights had
meant he may not have understood his right to silence. The night
before Tony Mullagully and Jacob were due to appear in court both
men had their jaws broken. The written statements of the two trackers were accepted as they were unable to give oral testimony. They
either didn't know or wouldn't say who had done it to them.

Larry Boy was sentenced to thirteen years gaol but died just
four years later on 13 June 1972. He was suffering from a parasitic
illness, meliodosis, probably contracted during his years of living
in the Jungle. He was aged only twenty-seven.

Postscript

The cases detailed in this volume tend to be those that are famous
or notable in some way. The murder committed by Larry Boy, however, comes closest to the violent crimes that happen in outback
Australia but are all too rarely reported. Assaults and murders
are disproportionately high (ten to twenty times higher than the
general population) in Aboriginal communities. The victims are
predominantly women. Often the reasons can be traced to cultural
dislocation, caused by relocating people away from their traditional
lands.

In the 1960s the Larry Boy case was regarded as a straightforward case of murder. However, since then increased understanding of Aboriginal culture by the European legal system has led to the gradual realisation that a great deal of Aboriginal crime relates to the social and cultural dislocation caused by the European impact on traditional life. In the 1980s, for example, lawyers in the case of Queenslander Alwyn Peter successfully argued for a reduced sentence because the murder of his girlfriend was a consequence of that dislocation. Peter and his community were living on their tribal lands at Mapoon on Cape York when a mining company decided it wanted the land. The whole community was forcibly removed to a reserve at Weipa where unemployment, social tensions between tribal groups, alcoholism and violence were chronic problems. The killing was not in any way condoned, not even by the remorseful perpetrator, but the circumstances were taken into account in sentencing.

It is also worth noting that one of the great Aboriginal warriors of the Northern Territory, Nemarluk, opposed the coming of Europeans because he thought it would be to the detriment of his community – socially and culturally. In 1931 he and his followers started to actively resist incursions by any foreigners who trespassed on their tribal lands around Port Keats and on the Moyle Plain on the north-west coast of the Northern Territory. Several were killed and Nemarluk was eventually captured in 1934. He was spared the death sentence, dying in gaol in 1940. However, the community that now exists on his tribal lands, Wadeye, has experienced profound social problems that continue to this day.

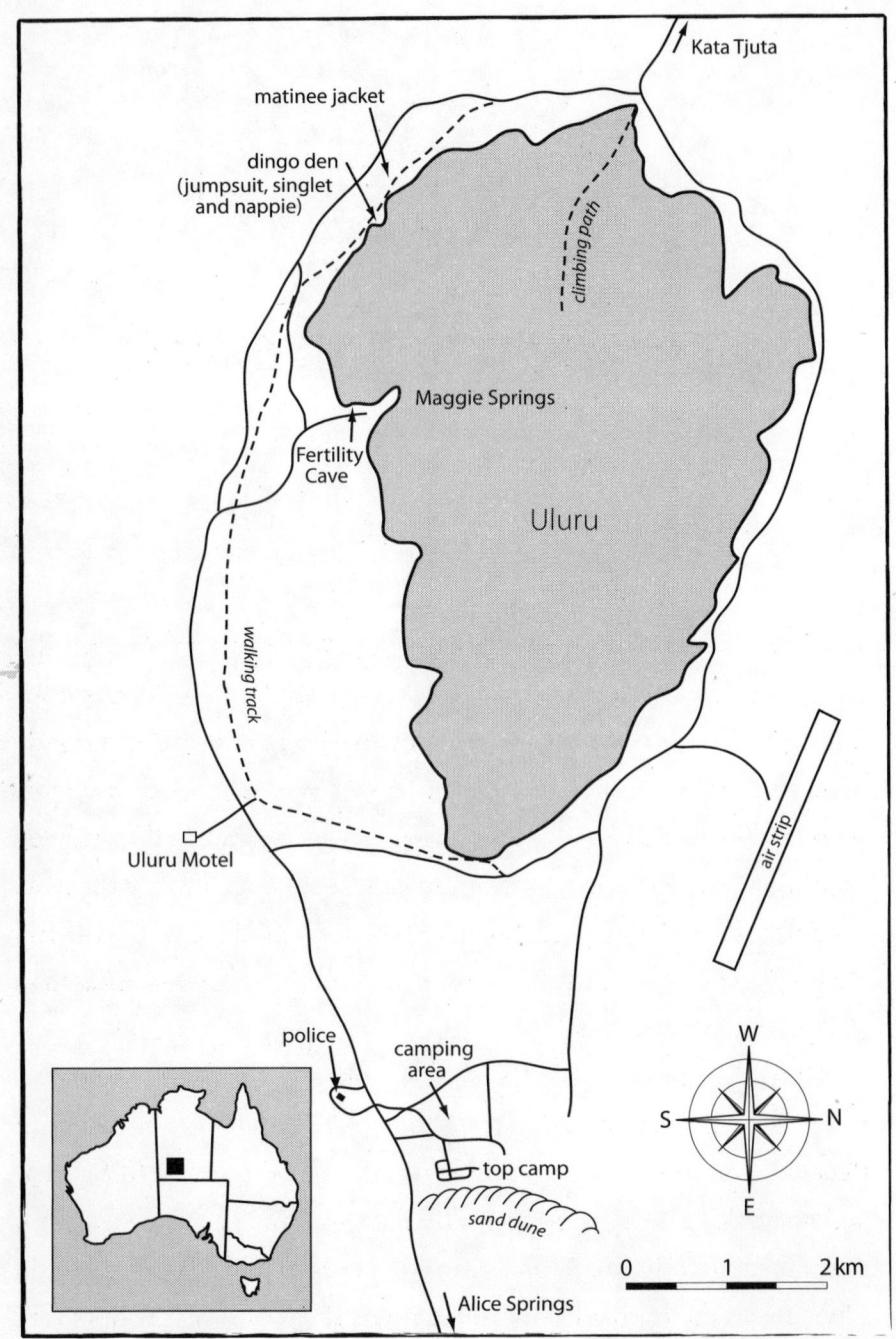

matinee jacket

dingo den
(jumpsuit, singlet
and nappie)

Kata Tjuta

climbing path

Maggie Springs

Fertility
Cave

Uluru

walking track

Uluru Motel

air strip

police

camping
area

top camp

sand dune

W

S   N

E

0   1   2 km

Alice Springs

RED IN TOOTH AND CLAW

In the red centre, ignorance can be lethal. Fail to appreciate the dangers of heat, lack of water, deadly reptiles and immense unpopulated areas where a cry for help will go unanswered, and tragedy is sure to follow. Such knowledge isn't gained easily, yet it seems reasonable that two centuries of European experience in the outback would be enough to be aware of its many hazards. Unfortunately, as recently as 1980, that was shown to be wrong. Sadly, death was only the beginning of what was to become one of the darkest chapters in Australian crime history.

On the afternoon of 17 August, Michael Chamberlain and his wife Alice Lynne (known as Lindy), their two sons Aidan and Reagan, and their new-born daughter Azaria (pronounced Az-aahria) arrived at Uluru, the enigmatic red monolith in the geographic centre of Australia. The Chamberlains were typical of a new breed of visitor to the outback. Improved roads meant more tourists were tackling the huge distances involved to discover 'the real' Australia. But they were also being brought closer to dangers they barely comprehended, if at all.

The Chamberlains knew the country better than most. Michael was a pastor of the Seventh Day Adventist Church (a comparatively strict branch of Christianity) in the tough outback mining town of Mount Isa, and Lindy had visited Uluru with her parents some years before. Lindy thought that her husband, a keen photographer, would find the Rock an ideal subject. Plus the family loved to get away camping on those rare occasions Michael got leave from his religious duties. Although it meant travelling with a babe in arms, the resourceful outback pastor's wife believed she could take it in her stride.

In the quieter top campsite, adjacent to Uluru's main campsite, the Chamberlains pitched their small tent beside the driver's side of their car. Just twenty metres away, they prepared their dinner at a well-lit barbecue area and socialised with another couple, Greg and Sally Lowe from Tasmania. The Lowes were visiting Uluru with their eighteen-month-old daughter Chantelle.

All around the camping ground, families were engaged in similar routines. Many were aware of the wild dingoes patrolling the area, on the lookout for any opportunity to scavenge food. Indeed, the Chamberlains' six-year-old Aidan had been spotlighting a desert mouse near the barbecue area when a dingo pounced from the darkness and snapped up the tiny rodent. The Chamberlains had seen signs around the campsite warning people not to feed the dingoes; however, there was no suggestion they were anything more than a nuisance. Why should there be? Even the Latin name *Canis familiaris dingo* suggests a close relationship with the common dog. Yet the dingo's nearest relative is the Indian wolf, *Canis lupus pallipes* – even zoologists have difficulty telling them apart. There's no such difficulty when it comes to understanding the difference between a dog and a wolf. To a dog, we're a friend. To a wolf, we're prey.

The Chamberlains' youngest son Reagan had already eaten and been put to bed. Aidan was waiting for his mother to get his tiny sister Azaria ready; however, Azaria had other ideas. She kept kicking and wriggling in her mother's arms. Eventually Lindy, wrapping her closely, nursed her on her lap until she fell asleep. Lindy sat quietly for a moment before heading to the tent with Aidan to put them both to bed.

Scrub partly obscured the tent but Greg Lowe saw Lindy kneel to enter it. Inside Azaria was further wrapped against the winter cold. As the baby was being put in her carry basket, Aidan announced that he was still hungry. Lindy hadn't eaten but it had been such a tiring day sightseeing around the Rock that she decided to turn in after feeding Aidan. Thinking she wouldn't be away long, she left the tent flap unzipped when she went to get some baked beans from the family's Torana hatchback. She got them and then raced Aidan the short distance back to the barbecue area.

In the tent next to the Chamberlains', the Wests – Bill, Judy and ten-year-old Catherine – a farming family from Western Australia, had finished their dinner and settled down to quiet evening pastimes. Bill and Judy both heard the low growl of a dingo. Bill thought it sounded like a dog warning another to keep off its property. Just the day before, their daughter had been gripped on the arm by a dingo. The animal had only let go when her parents chased it away.

At the barbecue area Aidan asked, 'Was that bubby crying?'

Sally Lowe replied, 'Yes, it was.'

Lindy was sure Azaria had been sound asleep when she put her to bed but Michael, who had heard the sound as well, suggested she go and check. As she walked ten metres towards the tent, she saw a dingo coming out of it. The animal was partly in the shadow cast by the low bushes, but it looked like it had something in its mouth. The dingo struggled to get past the tent flap, then shook its head vigorously.

Thinking it had one of Michael's shoes, Lindy shouted something like, 'Go on, get out.' The dingo bolted. Then she thought Azaria might have cried because the dingo had bitten her. She turned to the tent, and pulled open the flap.

'My God! My God! The dingo's got my baby!'

Lindy's scream came from the depths of a mother's worst nightmare.

Michael and the Lowes rushed towards the tent as Lindy dived inside. Azaria's carry basket was empty. She checked Reagan to make sure he was alive, and then was out of the tent, moving in the direction she thought the dingo had gone. She saw a dingo behind the car and chased it into the dark scrub, then lost sight of it. Even in the midst of the horror surrounding her, she thought there was nothing in its mouth. It didn't make sense. Her husband and Greg Lowe ran past, plunging into the impenetrable black of the desert night.

Lindy's screams brought the Wests from their tent and people from nearby converged as well. Michael, in shock, returned to get a torch from the car but he couldn't find his keys. He didn't need them; the car was unlocked. The torch was useless anyway, the batteries were flat. Car headlights were turned on the scrub but they only cast shadows that added to the confusion. Men and women came from everywhere.

A nearby camper, Murray Haby, ran up to Lindy, 'Which way did the dingo go and how big is the baby?'

'I didn't see Azaria in its jaws,' she said.

Michael rushed up to the tent of the Whittaker family, who were listening to hymns on their radio. Illogically, under the circumstances, he asked them why. They explained to Michael that they were Christians.

'Then pray, please pray. A dingo has taken our baby. She is probably dead by now. She was nine weeks old,' he replied.

Instead of praying, Max Whittaker and his daughter Rosalie grabbed torches and jackets and headed into the darkness to help.

Michael cried out, 'I am a minister of the gospel.'

Prompted by not seeing Azaria in the dingo's mouth, Lindy rushed into the scrub, checked and rechecked the tent and then searched the immediate vicinity, fearing her daughter might have been dropped, injured, and was lying unnoticed in the shadows. More and more people arrived and moved out into the scrub with torches, covering a wider and wider area, criss-crossing the red desert sands with countless footprints. Someone went to alert the police and park rangers.

Sally Lowe noticed Aidan, intensely upset, crying, 'The dog has bubby in his tummy.'

Sally took Aidan to the Chamberlains' tent, where she found a pool of blood. Recalling the foreshortened nature of Azaria's cry, she began to suspect Azaria might have been dead before being taken from the tent. There was more blood on clothing and sleeping bags. Aidan, seeing it, cried out terrified that Reagan had been killed, too, but he was unharmed and 'sleeping'. In fact he'd gone into an almost catatonic state, neither moving nor making a sound, trying not to attract attention – an instinctive reaction by the young of some species as a last defence against the presence of a predator.

Amy Whittaker, a nursing sister and trauma counsellor, arrived to take care of a profoundly distressed Lindy Chamberlain. Her husband was still searching the dunes with Greg Lowe, concerned that, in the freezing night air, a child only nine weeks old and suffering blood loss could not survive long. Camp lights on stands were brought in to illuminate the area around the tent.

An official-looking vehicle pulled up, containing Senior Park Ranger Derek Roff. This was the realisation of his worst nightmare. Earlier that month he'd written to his superiors warning them that the behaviour of a group of dingoes was becoming increasingly aggressive towards the tourists visiting Uluru. He'd had four reports of attacks and several complaints. And now this.

Roff told Lindy not to disturb the tent as the police would need it for evidence. This was easier said than done as Reagan and Aidan were 'sleeping' inside.

The senior police officer at Uluru, Constable Frank Morris, arrived, also warning that the tent needed to be preserved for evidence. In between coordinating the search he grabbed moments to question Lindy, gaining a fragmented understanding of what Azaria was wearing. There was a jumpsuit, a singlet and a nappy inside the jumpsuit. Lindy might or might not have mentioned (in later interviews she stated that she had) that there was a matinee jacket outside the other clothing, but Morris took no notes. What seemed particularly confusing was that she said a dingo had taken Azaria, but she couldn't say if she'd seen her baby in the dingo's mouth. In part, that was why she had searched the vicinity of the car repeatedly. Perhaps the dingo had dropped Azaria. The possibility that there might have been two dingoes hadn't occurred to her.

A group of searchers had gathered and Michael addressed them. 'I want to thank you all for what you're doing,' he said. 'I'm a minister of religion and I know that nothing happens in the world unless God allows it. I know our baby has passed from us into heaven. My wife and I must not be sad, but jubilant that our little daughter is safe in the arms of Jesus.' One of the searchers embraced him to comfort him. When they parted, Michael was crying.

Two dogs were brought in to track Azaria's scent. Standing beside, then sitting in the front passenger seat of the family car, Lindy presented one of Azaria's garments for each dog to smell. Neither dog gave any sign that there was anything suspicious in the front seat of the Chamberlains' car.

Out in the dunes Murray Haby was having some success. Haby was an amateur tracker, a skill he'd acquired in childhood and had kept up ever since. Searching on his own he'd found the tracks of a large dingo. The depth of the front-paw prints in the red sand of the desert suggested it was carrying something heavy. The tracks led up a big sand dune that extended in a north-south direction to the east of the camping area. He saw what he thought were blood spots in the lighter red sand, and there was a small furrow where, what-ever the dingo was carrying, had been dragged along the ground. Near the top of the dune Haby found a shallow depression in the sand. The dingo had laid its burden on the ground. Haby could see the imprint of knitted fabric and knew he was on the right trail. Unfortunately, as he went on the sand became more densely packed and the tracks less distinct. Then they disappeared altogether. Haby had arrived at the car park of Uluru's sunrise viewing area. On the hard ground the tracks he'd been following were gone.

Haby backtracked, following the paw prints, and was led directly to the Chamberlains' campsite. He sought out the ranger and reported his findings. Roff had found countless dingo tracks criss-crossing the area but none as hopeful as Haby's. He'd been joined by Aboriginal trackers Nuwe Minyintiri, his daughter Barbara (wife of tribal elder Nipper Winmatti who was too old to search in the cold winter night) and Daisy Walkabout. While most campers could scarcely believe that a dingo had killed a baby, Uluru's traditional custodians, with thousands of years' experience in the outback, weren't surprised at all.

Minyintiri led the other trackers and Roff, following the dingo tracks Haby had found through the maze of others until he reached the small depression where the animal had laid something down. He found two more similar marks nearby. Looking at the marks he made a grim observation, 'Not move any more.'

Minyintiri managed to follow the tracks further than Haby, but he lost them where a group of searchers had climbed the ridge in a line, obliterating the trail entirely. He thought he might have more success when daylight came.

When Constable Gordon Noble arrived with local bush nurse Bobbie Downs, she immediately recognised that Lindy Chamberlain was in deep shock and that staying at the source of that shock was only making matters worse. Accommodation was arranged at a nearby motel, the Uluru, and the Chamberlains' belongings were loaded into their car, including items from the tent that were spotted with blood from Azaria. Noble did so despite the suggestions of Ranger Roff and Constable Morris that the tent scene should be preserved as evidence.

Word had spread concerning the incident at the camping area. In the bar of the Uluru Motel, late-night guests were among the first to express doubts that a dingo could have taken a baby. Their view grew from ignorance of the true danger a dingo posed. Because they had never heard of this happening before, it seemed inconceivable that it had happened for the first time now. This perspective would soon influence the judgment of an entire nation.

Early next morning, when radiophone communications opened, news of what had happened spread to the outside world. The night before, a radio message had been relayed to Police Inspector Michael Gilroy at Alice Springs that an Aboriginal child had been taken by a dingo from a camp. Now, Constable Morris reported that, in fact, it was the child of a tourist. Inspector Gilroy decided he and Duty Sergeant John Lincoln should fly to the Rock to supervise the investigation.

Morris had already visited the Chamberlains at the motel early in the morning to tell them nothing had been found. They were sorting through numerous belongings that had blood on them to give to the police to assist their investigation. Aidan's parka had blood on it but without it the boy would freeze, so he was allowed to keep it.

The *Adelaide News* called Michael. He agreed to take photos as a way to publicise the danger. Geoff de Luca, the newspaper's police roundsman, spoke to him about the possibility of doing an interview with them both at Uluru. Michael also did a brief interview with the paper's managing editor, Greg Reid, warning of the dangers of dingoes at Uluru.

Morris picked up Inspector Gilroy and Duty Sergeant Lincoln from the airstrip and briefed them on what he knew. Asked if he had taken notes, Morris replied that he'd had too much to do. At the campsite Gilroy and Lincoln found what appeared to be saliva on a corner of the tent and on the ground nearby, and saw what seemed to be a spray of blood on the tent.

Less than twenty-four hours after Azaria Chamberlain disappeared, the problems for the police investigation were already emerging. Gilroy and Lincoln were required to gather evidence for a coronial inquest into the incident; however, in the chaotic early hours of the search, while a young life might still have hung in the balance, considerations such as preserving evidence, let alone establishing a crime scene, were not paramount. All the two men had to go on were the few fragments of the scene that remained intact. Even the eyewitnesses were disappearing. No one had taken down names and addresses, so once the initial search had scaled down most resumed their holidays and drove away. The only record of their presence was a list of car registration numbers, given when they had booked to stay in the camping area.

That day the Chamberlains gave statements to Gilroy and

Lincoln. Lindy's was detailed and thorough, Michael's veered off on tangents and into theorising. His calling as the spiritual leader of a congregation had trained him how to advise and guide people whose lives were in crisis. In his own crisis he clung to that role, and his behaviour came across as strange. Journalist Geoff de Luca came to a similar conclusion after he'd interviewed both the Chamberlains for television.

That night the three policemen – Gilroy, Lincoln and Morris – and the journalist De Luca discussed the case over a few beers. There'd been no sign of Azaria, not even her clothes, found in any of the known dingo lairs around the Rock. There was a feeling that the Chamberlains' story didn't add up and Lincoln in particular was suspicious. A key reason was Azaria's weight. Lindy maintained that Azaria weighed six kilograms. Lincoln didn't believe a dingo could carry a child weighing that much, and certainly not over any distance. In fact, none of the men had any experience of what a dingo could or could not do.

A week after Azaria's disappearance the Chamberlains were back home in Mount Isa, fending off an increasingly fascinated media, when they learned from a news team, first, that they were suspected of killing their daughter; and, second, that her clothes had been found, folded, at a dingo lair at Uluru.

Birdwatchers Wally Goodwin and his daughter had found some of Azaria's garments in a dingo lair unknown even to park rangers and Aboriginal trackers. The initial impression was that Azaria or parts of her were still inside the clothes. Around the scene her nappy had been shredded.

Goodwin called Constable Morris, who appeared disconcerted by what looked like a grim discovery. He picked up the garments with his bare hands, which surprised Goodwin. Like anyone who's ever watched a cop show, he thought it a strange way to handle evidence, and said so. Morris answered he was checking they were the right clothes, and eventually replaced them in the position he thought he'd found them. Later, on television, other police were shown openly handling the clothing prior to it being forensically tested.

The area around the dingo lair was searched. However, the matinee jacket that Lindy Chamberlain maintained Azaria was wearing outside her other clothing wasn't found. The discovery of the clothing added fuel and provided yet another twist to a story that was growing day by day. From the media's point-of-view it had everything: an innocent child missing, an isolated location, an implausible and shocking explanation, suspicions about what really happened and a mother and father who didn't fit the expectations of how grieving parents should behave. Did the dingo do it? If a dingo couldn't do it, was it the Chamberlains? As opinion started to polarise, the controversy grew. To the delight of media proprietors, so did their circulations.

Extraordinary rumours began to spread: Azaria was retarded, which was why her parents got rid of her; she was used in a ritual execution to atone for the sins of her parents' religion; Lindy dressed her child entirely in black; she starved her daughter, on one occasion for at least eight hours; Azaria's name meant sacrifice in the desert. Then there were the jokes: How do you bring up a baby in the desert? Stick your finger down a dingo's throat.

On 28 August the case was reassigned to Alice Springs Detective Sergeant Graeme Charlwood. One of Charlwood's first tasks was to begin the time-consuming process of tracking down the eyewitnesses who had dispersed to the far corners of the country.

The clothing found at the dingo lair also had to be sent to forensic science laboratories in Adelaide to be checked for samples of vegetation that might have been picked up while it was being carried to the lair, along with dingo hair, saliva and damage consistent with a dingo attack. When it came to testing for dingo saliva, however, there was no such test in existence. Biochemist Dr Andrew Scott had to devise one.

In Mount Isa the Chamberlains, still dealing with their grief, were finding more items marked by that fateful night in the desert. Several blood-stained items that had not been considered important by police were taken to a dry cleaner. However, a space blanket that had been covering Reagan was marked by paw prints – which Lindy's mother and her sister-in-law both believed they could see. Suspecting it to be important evidence, they called the police. An officer, who Lindy and her parents later described as a uniformed blond policeman, no more than twenty-four years old, came to collect the space blanket. When Lindy explained its significance and pointed out the paw prints, she recalled that he said, 'Oh yes, there's no dou—', then checked himself.

In late September 1980, Charlwood travelled to Mount Isa to re-interview the Chamberlains. He found them packing as they'd been transferred from Mount Isa to the Seventh Day Adventist College at Cooranbong, on the New South Wales Central Coast. Among their belongings Charlwood was surprised to see a small coffin, which Michael explained was used as part of his quit-smoking presentations.

The interviews of the Chamberlain family were conducted at Mount Isa Police Station. Charlwood attempted to secretly record them, but only succeeded in recording parts of the interviews. He did manage, though, to record himself referring to Michael Chamberlain as 'a fucking little weed'. Once again, Lindy and Michael were asked to relive the agonising moments of their daughter's disappearance. The boys were interviewed as well. Aidan gave a lucid statement that corroborated his parents' version of events, but young Reagan was so intimidated that he retreated into silence.

Graeme Charlwood revealed to Lindy that the tests done on Azaria's clothing had concluded that, whatever happened, a dingo wasn't involved. Dingo saliva: negative. Damage caused by a dingo: negative. Dingo hair: probably cat. This was the first time Lindy had been officially informed about the results of the tests, but they'd already been leaked to the media and reported widely. It was becoming increasingly obvious that, while many in the community thought the Chamberlains had killed their daughter, an increasing number of investigators were also coming to a similar view. And Lindy – attractive, smart, always seeming to be in control – the last person to see Azaria alive, had become the prime target.

While the Chamberlains were being interviewed, from mid-afternoon and into the evening, their car was checked for blood by two local police. No blood was found, nor any sign that the car had been recently cleaned.

Police were also slowly building the list of eyewitnesses who might be relevant to their investigation. As the weeks passed they started to contact people like the Lowes, Wests, Habys and Whittakers. Some, like the Wests, were oblivious to the suspicions swirling around the Chamberlains. When they learned of the accusations they were shocked. Nothing they'd seen on that night suggested anything but a horrific tragedy.

Until the statements from eyewitnesses were gathered, police only had the Chamberlains' accounts of the events surrounding Azaria's disappearance. The lack of corroboration allowed a range of alternative scenarios to present themselves to the investigators. For example, the Chamberlains had admitted to and had been observed sightseeing just 400 metres from the dingo lair where Azaria's clothes were found. So it was suggested that Azaria had been killed at Uluru during the afternoon, her clothes left in the lair to make it look like she'd been taken by the dingo and the alarm raised later that night.

However, as the eyewitness statements came in, they completely contradicted such notions; in particular, Sally Lowe's recollection of hearing Azaria's cry immediately before Lindy screamed at seeing the dingo. Yet, by the time these corroborating statements were collected, the view that it wasn't a dingo had already been firmly planted in the public's mind. The eyewitness recollections also flatly contradicted the expert opinions of the forensic scientists. Who should be believed?

Azaria Chamberlain's disappearance continued to sell newspapers. It was in the media's interest to explore each fresh twist, because circulation increased with every new rumour, suspicion, opinion and leak. Until the Chamberlains were actually charged with something (the media would then be restricted to reporting only the 'facts of the case'), suspicion alone meant it was open season. Meanwhile, anonymous forensic scientists doing valuable but largely unrecognised work suddenly found their names headlining television news and front pages, and reporters calling them for the latest angle. The case was debated in offices, pubs, restaurants, sporting venues and homes in every corner of the land.

On 15 December 1980, when Coroner Denis Barritt opened the inquest into the disappearance of Azaria Chantel Chamberlain at Alice Springs, the media attention had few precedents in Australian history. Every day the court room was packed to overflowing. To accommodate the media, the jury box was pressed into service, an irony not lost on many. The Chamberlains had been subjected to trial by media, and many journalists had openly concluded that the Chamberlains had killed their daughter.

The Chamberlains were represented by lawyer Peter Dean. For the second half of the inquest he was joined by Philip Rice QC (costs for both were met by the Chamberlains' church). Ashley Macknay was counsel assisting the coroner. Lindy was the first witness and went through the distressing task of detailing what had happened, moment by moment, for what was at least the fourth time. Lindy was also asked to comment on forensic dentist Ken Brown's conclusion that the tears in Azaria's jumpsuit and singlet were not consistent with a dingo attack. Lindy replied that she was no expert but his tests were on zoo or semi-domesticated dingoes, not wild ones. Later she challenged many of the forensic reports saying that they gave no hard evidence.

'It is interpretive depending on who is reading it,' she said.

However, the lack of saliva and plant material on Azaria's jump-suit could only be explained if it was covered by the matinee jacket that Lindy claimed Azaria was wearing at the time – or if Lindy had killed her daughter and disposed of her clothing but hadn't been clever enough to outwit the forensic scientists. But the matinee jacket hadn't been found, despite what police maintained was an extensive search. If it was a fabrication, it meant Lindy was trying to cover her tracks.

When forensic scientist Ken Brown took the stand, he explained how in one of his experiments he'd used a dingo skull from a museum in an attempt to replicate the bite marks caused by a live wild dingo. The revelation provoked laughter in the courtroom, and reports in the media added to Brown's public embarrassment. However, the unusual experiment demonstrated the new forensic frontiers that the Chamberlain case was presenting to scientists.

As the inquest progressed, there were many disturbing instances of evidence being mishandled. When the space blanket that had covered Reagan was produced as evidence, it no longer bore anything that resembled paw prints. According to Lindy, who had inspected them before delivering the blanket into the hands of the police, the marks were so embedded into the material they could only have been removed deliberately.

With regard to the finding of the clothing, the rangers maintained that it was impossible that they would have been found in that manner if dingoes were involved. However, when Wally Goodwin took the stand, he looked at photographs of the clothing and promptly announced that the pictures didn't show the way they were found. It was the way they were replaced by Constable Morris after he'd handled them. Goodwin testified that his young daughter had screamed when she'd seen the clothes because they'd looked like the body might still be inside.

Far worse was to come when Police Forensic Section Officer Moira Fogarty gave her evidence. Fogarty was new to the forensic section (with only three months' on-the-job experience), but she had received only bald instructions when given items to test such as the Chamberlains' tent – 'look for hair, look for blood'. Inspector Gilroy had wanted part of the tent tested for saliva, but it was instead tested for blood and naturally came back negative to saliva. Fogarty had taken the clothes (already handled by police on at least two previous occasions) from their boxes and swept anything that dropped off onto the floor. She vacuumed the clothing and put anything that came off into containers in a cupboard. Anything that had come off in the boxes the clothes had been transported in remained there, in a cupboard somewhere in the Forensic Section. Everything eventually was sent to Dr Andrew Scott in Adelaide but by then much of the evidence was damaged or lost. The arterial spray on the tent could only be identified as blood, not the blood of a child of Azaria's age.

Adelaide hair specialist Dr Harry Harding, on learning the forensic procedure, requested an opportunity to change his evidence. When he'd examined the clothing he hadn't known that the clothes had been vacuumed. He was sent the vacuumings, which included hair, feathers and other materials, but the hairs remaining were so damaged that he could not derive a conclusive result.

The inquest also took evidence in sessions at Uluru. The coroner inspected the sites where the events occurred and where evidence was found. Aboriginal trackers were interviewed but much of their evidence concerning the presence of two dingoes was misunderstood by the lawyers conducting the inquiry, due to language and cultural differences. Nipper Winmatti was the tribal elder entitled to speak on behalf of the tribe, and he was accustomed to speaking for other members using the first person 'I'. When it was learned that he had not been tracking on the night Azaria disappeared his evidence (when he was actually speaking about the tracking done by Nuwe Minyintiri) was largely discounted. Winmatti spoke some English but had a female interpreter assigned, a cultural insult, and the female trackers who testified had male interpreters.

When Winmatti was asked if dingoes ever took Aboriginal babies he denied any knowledge of such a thing, but the inquest hadn't realised the question touched on a taboo subject. The birth of twins presented a difficult situation for desert Aboriginals living on the knife edge of survival. If there were only enough resources to support one baby, a mother who tried to raise two might condemn both to death. The heart-rending solution for the extremely family-oriented Aboriginal people had long since been abandoned but it remained a painful secret memory. One they were unwilling to even acknowledge, let alone discuss.

To those who knew something about dingoes, much of the evidence presented at the inquest demonstrated a continuing ignorance of what the animals could do. Les Harris, president of the Dingo Foundation, had rung Inspector Gilroy shortly after Azaria had disappeared to set him straight, apparently without success. Before the inquest he also wrote to Coroner Denis Barritt. His report 'On the Propensity of Dingoes to Attack Humans' explained that a solitary dingo would totally consume a six-kilogram mammal in less than twenty minutes, not even leaving the bones, and that such a mammal is smaller than a dingo's usual prey, such as wallabies. Dingoes are fussy eaters and would be smart enough to easily remove Azaria's clothing without causing extensive damage. Being desert dwellers, they need to conserve moisture, so they don't salivate much, even when eating.

In summing up, Ashley Macknay, counsel assisting the coroner, made the assessment that the whole case came down to one simple question: was Lindy Chamberlain telling the truth? He noted that significant forensic bungling had put scientific confirmation in doubt, and in the case of the supervision of Moira Fogarty he noted that: 'It really shows almost derogation of responsibility on the part of the supervisor.'

When he brought down his finding on 20 February 1981, Coroner Denis Barritt went much further. Such was the interest in the case that he took the unprecedented step of allowing the presentation of his findings to be televised live. His summation was a systematic demolition of the culture of suspicion and rumour that had surrounded the Chamberlains, the Seventh Day Adventist Church and the death of Azaria. He extended his deepest sympathy to the Chamberlains, who, he said, had 'been subjected to months of innuendoes, suspicion and probably the most malicious gossip ever witnessed in this country. I have taken the unusual step of permitting these proceedings to be televised today in the hope that, by direct and accurate communication, such innuendoes, suspicion, and gossip may cease.'

For many of those watching, including this writer (at the time a final-year journalism student), it was a stinging rebuke for all the gossip, jokes and speculation we'd readily indulged in over the previous six months.

Barritt found that Azaria had been killed and taken by a dingo. Yet he also found that 'after her death the body of Azaria was taken from the possession of the dingo and disposed of by an unknown method, by a person or persons unknown'. Barritt's sharpest words were directed at the forensic investigation:

> *Once again during this inquest I have had occasion to criticise the work performed by the Northern Territory Police Force Forensic Science Section. Police forces must realise, or be made to realise, that courts will not tolerate any standard less than complete objectivity from anyone claiming to make scientific observations. This standard must be attained, and maintained, whether the examination in question is of a simple or complex character.*

His words, now largely forgotten, were apt then and prescient in respect to subsequent investigations of the Azaria Chamberlain case that followed. They were an unequivocal public humiliation of the Northern Territory Police Forensic Science Section, and had they been taken to heart the Chamberlains and several forensic scientists could have been spared the far worse pain that was to come.

Instead, Northern Territory Chief Minister and Attorney General Paul Everingham came out in defence of his police force, whose performance reflected poorly on the fledgling Northern Territory government. Forensic scientist Ken Brown was particularly stung and said so in a press release. When he applied to carry out further tests on Azaria's clothing, permission was promptly given by a Northern Territory government in damage control. In their view the case was far from closed.

Brown, himself a Seventh Day Adventist, sent the clothes to the highly credentialed London forensic pathologist Professor James Cameron. Despite having precisely zero experience of damage inflicted by dingoes (but with a museum's dingo skull provided by Brown), Cameron arrived at the opinion that Azaria's jumpsuit was cut by scissors or a knife, not dingo teeth. He ascertained that the jumpsuit had been buried with the child still in it. His remarkable skills with ultra-violet photography also revealed the bloodstained imprint of a female hand. He concluded that Azaria had died by having her throat cut by a woman who held her upright.

Cameron's sensational new findings changed everything. Paul Everingham became personally involved in the running of the police task force, Operation Ochre. On 19 September 1981, police, led by Graeme Charlwood, raided the Chamberlain home at Cooranbong, followed hotly by a large media contingent that had been updated on developments at Paul Everingham's simultaneous press conference announcing the reopening of the case. The raid took place on a Saturday, the Sabbath for Seventh Day Adventists. Dozens of items were taken from the Chamberlains as evidence, including their car. Twelve months after Azaria's death at Uluru it was to be tested again. At the same time, police were visiting a select list of witnesses.

In November 1981, the Northern Territory Supreme Court quashed the findings of the first coronial inquest into Azaria's disappearance and ordered a new one. Even before it began in Alice Springs on 14 December (a day short of a year after the first inquest), some sections of the media were calling it a trial by ambush. Information about evidence and details of witnesses (including the order in which they were to be called) were with-held from the Chamberlains' defence as much as possible. The media, on the other hand, tipped off the Chamberlains' defence that the flow of information they received was noticeably superior, and at times, denied to the defence team. Some journalists passed material on.

The coroner for the second inquest was Gerry Galvin, with Brisbane barrister Des Sturgess counsel assisting. The Chamberlains' legal team now comprised senior counsel Phil Rice QC, junior counsel Andrew Kirkham and solicitors Stuart Tipple and Peter Dean. Again, the cash-strapped family was reliant primarily on the largesse of their church for their representation.

The ambush wasn't limited to Lindy and Michael Chamberlain. Sally Lowe, in particular, came in for a grilling from Des Sturgess. The day before she was to give evidence at the inquest, he'd questioned her closely on the possibility that Azaria was already dead when Sally saw her at the campsite. Sally Lowe refused to be shaken from her original testimony when asked if Lindy had made Azaria's legs kick when she was nursing the restless child to simulate life, and whether the cry she had heard from the tent might have been a tape recording.

Once again, the focus on Azaria's mother was most relentless. For those who were certain that Lindy Chamberlain was 'a mur-dering bitch' the justice system was simply doing its job. For those who thought she was a woman who had endured a parent's worst nightmare, it was a further descent into a legal obscenity as she was taken moment by moment through the events of 17 August 1980 yet again.

Among all the new evidence being presented, the hand print on the jumpsuit was one item that posed a significant problem for Lindy's defence team. If she refused to provide her hand print for comparison it would make her look like she had something to hide. If she did provide a hand print, even an inconclusive match would be enough to make her look guilty. She couldn't win, until her lawyers came up with the answer. She testified that she was perfectly happy to give a hand print but her defence team had advised her not to. Only a legal mind could come up with the perfect answer: 'Yes but no'.

Then there was the evidence of the experts. Professor Cameron, exuding the supreme confidence of an experienced expert witness, gave his evidence regarding cuts, bleeding and ultra-violet revelations of female hand prints. By then, however, his definite 'female hand print' had become a less absolute 'small hand', which few at the inquest could even make out from the vague smudge he offered.

A textiles expert from New South Wales University, Professor Malcolm Chaikin, was both animated and self-assured when he testified that the damage to Azaria's clothing was consistent with scissors being used to make the cuts rather than a dog or any other canine. Other experts confirmed his views.

Most compelling of all, however, was the evidence of blood found in the Chamberlains' car. New South Wales forensic pathologist Joy Kuhl presented her evidence with practised confidence, testifying that she had got positive reactions to blood from the door handles, the console, seats and carpet. It had also been found on the hinge of the passenger seat (where it folded forward), under the seat and, from what appeared to be an 'arterial spray', in the underdash area on the front passenger side. This and blood on a ten cent coin under the passenger seat tested as foetal haemoglobin, the blood of a child under three months. Items taken from the vehicle also tested positive for blood – including a towel, nail scissors and Michael's camera bag.

Professor of Biological Science at the University of Newcastle, Barry Boettcher, was called as a defence witness and expressed considerable doubt about Joy Kuhl's testing methods and, therefore, the stated results. The defence also knew that Michael Chamberlain had a friend with the same model Torana as his, which also had an 'arterial spray' in the exact same place as the Chamberlain's car. Was it really possible that two identical Toranas had been at the scene of the slaughter of an innocent child? That information wasn't presented at the inquest, because the defence team decided to save it for the increasingly likely trial.

Des Sturgess's summing up presented an extraordinary scenario of the death of Azaria Chamberlain. What had come to be regarded as 'the dingo theory' was disregarded entirely. The Crown's case was that at some time during the day Lindy had cut Azaria's throat in the car, hidden the body in Michael's camera bag or some other place, and told him about it later. Then during the evening they'd taken the body away from the camping area and buried it. Later, with Michael's help, Lindy had dug Azaria up, removed her clothing, reburied the body, cut the clothing with scissors to make it look like a dingo attack and then taken the clothing four kilometres from the camping area to Uluru to plant it at the dingo lair.

By any measure it was quite a stretch. On 2 February 1982, Coroner Gerry Galvin brought down his finding. This time no television cameras were permitted in the courtroom when Galvin committed Lindy Chamberlain to stand trial for the murder of her daughter. Michael was charged as an accessory after the fact.

The problems for the Chamberlains' defence were many, including time and money. Their membership of the Seventh Day Adventist Church was a mixed blessing. Their faith was seen by a large section of the public and media as setting them apart. Yet their church, however reluctantly, continued to fund their efforts to defend themselves. If they'd simply been on their own, either of the two inquests would have bankrupted them, rendering them virtually defenceless. When it came to the trial, the massive resources of the Northern Territory government would have rolled right over them, guilty or innocent.

In the midst of the legal pushing and shoving, and the intense media scrutiny, the Chamberlains still struggled to maintain some semblance of a family life. Lindy in particular was keen to have another child, but had become savvy enough regarding the whims of public opinion to realise her pregnancy would be perceived as an attempt to gain sympathy during the trial. However, if she was found guilty and spent a substantial amount of time in prison, she'd be too old to have another child by the time she was released, if, indeed, she ever was released. She calculated that if she timed it right, her pregnancy wouldn't be showing when the trial took place. Unfortunately, the trial was delayed. Nature not being so accommodating, Lindy was only two months from full-term when the trial started.

The trial began in Darwin, on 13 September 1982, before Justice James Muirhead. The prosecution was represented by Ian Barker

QC, Des Sturgess QC, Tom Pauling and Michael O'Laughlin. For their defence the Chamberlains had John Phillips QC, Andy Kirkham QC and solicitor Stuart Tipple. They were also provided with legal aid solicitor Greg Cavanagh.

The case was dubbed by the media 'the trial of the century'. It was certainly the biggest thing in Darwin since the place had been levelled by Cyclone Tracy in 1974, and it was the most reported trial in Australia's history. The case could no longer be said to be polarising the nation. There was now a third group for whom the claims and counter-claims of the previous two years simply produced confusion and a gnawing doubt that the chances of the Chamberlains getting a fair trial were virtually nil. *Canberra Times* cartoonist Geoff Pryor captured the problem of finding an impartial jury with an illustration of a broken-down bushie in a remote out-back location asking two men who've landed in a chopper, 'Azaria 'oo?' One of the men replies, 'One down, 11 to go.'

At the trial the Crown case shifted once again. At the second inquest an element of premeditation had been suggested; now the prosecution alleged the murder to be spontaneous. Rather than bed Azaria down for the night, Lindy had taken her baby to the family car, sat in the front seat, cut the baby's head off using a pair of nail scissors, stuffed the body into her husband's camera bag, got out of the car, gone to the boot and got a can of baked beans for Aidan (who was either present or very nearby throughout the murder), then gone back to the campsite and heated the beans for the boy, who showed not the least trauma at seeing his baby sister butchered before his eyes. This all occurred in a well-lit area just twenty metres from the barbecue area where two independent

207

eyewitnesses were standing. The prosecution's case was presented as the scenario that was suggested by irrefutable circumstantial evidence. No motive for Lindy's behaviour was offered.

For all the foregoing to have happened, Azaria had to have been dead before Lindy returned to the barbecue area. If Sally Lowe had heard Azaria cry, it meant Azaria was still alive just moments before Lindy raised the alarm. To counter this and other weaknesses in its case, the prosecution adopted a tactic of questioning all the eyewitnesses first, then moving on to the forensic evidence. The eyewitnesses were dealt with in a few days; the forensic experts took weeks to contradict the eyewitness accounts, even as those accounts faded in the memories of the jurors.

During the murder trial, Mount Isa Detective Sergeant Brown took the stand and stated that he was the policeman who had picked up the space blanket the Chamberlains claimed had paw prints on it. He knew nothing of paw prints. However, Lindy Chamberlain, her mother and her father (who'd been present when the space blanket was picked up) did not recognise Detective Sergeant Brown. The matter wasn't followed up in the trial, but neither was it forgotten.

Lindy was asked to go through the distressing details of Azaria's death in intimate detail. It hadn't gotten any easier. When she saw the bunny rug her daughter had been wrapped in, she broke down in tears. Later she broke down again, as did some of the jurors. When Justice Muirhead asked if she wanted a break, she replied that she just wanted to get it over with.

The trial, and much of Lindy's cross-examination, revolved around blood. The Crown's case was that any blood in the car disproved 'the dingo theory' and established it as the site of the murder. However, an estimated seven millilitres of blood was found on just one item among many that were in the tent, but all of the blood found in the car amounted to only five millilitres. One explanation was that the blood found in the car came from an injured hitchhiker the Chamberlains had transported to hospital several years before. He'd had a head injury that had bled profusely. Further refutation came from the technical evidence given by Professor Boettcher. He all but demolished the case for foetal blood being present in the car, if only you could understand what he was talking about.

A similar demolition job was done on the evidence of Professor Cameron by Victorian forensic pathologist Professor Vernon Pleuckhahn. It was also revealed that evidence by Cameron had resulted in false convictions in England. In one case, Cameron had claimed he could see the perpetrator's initials written in blood on the victim. Lindy herself demolished the evidence of the blood-stained hand. Each of her fingers had the two joints and three bones that are normal for most of the population; however, the middle finger of the image Cameron had discovered clearly had an extra joint. The hand, if it was a hand, was definitely not Lindy's.

The trial ground on through September and all of October 1982. It went on so long that there was a chance Lindy would give birth during her trial. Finally, towards the end of October, the summing up began. For the prosecution, Ian Barker stated that there was no recorded instance of a dingo killing a human being. 'They're not man-eaters,' he said. The evidence against the Chamberlains was circumstantial but compelling. If a dingo didn't do it, and a dingo couldn't do it, then it had to have been the Chamberlains.

In his summing up, Judge Muirhead highlighted the conflicting points of view regarding the forensic evidence, then went to the point that the whole case hinged on – Azaria's cry. If the jury believed Sally Lowe had heard it, then all of the expert opinion was only that – opinion – and they should acquit. It was reported after the trial that Justice Muirhead concluded early in its course that the Chamberlains were not guilty. He is also reported as saying that he thought he summed up in their favour.

However, the verdict wasn't up to him. On 29 October the jury adjourned to consider what they had learned during a seven-week trial that had seen seventy-three witnesses, 145 exhibits, 2800 pages of transcripts, plus the evidence from two inquests (if they'd read it). While they were out Barker approached the defence team. He thought he'd lost the case and asked how much they'd be demanding in compensation.

As the evening wore on, the doubts grew. Finally, at around 9 p.m., word came through that the jury was ready. They, the judge, the prosecution and defence teams, and the Chamberlains returned to a courtroom tense with anticipation and filled to capacity with media and those members of the public who had managed to squeeze their way in. When the court was brought to order, the jury was asked for their verdict.

The foreman stood to address the court.

'On the charge of murder?'

'Guilty.'

'On the charge of Michael being an accessory?'

'Guilty.'

There was a stunned silence. Two female jurors and one male

juror were in tears. Ian Barker, the successful prosecutor, was ashen faced. *Sydney Morning Herald* journalist Malcolm Brown broke the spell.

'Bastards,' he shouted.

It was reported that around the country people in public places stood and applauded the verdict. Judge Muirhead eschewed any editorialising on the verdict. He simply did as he was bound to do. He sentenced Lindy Chamberlain to life imprisonment with hard labour. He reserved sentencing on Michael Chamberlain to a later date (he was given an eighteen-month suspended sentence).

The Northern Territory Police Force had been vindicated, or so it seemed. While those who were sure Lindy was guilty were satisfied, many who thought she was not guilty found that their disquiet over an innocent woman being jailed wouldn't let them rest. In particular, some forensic scientists were uneasy about the quality of the evidence that had supported the conviction. In laboratories around the world, the tests the evidence was based on were put under the microscope. The wheels of the law are said to grind slowly, but where the wheels of forensic science are concerned they grind even slower still.

Shortly after the trial concluded, on 17 November 1982, Lindy Chamberlain gave birth to a daughter, Kahlia Shonell Nikari Chamberlain. Almost immediately after the birth the child was taken from her. According to the Northern Territory authorities it was to protect Kahlia from her mother. Within days, however, Lindy was released when a bail application was upheld pending an appeal against her conviction to the Federal Court. She was reunited with her daughter.

The appeal was set down for April 1983, giving Lindy precious months with her family and baby daughter. On 29 April, however, the appeal was unanimously rejected and Lindy was sent back to Darwin and imprisoned in the women's section of Berrimah Gaol. Knowing Michael would struggle with a young baby, Kahlia was placed in the care of foster parents Wayne and Jenny Millen.

The opportunity existed for Lindy to be transferred to a New South Wales prison so she could be closer to her family. It was an opportunity for the Northern Territory government to show some compassion, if not to Lindy then to her husband and children, but the request was blocked by Chief Minister Paul Everingham. Frustrating the children's access to their mother was perhaps the lowest point in the Crown versus Lindy Chamberlain case.

A year later an appeal to the High Court of Australia also failed, the judges split three–two. Their decision exhausted all possible legal avenues for Lindy Chamberlain, yet the case would not go away. The support that had existed throughout the long days of the inquests and trial continued to grow. In May 1984 a petition of 130 000 signatures requesting Lindy's release was presented to Australia's then Governor-General, Sir Ninian Stephen. In 1985 an Innocence Committee was formed, with the purpose of putting pressure on the Northern Territory government to re-examine Lindy's case.

In June 1985 the Innocence Committee submitted new evidence (including that the 'arterial spray' was actually sound deadener sprayed on all Toranas) that it felt warranted an inquiry. None of it moved the Northern Territory government's attitude in the least. Then, in late January 1986, everything changed.

Professor Barry Boettcher had been frustrated in his attempts to get hold of some of the chemical batch that Joy Kuhl had used to test for foetal haemoglobin in the Chamberlains' car. Her laboratory and the Northern Territory police flatly refused to help him. So Boettcher went direct to the German manufacturers of the test, Behringwerke. He used it to test for foetal haemoglobin but couldn't get it to work. So he went back to Behringwerke to discuss his results.

In response to Professor Boettcher's concerns about the test for foetal haemoglobin that Joy Kuhl had carried out, Behringwerke issued a clarification. It could only be used as a test for foetal haemoglobin if specific controls were used. In the Chamberlain case, that hadn't been done. So the 'blood' Kuhl had found in the car, if it was blood and not sound deadener, could not be identified as Azaria's. It could just as easily have been the hitchhiker's, or it might not have been blood at all.

When Northern Territory Labor politician Bob Collins received a copy of Behringwerke's report, the evidence hit the fan. He sent it to Adelaide forensic biologist Dr Andrew Scott, who promptly wrote back attacking the Northern Territory government's irresponsible evaluation of scientific evidence.

Meanwhile, out at the timeless red monolith of Uluru another tragedy was unfolding. A young Englishman, David Brett, had decided to climb the Rock on his own just on dusk and had failed to return. Exactly what happened will never be known but suffice to say Uluru is no place to climb up or down in darkness. Eight days later, David Brett's body was discovered at the bottom of Uluru, in close proximity to the dingo lair where Azaria's clothing was found five years before. The natural predators of Central Australia had scattered parts of David's body over a wide area, and a search was organised to locate them. One of the local volunteers, who'd been at Uluru during Azaria's disappearance, noticed a piece of clothing partially buried in the dirt. When he pulled it free, he saw it was a baby's matinee jacket. It was only 150 metres from where Azaria's other clothing had been found.

A few days later, on 3 February 1986, the Chamberlains' solicitor, Stuart Tipple, got a call that the matinee jacket had been found. This was the jacket the prosecution said didn't exist and therefore didn't protect Azaria's other garments from damage consistent with 'the dingo theory'. Lindy's insistence that it did exist was one of the flaws in her story that had been exploited by the prosecution. The discovery of the matinee jacket meant she'd been telling the truth.

Four days later, Bob Collins summoned *Northern Territory News* journalist Frank Alcorta, a former speechwriter for Paul Everingham, and gave him the news that the tests on blood in the car couldn't prove it was Azaria's blood. He went further and made Alcorta ring the German manufacturer to get the story from them, on the spot, from his office. When Alcorta hung up, Collins forcefully impressed upon him the importance of reporting the truth.

Alcorta wrote the story but before publishing it he sent a copy to the Territory's new Chief Minister Ian Tuxworth. Alcorta told Tuxworth's office he would run his story unless Lindy was released or an inquiry was called. He gave the government until noon the next day to decide. At lunchtime Tuxworth rang to say he'd decided to free Lindy and call a Royal Commission. After three years in prison and five years of accusation, suspicion and vicious rumour, Lindy Chamberlain was finally being believed.

The Royal Commission was conducted by Federal Justice Trevor Morling and commenced hearings on 5 June 1986. It extended over almost a year, taking the Chamberlains through all the evidence once again, but also exposing the workings of police and forensic scientists to a scrutiny that found many of them wanting.

The Aboriginal trackers were questioned in detail, and demonstrated that they were aware that two dingoes had been present at Azaria's disappearance. They could identify the one carrying Azaria from the deeper impression created by its paw prints after it left the tent. Through an interpreter Barbara Winmatti was probed by pedantic commission lawyers on how she knew the dingo was carrying Azaria. Commissioner Morling tried to be helpful by asking if the dingo might have been carrying a joey, or a baby kangaroo. Schooled in basic common sense, Barbara replied, 'Was a kangaroo living in the tent?' The court broke into embarrassed laughter.

Dingo trainers proved a dingo could carry a six-kilogram baby. The arterial spray inside the car was exposed as sound deadener. One of the tests used to find blood in the Chamberlains' car was shown to react to things other than blood, in particular to copper. At the time of Azaria's disappearance the Chamberlains lived in Mount Isa, where copper is mined. The town is coated in a thin film of the stuff, and the blood tests that were tried on several surfaces in the town all gave a positive result. Joy Kuhl's evidence was described as 'just plain wrong'.

It was also found that Detective Sergeant Brown's police diary for the period covering the date when he had picked up the space blanket from the Chamberlains, and only for that period, had gone missing. The young blond uniformed policeman was never identified.

For the first time, Greg Lowe gave some startling evidence. At the Royal Commission he revealed that he had seen Lindy come out of the tent, without Azaria, before she went to the car to get the baked beans. He hadn't mentioned it in earlier statements, thinking it would distract from his wife's evidence about hearing Azaria cry. Then he'd taken legal advice on what would happen if he mentioned it at the trial. A Hobart solicitor advised him to say nothing unless specifically asked. His eyewitness account, however, would have seriously damaged the prosecution's contention that Azaria had been killed in the car.

If the Northern Territory government didn't like the flaying it had got at Coroner Barritt's hands after the first inquest into Azaria's death, Morling's findings were an even worse indictment. The fundamental criticism was again directed at the quality of the forensic science.

Some of the experts who gave evidence at the trial were over-confident of their ability to form reliable opinions on matters that lay on the outer margins of their fields of expertise. Some of these opinions were found to be of doubtful validity or wrong. Other evidence was given at the trial by experts who did not have the experience, facilities or resources necessary to enable them to express reliable opinions on some of the novel and complex scientific issues which arose for consideration.

The Commission also regarded the failure to protect evidence at the scene as inexcusable and the loss of vital evidence in a number of instances as disturbing. Morling noted the failure by police to inform the Chamberlains of witnesses who supported their defence or negated the prosecution. He concluded, 'Almost every facet of [the Crown's case] is beset by serious difficulties.'

Commenting on the findings, the then Northern Territory Attorney General Daryl Manzie said he would ask the Commonwealth and other state governments to establish a national forensic science institute to standardise testing procedures and raise the standard of forensic investigations. To this day it hasn't happened. Indeed, most states still leave forensic investigation to departments within their police forces. And despite the criticisms of her forensic work Joy Kuhl was ultimately employed by the Northern Territory Police Force Forensic Science Section.

Even after the Royal Commission, the Northern Territory's legal representation maintained the body of evidence allowed possibilities other than a dingo taking Azaria. Nevertheless, the Chamberlains eventually received a compensation payment from the Northern Territory government estimated to be one-fifth of the legal costs they'd incurred (in a case estimated to have cost taxpayers $20 million). Their guilty verdicts were quashed, as were the findings of the second inquest. A third inquest was held in 1995. Coroner John Lowndes found that Lindy and Michael were not involved in their daughter's disappearance but returned an open finding on what actually happened.

By then, however, most Australians had included dingoes in the compendium of outback dangers. Sadly, the lesson had cost Azaria

Chamberlain's young life and devastated her entire family, especially her mother. Unfortunately, in 2001, the question of whether dingoes were man-eaters was answered beyond all doubt on Fraser Island, a major tourist destination on the Queensland coast, when a nine-year-old boy, Clinton Gage, lost his life after being savaged by a dingo pack. His six-year-old brother was also mauled but survived.

There may be some consolation in recognising that the loss of two young children helped shed light on a previously unknown facet of the outback. Yet the tragic lesson has even more value if it helps us realise that there are dangers that remain undiscovered.

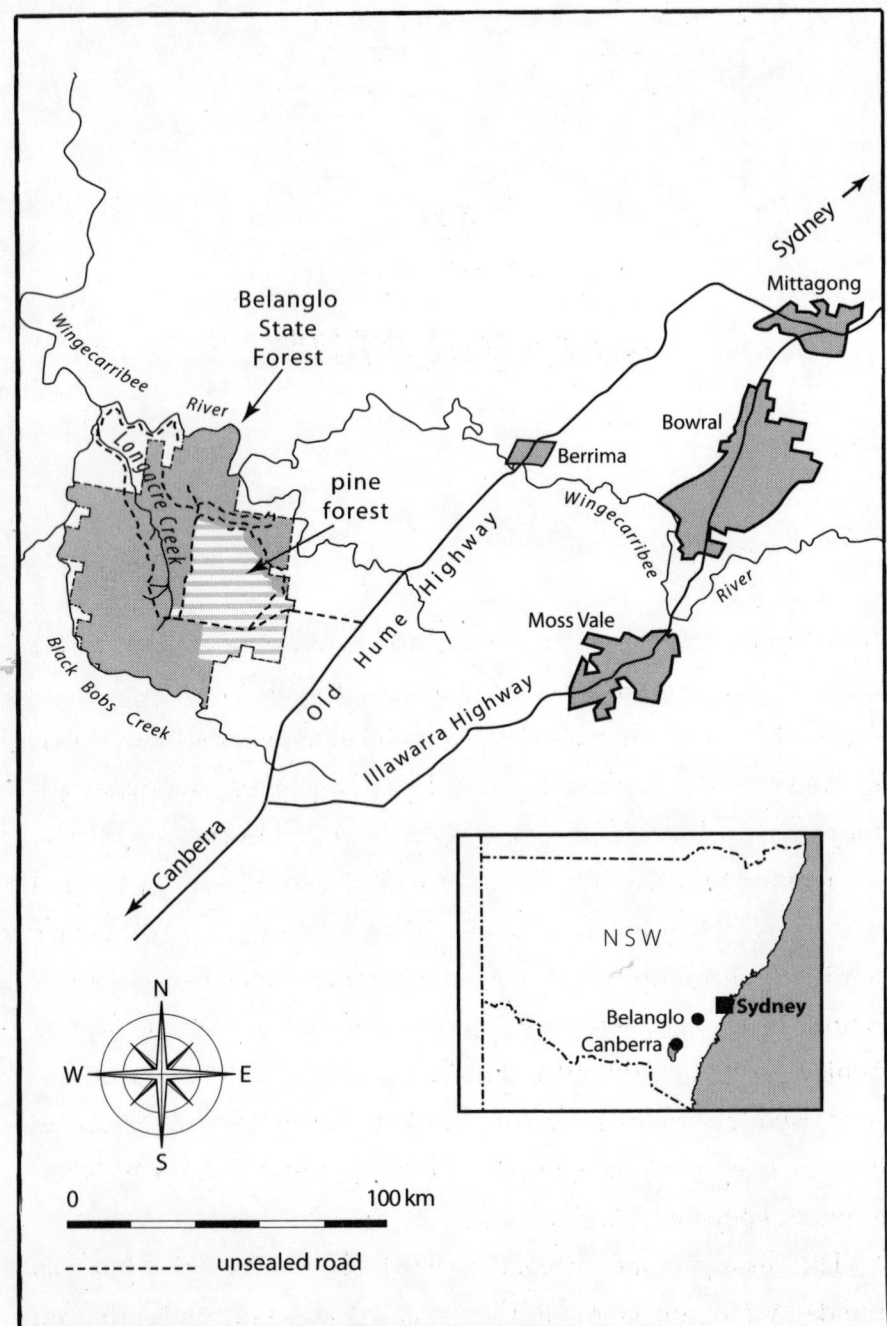

9

BACKPACKERS

In Australia, people disappear with such frequency that it rarely rates a mention in the national media. Of the 30 000 who go missing every year, many choose to do so for personal reasons. When located by police (half within two days of being reported missing), they frequently express a desire not to be found by the people who are looking for them. Of the other half, almost all will be located within a year – some alive, some the victims of foul play. What's left is a small group, about one per cent of the total, who are never found. Every year, 300 people go missing without a trace, leaving behind baffled (and fearful) family and friends. Why they disappear usually remains a mystery. But between 1989 and 1992, one case gave a terrible insight into the kind of fate that could befall a missing person.

The disappearances began on 30 December 1989. That was the day Victorians Deborah Everist and James Gibson (both aged nineteen) decided to hitchhike from the home of friends in Sydney to a music concert on the New South Wales/Victorian border. Their friends had already set off before them, so they left on their own, early in the morning. Back then, the best way out of town was to take the train to Liverpool, a suburb on Sydney's south-western outskirts, walk to the nearby Hume Highway and pick up a lift from there.

That night, Deborah's mother, Patricia Everist, started to worry. Her daughter had promised to call to set her mind at rest, and she could be relied upon. By New Year's Day she still hadn't heard anything so she rang James's mother Peggy, who'd heard nothing from the easygoing James but wasn't worried. When travelling around before, James sometimes hadn't called for a couple of weeks. Nevertheless, on 15 January, when the Gibsons and Everists still hadn't heard anything, they went to Frankston Police Station in Melbourne to report their children missing. To the police it was just another report with very little to go on. But a week later, when James didn't turn up to his sister's wedding, Peggy and Ray Gibson were certain something had happened to him.

As the days wore on, the two families travelled the Hume Highway putting up posters wherever they could, hoping to prompt anyone with information to come forward. There was something unusual about two sensible young adults from caring families going missing that tweaked media interest from Melbourne to Sydney, and when they ran the story the police started to take it more seriously. On 13 March they took it a lot more seriously when a motorist, Wendy Dellsperger, picked up a red backpack that had been lying beside Galston Road, on Sydney's northern outskirts, for several weeks. Inside she found a name, a Melbourne address and a telephone number, which she rang. Peggy Gibson answered. She told Dellsperger that her son was missing and to take the backpack to the police.

A search of the area where the bag was found revealed no clues. Eventually inquiries established that the backpack had been beside the narrow road, at a point where it was dangerous to stop, since the beginning of January 1990. There was no sign of James or Deborah.

A year passed. The story faded but never quite disappeared. The Christmas holidays rolled around again. At 8.15 a.m. on 20 January 1991, 21-year-old Simone Schmidl from Regensburg, Bavaria, left the home of her Australian friend Kristine Murphy in Sydney's Guildford intending to hitchhike to Melbourne to meet her mother, who was flying out for a campervan holiday with her daughter. Simone agreed to ring Kristine when she got to the southern capital. The call never came. The last known sighting of Simone was around nine o'clock that morning. Simone had been a remarkable sight carrying a heavy backpack along the Hume Highway at Moorebank.

When Erwinea Schmidl arrived in Melbourne she was met by a friend who told her Simi hadn't arrived. The next day, 25 January 1991, Erwinea reported Simone missing to both New South Wales and Victoria police. Days went by with no sign of Simone, who, like Deborah Everist, was described as very responsible. Erwinea was a stranger in a strange land but with her worst fears gnawing at her she tried to get the media to publicise her story. Eventually the multicultural broadcaster SBS put out bulletins on television and radio, requesting any information from the public. During the month of February, the publicity through SBS and a number of other media outlets resulted in a number of reported sightings. Two were from Albury, on the road from Sydney to Melbourne, and sounded like Simone; however, all the leads came to nothing. Erwinea spent six weeks in Australia, waiting by the phone, giving interviews, before giving up and returning to Germany. Erwinea's ex-husband Herbert, Simone's father, organised posters to be made and displayed in backpacker hostels, and anywhere else that might prompt someone to come forward with information. Weeks and then months passed with no leads and no word from Simone.

Then it was Christmas holiday time again. For Gabor Neugebauer, twenty-one, from Heimerzheim near Bonn, and Anja Habschied, twenty, from Munich, it meant six days of flat-out hitchhiking. Leaving Sydney on Christmas Day 1991, they had until 1 January to reach Darwin and catch their flight to Indonesia, for a few weeks' holiday before returning home at the end of the month. They called their parents before they left Sydney, and then there was nothing.

On 24 January 1992 Anja's father, Guenther, went to meet them at Munich Airport. They weren't on the plane. Three days later Anke Neugebauer went to the German foreign office to seek assistance and was told there wasn't much they could do. On 30 January the Neugebauers and Habschieds reported their children missing to the German police. The German Consul in Germany checked with the post office in Darwin for a parcel sent poste restante to Gabor. It hadn't been picked up.

Gabor's family enlisted a Sydney private investigator to check around backpacker hostels in Kings Cross. He found a woman at the Original Backpackers hostel who remembered the strikingly beautiful Anja changing money to ring her parents. She checked the hostel's records. Anja and Gabor had definitely booked in on 23 December 1991 and left two days later. The woman thought they were heading north.

The investigator reported the snippets he'd found in March and April. With little to go on, Manfred and Anke Neugebauer with Anja's brother Norbert flew in to Sydney on 10 April 1992 and started canvassing backpackers around Kings Cross – showing photos and asking for any information. The parents appeared on television shows and in news bulletins, saying it was unlike Gabor and Anja not to call and asking for anyone who recognised their children to contact them.

Two more missing kids. Where do you start looking for them in Australia's vast outback? In the first week police logged 200 calls from people with 'information', but none of it led them to Gabor and Anja.

As the relatives of Gabor and Anja were pleading for any news that might help locate their loved ones, other backpackers were travelling around the country, oblivious to the potential dangers of hitchhiking. It was early on Easter Saturday morning when Joanne Walters and Caroline Clarke left the room of fellow backpacker Steve Wright after scamming a free night's accommodation in Sydney. He thought their intention was to hitch to Melbourne, then head west along the Great Ocean Road, ending up in Kununurra in Western Australia for some crop-picking work. Joanne, from Maesteg in Wales, was twenty-two. Caroline, from Farnham in Surrey, was twenty-one.

The Neugebauers and Norbert Habschied, meanwhile, had hired a campervan and were driving up the east coast looking for anyone who'd had contact with Anja and Gabor. In Brisbane they did a radio interview that was heard in Darwin. A woman who ran a caravan park rang to say she'd had Gabor and Anja stay with her. Norbert had to fly home but the Neugebauers tackled the long drive to Townsville, across to Tennant Creek, then north to Darwin. When they got there, it turned out the woman was mistaken. So the road-weary Neugebauers drove south to Alice Springs. In several places they found bookings made by Anja and Gabor, from trips they'd made before their disappearance. They arrived back in Sydney on 9 May 1992 no closer to finding their loved ones.

By late May, Joanne Walters's father Ray had grown increasingly worried. He hadn't heard from his daughter, a well-organised and considerate young woman, for weeks. A methodical man himself, he rang her bank to find out if she'd been using her account – she hadn't made a withdrawal since 16 April, a month before. Joanne's plane ticket home was for 27 May and her visa ran out the next day. The 27th came and went and she hadn't returned. Concerned, Ray rang Jean Jensen, the grandmother of a child Joanne had nannied for in Sydney. She, too, had expected to hear from Joanne before she returned to England. While Ray reported her disappearance to police in Wales, Jean reported her missing at North Sydney Police Station.

In the north of England, Caroline Clarke's parents were less worried by her lack of phone calls but they had thought it strange that she'd missed calling for her sister's birthday on 8 May and her father's on the 24th. Then Ray Walters tracked down the Clarkes and expressed his concerns. Ian Clarke was the manager of the Bank of England in the north of the country, and took Ray seriously enough to put him on to his chief of security, a former head of the International and Serious Crime Branch of the Metropolitan Police. Caroline was officially reported missing on 5 June.

Ian Clarke contacted the London offices of News Ltd regarding the disappearance, and a story appeared in the Australian papers on 10 June. The story was picked up by Australian television as well. In a television interview, Ian Clarke unconsciously echoed the sentiments of the parents of the other missing backpackers when he said, 'We hope that she's having a good time somewhere and will surface in due time, but it is a long time and she is a responsible girl and I would have expected her to have spoken to us before now.'

With yet another pair of missing backpackers, and another clutch of distressed parents protesting that these weren't the kind of kids to stop calling home, was it possible that something terrible was going on? Reports of sightings of Joanne and Caroline came in from all over Australia. Sightings in Darwin, Mount Isa and Uluru were all checked and found to be incorrect. There were suggestions the pair had gone to work in the skifields. They hadn't. By July, New South Wales police had established an investigation to look into the growing number of backpackers who had inexplicably disappeared.

Ray and Jill Walters flew to Sydney on 25 August 1992. The Clarkes intended to follow soon after. Ray and Jill did a number of media interviews expressing their hopes and fears. They also talked to two women from Thirroul, who thought they'd dropped off the girls at Bulli Tops, on the New South Wales south coast, three days after they'd left the backpackers' hostel in Sydney. Their story sounded like it might be right, except for the timing.

Ray and Jill were still in Australia on Saturday, 19 September 1992, when orienteerers Keith Siely and Keith Caldwell were practising their sport in Belanglo State Forest in the Southern Highlands, just over 100 kilometres south-east of Sydney. The pair caught the pungent odour of decomposition and sought out the source. The smell led them to a pile of sticks and other debris wedged under the ledge of a sandstone outcrop. Beneath the sticks they saw hair, a boot and an arm. The two men took only a moment to realise what they were looking at and set off to alert local police at Bowral.

The body lay ninety metres off the Longacre Creek Fire Trail in an area of rugged bush seldom disturbed except for the occasional fire-fighting tanker sent to protect the pine plantation, which separates the forest from the nearest houses, several kilometres away. The sticks were almost as long as the body and arranged horizontally down its length. Beneath the sticks police crime-scene investigators found a layer of smaller sticks, twigs and leaves. The body, identifiably female, was face down, still clothed in a dark blue T-shirt, jeans and black shoes, and wearing two rings and a bracelet. When the body was rolled over, it was found that her T-shirt and bra had been pushed up over her breasts, the buttoned fly of her jeans was open, but the top button was still done up, and her mouth was gagged.

The jewellery enabled the body to be quickly identified as that of Joanne Walters. Her remains were in remarkably good condition considering she'd been missing since April. The cold of a Southern Highlands winter and the placement of her body under the shelter of a rock ledge may have slowed the process of decay. After the body had been removed, a search was conducted for her companion, Caroline Clarke. A line of police and members of the Berrima Volunteer Rescue Squad carefully searched the ground in a pattern that radiated out from the location of Joanne's body. They found Caroline just thirty metres away under a fallen gum tree.

Her body was also covered with sticks that were almost as long as her body. Beneath the sticks there was a layer of twigs and leaves. However, Caroline's head was wrapped in a red cloth. The cloth appeared to have bullet holes in it. She, too, was face down. The position of the body was more exposed and, as a result, it was in an advanced state of decomposition.

At the scene, six cigarette butts were found (later determined to be the brand that Caroline smoked) and one .22 Winchester cartridge case. An area of damaged vegetation between the two bodies suggested a 'struggle area'. The distance between the bodies, and the different ways they appeared to have died, signified that the murders may have been committed by two people. The police were surprised not to find any of the backpackers' belongings; however, a search along both sides of the forest trail leading to the bodies uncovered nothing.

Forensic pathologist Dr Peter Bradhurst conducted the post-mortem examinations, starting with Joanne Walters. Around her neck he found a loose piece of rope that suggested she might have been strangled. She'd been stabbed three times on the right side of the chest, once on the left and once on the right side of the neck.

On her back were two wounds on the left side, five on the right. There were two stab wounds to the spinal cord at the base of the neck. One of them would have left her paralysed, but they probably didn't kill her. Her hands showed no signs of defensive wounds, suggesting she may have been bound or incapacitated during the attack. The cause of death was given as multiple stab wounds to the neck and chest. Because her body had not decomposed as much as might have been expected, Bradhurst was cautious about the time of her death, placing it between April and June 1992.

The following day Bradhurst did the post-mortem on Caroline Clarke. X-rays suggested there were four bullets lodged in her head. When Bradhurst peeled back the red cloth wrapped around her skull, he counted entry wounds from not four but ten bullets. There were four exit wounds (indicating some bullets had not exited the skull, while others had exited through wounds already made). The bullets were probably .22 calibre. The four bullets remaining in Caroline's skull had markings that suggested a silencer may have been fitted to the weapon used to shoot her. The entry wounds were clustered at three points, suggesting the killer had shot at her from three different directions, or had rearranged the position of her head between bursts of fire.

There was one stab wound to her back, probably from the same knife that had been used to paralyse Joanne. Caroline may have received more stab wounds but the decomposition of her body made it impossible to identify them. The hyoid bone was missing from her throat, indicating she may also have been strangled. The cause of death was given as gunshot wounds to the head and stab wounds to the chest. It wasn't possible to ascertain which had actually killed her. The time of death, however, was more accurate: around April, the same time that she'd disappeared.

There was no clear evidence of sexual assault on either Joanne or Caroline (whose bra was opened at the front), but decomposition made the assessment uncertain. Swabs for sperm were taken, but the results were inconclusive.

While police had only just begun to fathom what they were dealing with, the media were already well advanced with their investigations. Newspapers in Australia and Britain quickly made the connection between the two deaths and the other reports of missing backpackers from the previous two years. No other bodies had been found but that didn't stop speculation that a serial killer was preying on backpackers. In England, the *Sun* reported that 'Two British girl backpackers were murdered by a serial killer who held them prisoner for three months in the Australian bush.'

The Belanglo State Forest was an isolated location. The killer or killers would have been confident there was little chance of being disturbed as they carried out their horrific crime. And the chance of the bodies ever being discovered was just as insignificant. The frightening fact was that this hadn't taken place in a remote and lonely place in the middle of the outback. It was only a two-hour drive from the most populated city in the country, and just fifteen minutes down a dirt track from the Hume Highway, the busiest road in the country.

From the scene of the killings, ten cartridges were eventually recovered, matching the ten bullets found in or on Caroline's body. Ballistics expert Gerard Dutton reported that every cartridge had a distinctive curve on the heel of the case, left by the firing pin of the weapon that had fired them. Other characteristics of the cartridges and bullets indicated they'd all been fired by the same weapon. Not only that, but the curve was a pronounced version of a manufacturing defect in the firing pins of Ruger 10/22 rifles. Rugers have a magazine that holds ten cartridges, so it appeared Caroline's killer had stopped shooting only when he'd run out of bullets.

Unfortunately, Rugers are extremely common, with thousands sold in Australia every year. Tracking down the exact weapon could take years, assuming the killer didn't dispose of it long before the police got to them. Yet it was the strongest lead in a case where appeals to the public initially produced many calls but few strong leads.

One Southern Highlands local, Bruce Pryor, a potter and house-husband, couldn't get the case out of his mind. He had a licence to gather firewood from state forests and started collecting wood from Belanglo, although it wasn't particularly handy. He was, in reality, scouring the bush looking for more bodies. He suspected and dreaded that the forest hadn't revealed all of its dark secrets.

In early October 1993, he drove down the Morice Creek Fire Trail for the first time, stopping where the trail traversed some rocky outcrops. He was just fifty metres from his car when he saw what looked like a femur at the bottom of a slope. When he started to climb the slope he saw something else. A human skull.

Fearing he wouldn't be believed or that the perpetrator might choose that day to return and clean up the murder scene, Pryor took the skull with him and backtracked. He reached a bush hut that belonged to the orienteering club whose members had discovered the first two bodies, and used the phone to call the police.

The police found bones strewn all over the slope, probably by foraging animals. Most of the remains, however, were at the base of a tall gum tree. Then, as more police converged on the scene, someone noticed a piece of bone protruding from the ground twenty-two metres from the gum tree. It was another skull. There wasn't one body. There were two.

A felt hat found at the scene provided an early clue to the identity of one of the bodies. A check of missing persons matched it with James Gibson. The other body was soon confirmed as that of Deborah Everist. It was nearly four years since they'd disappeared; most of their clothing had rotted away and their remains were mainly skeletal. The examination of the scene went into the night and then resumed the next day.

The post-mortem on James Gibson put his time of death at more than two years before, probably four – about the time of his disappearance. Knife-wound marks on his bones showed that his spine had been cut, paralysing him. There was evidence of several other stab wounds, which were given as his cause of death. Peter Bradhurst couldn't confirm how many wounds might have been inflicted because the soft-tissue injuries had long since decomposed. The post-mortem on Deborah Everist revealed fractures to her skull and jaw, and that she'd probably been bound when she had been attacked. The injuries suggested she may have been attacked with a sword. Her cause of death could only be given as multiple injuries.

Faced with the discovery of four bodies in the Belanglo State Forest, and the possibility that there could well be several more, a special task force was established to take over the investigation, under the command of Liverpool District Superintendent Clive Small. It was named Task Force Eyre, after the Australian explorer, but it was soon renamed Task Force Air. In Sydney and the Southern Highlands, Small's officers started pulling together the resources needed to deal with what they expected would be a long and complex investigation. But the first job was to search the rest of the forest.

When the bodies of Joanne Walters and Caroline Clarke were found, police searched for evidence along most of the Longacre Creek Fire Trail. Now that bodies were found in a different section of the forest, about one kilometre away cross-country, police realised they would have to search the whole forest.

They questioned members of the Bowral Gun Club, which had a shooting range close to where the murders had occurred. Perhaps one of their members had seen something. As it happened, one of them apparently had. Alex Milat gave police a detailed statement that he'd seen two girls, gagged and looking frightened, being driven in two cars full of men into the forest around April 1992. The statement included details of the vehicles, a sedan and a 4WD, and several of the occupants. He even identified the model of the shotgun that one of the men was holding. Alex Milat explained he hadn't reported the incident because he thought it was just some young blokes taking some girls into the forest to have a good time. Police showed him photos of Joanne Walters and Caroline Clarke. He said the photos didn't do them justice.

It was a potentially excellent lead, almost too good to be true. If it was true, it did beg the question why Alex Milat had done precisely nothing to help the girls or to report the incident. Nevertheless, there was no doubt the story warranted closer scrutiny, but for now it joined a list of matters to be investigated, a list that was rapidly expanding thanks to an increasing mountain of information being supplied by the public.

By 1 November, the police search of Belanglo State Forest was almost complete. It had covered almost twenty-two square kilometres, with lines of police edging through thick scrub, combing gullies and checking every rock outcrop. With just a few small pockets left to be searched it seemed that there were no more bodies in the forest. Then they found Simone Schmidl.

The scene where her body was found bore the same characteristics as those where the other four backpackers had been discovered. The clothing on Simone's body helped identify her, but there was something odd about some of the clothes strewn nearby. They didn't belong to Simone. A check soon revealed they belonged to Anja Habschied. There was no sign of her body in the immediate vicinity but the police believed they had located not one crime scene, but two.

Two days later, Bradhurst conducted the post-mortem on Simone. The results were all too familiar. There were two stab wounds to the spine that would have caused paralysis, and there were no defensive wounds, again suggesting she may have been bound. The cause of death was given as stab wounds and the time of death as two to three years previously. Bradhurst had almost finished when he was interrupted by a phone call. The searchers had found the bodies of Anja Habschied and Gabor Neugebauer, fifty metres apart and just 200 metres from Simone.

Anja had been decapitated, but her head was missing. The post-mortem on Anja indicated she may have been decapitated by a sword, machete or axe. The marks at the top of her spinal column gave the impression that her head had been pushed forward onto her chest, suggesting an execution-style killing. She was naked from the waist down.

Gabor had been gagged and possibly strangled. His head, which was wrapped in a manner similar to that of Caroline Clarke, had six gunshot-entry wounds. He also had fractures to the skull and upper jaw, caused by the bullets. There were no other bone injuries, nor signs of defensive wounds. The cause of death was given as gunshot wounds, strangulation and gagging. Analysis of the bullets taken from his skull revealed they were .22 Winchester bullets, but none of the bullets that had exited his skull could be found near his body. There were no cartridges. So, unlike Caroline Clarke, who'd been shot where she was found, Gabor had been shot somewhere else. Unfortunately, the bullets in his body were too damaged to be useful in identifying the gun that had fired them.

However, an examination of the area surrounding all three bodies, located a number of spent cartridges of two types: .22 Winchester cartridges and Eley .22 subsonic bullets. The .22 Winchester cartridges had the distinctive crescent-shaped mark, which meant they were fired by the same weapon that was used to shoot Caroline Clarke.

It was now abundantly clear that police were dealing with a serial killer who was targeting hitchhiking backpackers. All of the victims were young and, apart from James Gibson and Deborah Everist, they were from overseas. The kind of independent traveller who wouldn't be missed for some time. When the deaths were considered in the order that the victims had disappeared, a chilling progression became clear. From James and Deborah, to Simone, then Gabor and Anja, and finally to Joanne and Caroline, all the attacks were frenzied, but the area involved in the crime scenes grew larger, and the time the killer spent at the scene became longer. The method of killing progressed from ropes, knives and possibly swords to include guns. At the last scene the presence of six cigarette butts suggested the killer (or killers) had taken time to smoke or to allow a terrified Caroline to do so.

The seriousness of the crimes prompted the government to offer a reward of $100 000 for information leading to the arrest of those responsible, and certain newspapers were motivated to add to the reward as well. Not that anyone needed a financial incentive where such an appalling series of crimes was concerned.

It wasn't surprising that, when police opened a hotline for anyone who might have any information, over 5000 calls in twenty-four hours were received. The substantial resources allocated to Task Force Air were immediately overwhelmed. Countless people were accused. All had to be logged as 'persons of interest' and resources allocated to investigate them. Even if one of the accused was the killer, it looked like it might take years to find them in the backlog. In the days after the hotline was set up, Task Force Air's primary function was answering the phones. Officers found that the sheer volume of information meant even promising leads were difficult to follow up. Some were noted and passed up the chain of command, joining the other leads competing for the resources of the investigators.

Numerous criminals with violent histories were among the

persons of interest. By the end of 1993, police were looking at 2000 people who might be the killer or know something about the murders. There were 10000 running sheets, covering leads provided by the public and lines of inquiry that had to be followed up. The computer software keeping track of it all had to be redesigned to cope, which meant re-entering the data collected on guns, addresses, vehicles and much more.

It was while evaluating running sheets to be re-entered that senior analyst Detective Senior Constable Shaun Gagan noticed the name Paul Onions on one sheet and thought it funny enough to tell a colleague, Detective Constable Paul Martin. Paul Onions had phoned the hotline from England on 13 November 1993. Gagan thought his statement was worth following up and marked it for the attention of the investigators. A few weeks later, still processing running sheets, Paul Martin came across a statement from a woman named Joanne Berry that referred to the guy with the funny name, Onions. It too was forwarded to investigators.

Early in January 1994, ten more detectives joined Task Force Air. Detective Senior Constables Paul Gordon and David McCloskey were given the long overdue task of checking out a promising lead from a woman named Lynn Butler. It was about a man named Paul Miller. In fact, another detective had already discovered that the name was actually an alias for Richard Milat – a brother of Alex Milat from the Bowral Gun Club. However, Lynn Butler's story was very different: 'Paul Miller' worked at the same road-building company (Boral) as her husband and when Caroline Clarke and Joanne Walters' bodies were discovered he'd said, 'There's more bodies out there. They haven't found the Germans.'

As Gordon and McCloskey looked further into Richard Milat's background, they found a family obsessed with guns, a family feared by many who knew them. Milat and his brothers (there were ten Milat boys) had properties near the Belanglo State Forest, where they frequently went shooting. However, when they checked Richard's work records, they found that he was working when James Gibson and Deborah Everist disappeared. Then Gordon checked on Ivan Milat, who also worked in road construction. He was off work on all the dates that the backpackers had disappeared.

Gordon's investigation into Ivan Milat's background proved fruitful. Born in 1944, Ivan was the fifth of fourteen children, from a home ruled by a strict and often violent father. Several of the sons went off the rails early, stealing cars, fighting with other kids and harassing neighbours before progressing to armed robberies. Ivan's budding criminal career was soon eclipsed by his prison career, which saw him spend most of the 1960s behind bars, including a spell in the notoriously brutal Grafton Gaol.

Yet there was no sign of a progression to more serious crimes. District Superintendent Clive Small advised Gordon to go back and look through the records again. And there, among the numerous minor criminal charges and convictions, Gordon discovered that in 1971 Milat had been acquitted in a rape case.

Convinced he was onto something, Gordon went back to Small and sought permission for listening devices to be placed in Milat's house and car. To his surprise, Small said no. Indeed, he told Gordon to go back and keep digging, in particular to find out if there was any reason why Milat couldn't be the killer. Small's attitude made no sense to Gordon. In fact, it reflected a cultural shift in the approach to policing that had been taking place since the disasters of high-profile cases like the Chamberlains where police had leapt to conclusions, and couldn't or wouldn't consider any other possibility.

The terrier-like Gordon had homed in on his suspect and was ready to pounce. Small, however, overseeing the whole investigation, wasn't about to succumb to tunnel vision. In a case where there were no eyewitnesses, a conviction would depend on circumstantial evidence. If there were any holes, or if there was an even more likely suspect that a defence team could point to, then the culprit could walk. Alternatively, an innocent person could go to gaol.

So Gordon and McCloskey delved deeper into Milat's rape case. The more they read, the more certain they became that Milat was their man. The rape had occurred after Milat had picked up two girls on the Hume Highway, near Sydney. He'd used knives and rope during the attack and the girls only escaped after one of them agreed to have sex with him. At his trial, Milat got off only when the victims changed their evidence.

The information moved Ivan Milat up the list of the suspects, and more resources were allocated to investigate him, but it still didn't put him at the top of the list. He was just one of a number of other suspects with alarming criminal histories whose whereabouts at the times the backpackers disappeared weren't able to be verified.

Meanwhile, throughout the early months of 1994, Task Force Air continued to struggle with the mass of information pouring in. It was so overwhelmed that one crucial lead was revealed by a journalist, although it had been reported to the investigation months before. The highly respected reporter for the ABC's *Four Corners* television program, Chris Masters, learned that in July 1977 two young women on their way to Canberra had been picked up by a man on the Hume Highway on the outskirts of Sydney. The man had turned off the Hume Highway onto the Wombeyan Caves Road near Belanglo Forest and attempted to rape them. They'd fled and hidden in the bush for several terrifying hours while their assailant drove back and forth.

After the story was shown on television, Paul Gordon located the statements the women had given to Task Force Air and then interviewed them. Although seventeen years had passed since the attack, they immediately identified from a series of photographs the brothers Wally, Richard and Ivan Milat as their possible attacker. Some years later, Wally and Richard had bought a property on the road where the attack took place. It was one of the places the Milat brothers went to practise with their guns.

Gordon checked the details of Ivan Milat's motor vehicle ownership and discovered that two months after the deaths of Caroline Clarke and Joanne Walters he'd sold a silver two-door Nissan Patrol. It turned out to be nothing like the 4WD described by Alex Milat, which was increasingly looking like a red herring. When Gordon interviewed the new owner, he was shown an unfired bullet that had been found under the driver's seat shortly after the vehicle had been bought. It was a .22 Winchester, the same type as the bullets found at the Clarke murder scene.

Then Gordon stumbled on something even more significant. The computer system had all but 'melted down' under the weight of data pouring into it, with many of the statements and running sheets still waiting to be entered. Some of the detectives on Task Force Air had taken to trawling through the statements manually. Gordon was one of them, and while doing so he came upon the statement from Englishman Paul Onions, the one that had piqued the interest of Shaun Gagan. It was now nearly five months since Onions had contacted the hotline.

Onions, a 23-year-old air-conditioning engineer fresh out of the Royal Navy, had set off from Sydney on the morning of 25 January 1990 to hitchike to Mildura to try his hand at fruitpicking. It was just weeks after Deborah Everist and James Gibson had disappeared. As many backpackers do, he caught the train to Liverpool, on Sydney's outskirts, and then started to hitch. He was offered a ride by a bloke who introduced himself as Bill. Onions remembered him as solidly built, fit, in his forties with a moustache similar to the Australian cricketer Merv Hughes. The vehicle he drove was a white or silver 4WD, possibly two-door.

Bill was heading to Canberra and as they drove they chatted – about Bill's recent divorce, his Yugoslav background, his home near Liverpool, his work on the roads. Onions talked about his service with the Royal Navy and answered no when Bill asked if he'd had any combat training. Bill had some pretty strong opinions, especially about Australia's immigration policies, but it was after they'd passed through Mittagong (which the highway now bypasses) that Bill's behaviour began to change. He started slowing down, speeding up, looking in his rear-view mirror, and then he stopped talking. He pulled over, saying he wanted to get some cassette tapes out of the back of the car, but Paul could see there were plenty of tapes already in the front. As Bill got out Paul began to plan what he'd do if Bill tried anything. He made to get out of the car, but Bill challenged him.

'Get back in there, you.'

'I just want to stretch me legs,' Paul said, but he did as he was told. Bill got back in, then opened the door again and stepped out. He rummaged beside his seat, producing a revolver. Paul Onions saw copper-tipped bullets pointed straight at him.

'This is a robbery.'

It was too much for Paul when Bill also produced a rope. He jumped from the car and ran, zigzagging, as he was trained to do in the armed forces when under fire.

He heard two shots but kept running. He tried to flag down a car but it swerved without stopping, and then he saw a family van, driven by Joanne Berry, with her four kids and sister as passengers. In her version, Joanne saw in the distance a man tackled to the ground by another man, then the tackled man broke free and ran towards her. Joanne didn't want to stop but Paul was right in front of her. She stopped about 150 metres up the highway from where the other vehicle had pulled over.

'Please help. He's got a gun,' Paul yelled through the window.

With her children in danger Joanne didn't want to know but Paul tore open the sliding side door of the van and threw himself into the vehicle. The children were crying but he refused to get out. Berry reversed, crossed the central median strip and drove straight to Bowral Police Station, where she and Paul Onions gave statements to the local police. A report was put out over the police radio to be on the lookout for the car and its driver.

As he read the statement Onions had given to Task Force Air,

Gordon realised that here was a backpacker who had been perilously close to becoming another of the serial killer's victims. Having got away, however, he was now a vital witness. Yet Onions' statement also raised questions about why the matter hadn't been investigated more thoroughly at the time. It was far from the police force's finest hour, especially when it was found that both Onions' and Berry's original statements to Bowral police had been filed and then lost. Fortunately, when he dug deeper, Gordon also found the statement that Joanne Berry had given to Task Force Air, which backed up what Onions had said.

Apart from detailing his ordeal, Paul Onions' statement provided valuable information about 'Bill'. It said 'Bill' was divorced, in his forties, of Yugoslav origin, with a white or silver Nissan or Toyota, two-door, 4WD. Ivan Milat, at the time in his mid-forties, owned a silver 1987 Nissan Patrol two-door 4WD (the one he'd sold); his father was Yugoslav; he had used the name Bill Milat (he had a brother with the same name) while working between 1988 and 1989; he'd been married from 1984 to 1987 and divorced in 1989. Not only that, Ivan wasn't working on the day of the Onions attack and a passport photo from the time showed he had a 'Merv Hughes'-style moustache.

Even with all this evidence, Small still refused to use listening devices at Milat's home or in his car, because he believed that a judge would only allow the bugs when all other investigative avenues had been explored. It was frustrating, but Gordon was still making progress.

It wasn't as though the Milat family didn't know they were being investigated. Indeed, in one of Chris Masters' televised interviews with police in the Task Force Air offices a whiteboard in the background with the words 'Air/Milat' written on it had been captured. The video was vetted by police before it was aired nationally but the highly confidential words had slipped through. As Gordon cast his net wider, talking to Milat's work colleagues and associates, word inevitably filtered back that the family was under investigation. This knowledge would have given Milat ample opportunity to destroy any incriminating evidence he might have still had in his possession. Yet the fact that there was no arrest, not even any questioning, might have also inspired a belief that he would continue to get away with murder.

Meanwhile, the investigation had also discovered things about Milat that didn't fit with what they knew about the killer. In particular, he was a strict non-smoker, while the six cigarette butts at Caroline Clarke's murder scene suggested the killer smoked. Or was it possible he'd allowed Caroline Clarke to smoke before her execution?

Despite these inconsistencies Ivan Milat kept climbing up the list of suspects. Towards the end of April, Task Force Air rang Paul Onions. After little police response to his initial report of the attack, and nothing following his call to the hotline five months earlier, the police now wanted him to fly back to Australia. He touched down on 2 May 1994. Two days later, Detectives Stuart Wilkins and Graeme Pickering took him for a drive down the Hume Highway, revisiting the scene of his attack. He identified the spot where he'd escaped: it was just 800 metres from the turn-off to the Belanglo State Forest.

On 5 May he was shown videotapes of thirteen possible suspects, with moustaches. He went through them thoroughly, identified two possibilities, then went through them all again. Finally, he settled on one as his attacker. It was Ivan Milat.

Now, at last, Clive Small decided it was time to move. Police surveillance of the house where Ivan Milat lived with his sister Shirley was stepped up, conspicuously so. In fact, his whole family knew there was a police observation post on a hill overlooking his house, just 400 metres away.

On 16 May, Milat's former wife, Karen Milat (nee Duck), was interviewed by detectives from Task Force Air at her home in the Hunter Valley. Karen, thirteen years younger than Milat, was only seventeen when they were married. She confirmed that he had a large number of guns and a knife with a ten-inch blade, and told them she'd gone with Ivan into Belanglo State Forest, where he'd shot two kangaroos. She also admitted to being raped by him when they first met, and anally raped when they were married. She'd been terrified while she was with him, but more terrified by what he might do if she left. She finally plucked up the courage in 1987, and her divorce was finalised in 1989. Not long after she left him, her parents' home was subjected to an arson attack.

In June 1992, three years after his divorce, Milat started going out with Chalinder Hughes. The disappearances of the backpackers all occurred in the period between the end of his marriage and the start of his relationship with Hughes.

Despite the strong indications that Milat was the backpacker killer, Task Force Air knew that the evidence was still only enough to have Milat charged for the armed robbery of Paul Onions. Raiding Milat's home in the hope of finding something incriminating was fraught with the possibility that they'd come up empty-handed – an embarrassing bungle that might mean Milat remained free. So, they continued the waiting game. However, there was one characteristic of serial killers that gave them hope that something would be found – they take souvenirs, trophies through which they relive the experience of their crimes. The souvenirs can have such potency that the killer will keep them no matter what. And, as time goes on, a criminal who doesn't get caught becomes increasingly convinced of their superiority. Each successful crime adds to their confidence and their contempt for the law. Eventually they think they can get away with anything.

On Saturday, 21 May 1994, Detectives Bob Benson, Stuart Wilkins and Tony Roberts flew to Brisbane to visit Alex Milat at his new home at Woombye, an hour north of the city. They said they wanted to go over aspects of his statement. Alex and his wife Joan were more than helpful, perhaps hoping they might be in line for a reward. When the police asked about backpacks, Joan said they had one that Ivan had given them. It was a Salewa brand backpack, identical to one that had belonged to Simone Schmidl. The significance wasn't lost on the detectives. It looked like someone had been collecting souvenirs.

At dawn the following morning, police raided the Eagle Vale house in western Sydney where Ivan Milat was living. The police weren't taking any risks: the search squad included ambulance officers trained in dealing with gunshot wounds. Police surrounded the house, then phoned Milat to tell him to give himself up. With him in the house was his girlfriend Chalinder Hughes. Three minutes and three phone calls later, Ivan Milat walked out his front door and was arrested for the armed robbery of Paul Onions on 25 January 1990. Police had a warrant to search the premises and told Milat he would also be asked questions in relation to the death of seven backpackers, questions he was not obliged to answer.

Once the home was secured and the search commenced, some of the squad moved on to Chalinder Hughes' nearby home and to Milat's mother's house in the Sydney suburb of Guildford, where he'd lived at the time the attacks took place. The homes of his brothers Richard, Walter and Bill, and the Milat property on the Wombeyan Caves Road near the Belanglo State Forest, were also raided that morning.

An hour into the search of Milat's house, all police had found was a bullet, a postcard addressed to 'Bill', and New Zealand and Indonesian currency (Simone Schmidl had visited New Zealand; Anja Habschied and Gabor Neugebauer had been bound for Indonesia). However, the search team had only looked in the obvious places. Up in the roof, Detective Senior Constable Peter O'Connor, while lifting insulation batts, had noticed something stuffed down a wall cavity. He got a stick and lifted it out. It was a shopping bag with some old rags, but, among the rags, he found gun parts.

Ballistics expert Gerard Dutton confirmed the parts were from a Ruger 10/22. He looked at the breech bolt with a magnifying glass: the firing pin had a distinctive crescent shape just where he'd hoped it would be. There was something else underneath where the shopping bag had been. O'Connor and Dutton tried to lift it with the stick, but it fell deeper into the wall. In the end, a hole had to be cut in the wall to get it out. It was a magazine for a Ruger 10/22.

In the house they found a foot-long bowie knife, a bayonet painted in camouflage colours, a water bottle with the name 'Simi' scratched out, Eley subsonic cartridges from the same batch as those found at the Neugebauer/Habschied scene, a camera similar to the one owned by Caroline Clarke, copper-tipped bullets for a Colt .45 like the ones Onions had seen when he was looking down the barrel of Bill's gun, and a photo of Chalinder Hughes wearing a Benetton top similar to one that Caroline Clarke had. The searchers in the garage found a Salewa sleeping bag cover. Inside was a homemade gun silencer and a tent wrapped in a Compact-O-Mat band. The tent was identical to the one owned by Simone Schmidl, the band identical to the one that had been found wrapped around her skull.

Police attempted to interview Milat at Campbelltown Police Station. He played dumb, denying all knowledge of any weapons. After half an hour, they were forced to give up.

At Richard Milat's Hilltop home, camping equipment belonging to Caroline Clarke and Joanne Walters was found. And at Wally Milat's place there was a veritable arsenal of weapons and ammunition that weighed a staggering 250 kilograms, some of it from the same batch found at the Neugebauer/Habschied scene. A small knapsack identical to the one belonging to Simone Schmidl was found. In the garage at Milat's mother's home police found a blue Next brand of shirt that belonged to Paul Onions. Drugs, mostly marijuana, were found at a number of properties, and several of Ivan's brothers ended up facing drug and weapons charges.

Eventually, so much incriminating evidence was found that it was hard to believe that someone would keep it all. The Milat family certainly struggled to explain the presence of so much evidence and suggested it was an attempt by the police to frame Ivan. Yet police believed that keeping so many souvenirs indicated the mindset of a serial killer at work. It was hard to understand but so was the slaughter of seven innocent people.

Ivan Milat's arrest prompted people who had known him in the past to come forward. One of them was Phil Polglase, a central-coast construction worker who had been friends with the Milat family when the murders began. Early one morning, around the time that Deborah Everist and James Gibson had disappeared, he'd been staying at Ivan Milat's mother's house. Ivan had returned very early one morning, saying he'd been hunting. He had a knife with what looked like blood on it.

'That's human blood,' Ivan told Polglase. 'I stabbed a bloke with it. I stabbed him through the spine.'

He also mentioned, unprompted, that there'd been a lot of unsolved killings in the Canberra–Queanbeyan area. Polglase wasn't sure whether to believe Ivan or not, but it made him steer clear of the Milats from then on.

In the lead up to his trial, Ivan Milat's legal representation changed on two occasions. He sacked his solicitor of more than twenty years, John Marsden, who'd got him off the 1971 rape charge, and appointed Queensland solicitor Andrew Boe. During his committal hearing he sacked his barrister Cate Holmes and appointed Queensland barrister Terry Martin. As happened in the Azaria Chamberlain case (and, indeed, all the way back to cases like Ned Kelly's), Milat struggled to scrape together enough money to mount an effective defence against the formidable resources of a state government. He did receive legal aid, but, guilt or innocence aside, his case highlights the continuing injustice of a legal system where governments don't fund prosecution and defence costs equally.

The trial of Ivan Milat on seven charges of murder and one of armed robbery began in Sydney's Supreme Court in March 1996, Justice David Hunt presiding. Terry Martin was defending Milat, Mark Tedeschi QC was the Crown prosecutor. Milat's defence was straightforward: he didn't do it. Then, as the case unfolded, it became clear his defence team would attempt to do exactly what Clive Small had feared – shift the blame onto another likely suspect. They tried to incriminate another member of his own family, Wally Milat. However, the evidence of Paul Onions, and the 'Aladdin's gold mine' found at Ivan's home (as Clive Small later described it) kept Ivan firmly in the frame.

One of the key elements in the prosecution's case was a blood-stained rope found in Ivan Milat's house. The blood was linked to Caroline Clarke. DNA evidence wasn't able to show it was specifically Caroline Clarke's blood; however, testing of her parents showed it was most likely that the blood came from one of their children, so by inference Caroline.

Faced with evidence such as this, plus a mountain of circumstantial evidence and the eyewitness account of Paul Onions, the defence needed to do something remarkable if Milat was to have any chance of walking from court a free man. They took a gamble, and Milat took the stand in an attempt to clear his name. It was a big risk and one that backfired.

Late on a long day of cross-examination, Tedeschi relentlessly probed Ivan about the possibility that he'd used the gloves to avoid leaving any evidence at the murder scenes. Milat became frustrated.

'I didn't wear no . . .' he finally burst out.

Milat's cut-short sentence was followed by a terrible silence.

'Did you mean you didn't wear them in the forest?' prosecutor Tedeschi said.

For Ian Clarke, sitting in the courtroom, it was the moment that removed any doubt in his mind. Ivan Milat was the backpacker killer.

After a trial that ran for fifteen weeks, called 151 witnesses and presented 331 exhibits (many of them weapons), the prosecution, in summing up, didn't discount the possibility that Ivan wasn't alone in the killings, and that his accomplice may have been a member of his family. However, their contention was that he was present on every occasion.

Near the end of the trial an anonymous phone call was made to one of the jurors. The words used were: 'If you find my . . . Look out, if you find him guilty, you're dead.' The juror was discharged before he contacted any of the other jurors, thus avoiding the possibility of a mistrial. On Wednesday, 24 July 1996, the remaining eleven jurors retired to consider their verdict. Day after tense day passed until finally, on Saturday, 27 July, they announced they were ready to return.

When the court had come to order, the foreman was asked his verdict on the charge of wilful murder of Deborah Everist.

'Guilty.'

Each time he was asked for his verdict on the charges of

murder he replied: 'Guilty.' On the charge of armed robbery of Paul Onions: 'Guilty.'

Ivan Milat was sentenced to seven life sentences for the murders of the seven backpackers and six years for the attack on Paul Onions. To date he has made no public admissions of guilt, although his brother George (the only one to acknowledge Ivan's guilt) maintains that he admitted his guilt to his mother, who has since died. Ivan Milat has appealed his convictions all the way to the High Court without success.

There has been considerable speculation that Ivan Milat may have been involved in several other unsolved murders that bear striking similarities to the backpacker murders. These deaths occurred in areas where he had worked on road construction projects. Clive Small expressed the opinion that Milat may have been involved in three other murders but there is insufficient evidence to charge him. His brother George says the number may be as many as twenty-eight or twenty-nine.

You don't see many people hitchhiking on the highways of Australia any more. It's likely that the extremely high media publicity of the backpacker murders had some impact on the number of people hitching. Though, as the last chapter of this book shows, when it comes to outback crime you're not safe even in your own car.

Postscript

While researching this chapter, I was reminded of when I was hitchhiking from Cooma to Canberra, back in 1982, then aged twenty. I got a ride for the 120-kilometre trip with a clean-cut, dark-haired man driving a relatively new blue sedan, bound for Sydney. Over little more than an hour, he stopped the vehicle three times, saying he wanted to get some tapes from the boot of the car. But each time he returned to the car without any tapes. By the third time, I felt he was building up to something and I had an escape plan in mind. I was going to leave my backpack and run – like Paul Onions, I was going to keep running no matter what. As we drove and continued to talk I made sure I agreed with everything he said, while making it abundantly clear that my family were expecting me that night for dinner.

The man eventually dropped me off on the outskirts of Canberra and I promptly dismissed all my fears, but after reading the statement of Phil Polglase (who died in a car accident before he was able to give evidence) that Ivan Milat had once said 'there's a lot of unsolved murders around the Canberra–Queanbeyan area', my blood ran cold. I've looked closely at photos of Ivan Milat and other members of his family but felt no spark of recognition. I can still remember the last thing the man said to me when I got out of his car: 'Have a good life.'

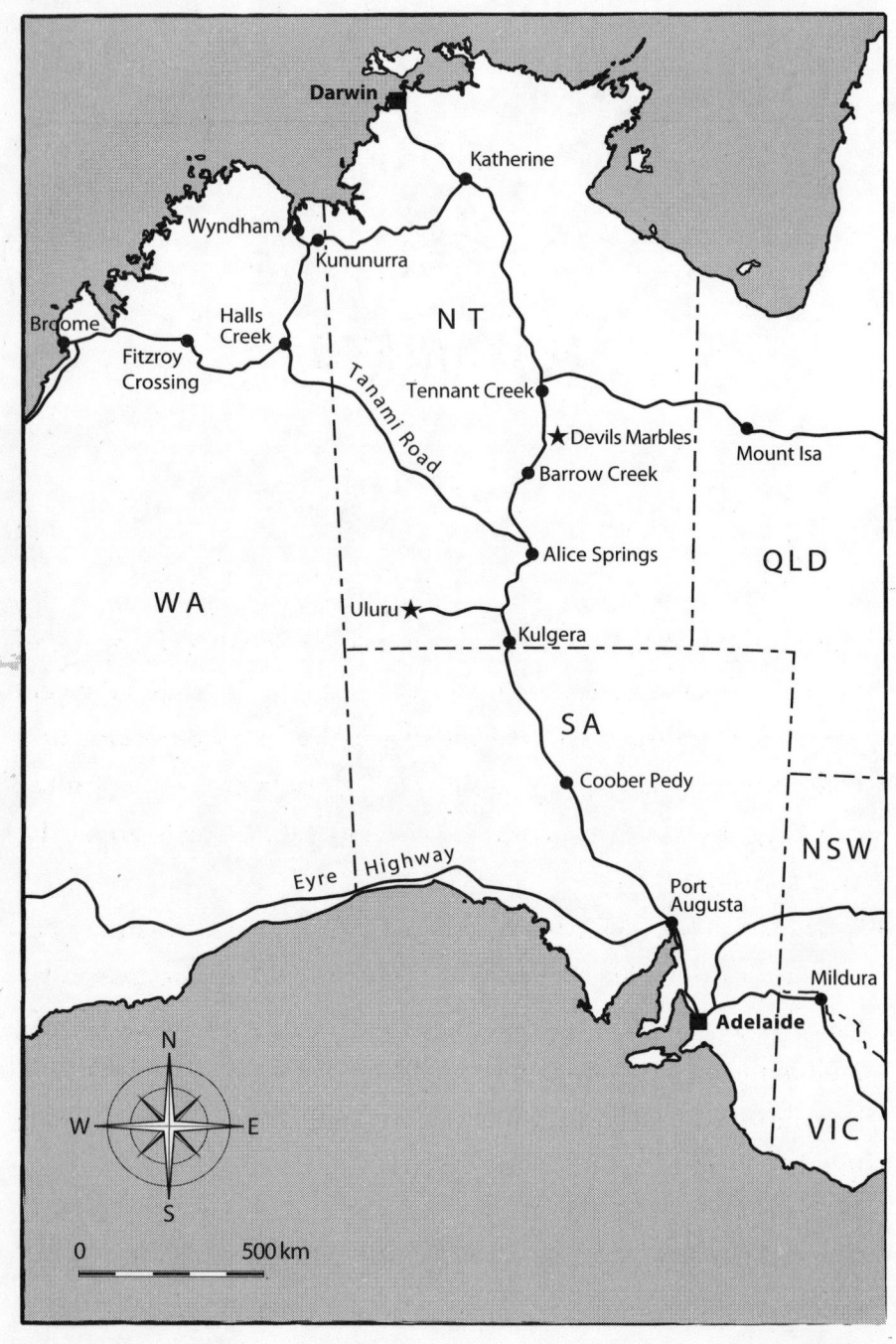

10

MOTORISTS

Don't drive at night. It's a standard piece of advice that can be found in many guidebooks to the Australian outback. The main dangers are wild animals and cattle wandering onto the road unseen, as a collision with a kangaroo, camel, water buffalo or even a wombat can have disastrous consequences. However, animals aren't the only danger.

In mid-2001, English tourists Peter Falconio and Joanne Lees were well aware of the risks of driving at night. But they were also starting to realise just how big Australia was. The logistics of taking it all in meant long hours at the wheel of the orange Kombi they'd bought for $1200 from another tourist in Sydney. It was tempting to take a few risks, just to stay on schedule.

Peter and Joanne first met five years earlier in a nightclub in Huddersfield, England, near where they both lived. He was twenty-nine; she was twenty-eight. Australia was part of an extended world trip they'd planned to do before they settled down to their careers, a mortgage and starting a family.

Joanne and Peter arrived in Australia in January 2001 and soon found work and a place to rent near the beach at Bondi. Both became seduced by Sydney, especially Joanne. The mixture of sun, beaches, parties and enough work to replenish their finances was just about the perfect lifestyle. They were having so much fun they extended their stay, but finally set off to see the rest of the country on 25 June 2001.

On their drive from Sydney to Canberra they'd have barely noticed the sign at the turn-off to Belanglo State Forest where Ivan Milat had taken his seven victims to their terrible fates in the early 1990s. Visiting the Barossa outside Adelaide, they drove near Truro, completely unaware that it was where serial killers Christopher Worrell and James Miller shot and stabbed seven women in the 1970s. Heading north, they passed Snowtown, where it was more likely they'd heard that bodies in barrels were discovered in a disused bank vault in 1999, leading to the conviction of John Bunting for eleven murders and his accomplice Robert Wagner for seven. They might have stopped at Coober Pedy, where in 1993 the body of German tourist Ann Neumann was located in one of the opal mining town's many mineshafts. To the east was Lake Eyre, where tourist Caroline Grossmueller died of heat exhaustion in 1998 trying to reach William Creek for assistance after her vehicle had become bogged in sand. Her partner, who stayed with the vehicle, survived. To the west was the vast desert region that claimed the lives of young, inexperienced jackeroos James Annetts and Simon Amos in 1986 when they'd become lost in a network of West Australian survey roads. Travelling deeper into Australia's red centre, Joanne and Peter visited Uluru, scene of the 1980 disappearance of Azaria Chamberlain, and where five people died in 1983 when disgruntled truck driver Douglas Crabb drove his rig through the crowded bar of the Inland Hotel after he'd been asked to leave.

On Saturday, 14 July, they decided to watch the Alice Springs Camel Races before continuing the long journey north to Darwin. The races are a major social and tourism event in Central Australia and the pair soon found themselves captivated by the entertainment, enthusiastically embraced by locals and tourists alike. Before they knew it the afternoon had ebbed away and it was four o'clock when they finally left, with Joanne at the wheel. It was only a couple of hours until sundown.

Their intended destination that night was the Devil's Marbles, a scattering of granite boulders that would be unremarkable if they weren't the only sightseeing opportunity in the straight, monotonous 531-kilometre drive from Alice Springs to Tennant Creek. Leaving late meant driving at night for much of the journey. They'd read the warnings in the guidebooks but they were keen to stay on schedule.

After refuelling at Ti Tree Roadhouse, they stopped and watched the sunset, smoked a joint and stretched their legs. Peter took over the driving and reached Barrow Creek Roadhouse, 120 kilometres south of the Marbles, around seven-thirty. The area was the scene of one of the last recorded massacres of Aboriginals, in 1928. In response to the death of a white man on nearby Coniston Station, three police constables rode through several Aboriginal camps, indiscriminately killing men, women and children as they went.

One constable was held responsible for thirty-one deaths, but the total massacre may have been as high as seventy. A board of inquiry found the killings were justified. The area is shunned by the local Aboriginal people, which to them remains a place of evil spirits.

Ten kilometres to the north of Barrow Creek it was now completely dark. Peter was driving carefully, alert for anything that might run onto the road. The traffic was virtually non-existent, showing just how seriously the 'don't drive at night' warning was taken. Headlights appeared on the road far behind them, relieving some of the tension – they weren't completely alone out there. The other vehicle quickly caught up to the sluggish Kombi. On the deserted road there was nothing to stop the faster vehicle overtaking, but, instead, it came up and sat right on Peter's tail.

'I wish this bloke would hurry up and pass me,' Peter said. 'He's blinding me.'

The vehicle pulled out and drove up beside them. The driver looked across at Peter and Joanne, then wound down his window and shouted what sounded like, 'Sparks . . . exhaust,' while gesturing at the back of the Kombi.

The man looked to be in his forties, with a drooping moustache (uncannily like Ivan Milat's Merv Hughes–style facial hair), a baseball cap and a dark T-shirt under a check shirt. A typical rugged Territorian, he drove the Territory's vehicle of choice, a white 4WD. He even had the standard-issue dog sitting up beside him.

Joanne didn't like the look of him but Peter was more trusting. 'We have to see what it is. It'll only take a minute.'

He slowed down, pulled over to the side of the road and got out. The 4WD, a trayback model with a canopy, pulled up behind.

The driver explained, 'I saw sparks coming out your exhaust. It's been happening for a while.' Peter and the other motorist peered at the exhaust.

Peter came back to Joanne and asked her to rev the engine, then returned to the back of the car. From the driver's seat she checked out what was happening in the rear-view mirror. As she did, the stranger's eyes met hers – an odd prolonged stare. She looked away. She revved the engine, listening at the same time for any instructions. There was a noise that sounded like a backfire. Thinking she might have done something wrong she turned to the window. Suddenly, the stranger was there, with a gun.

He wrenched her door open as she screamed, 'Pete! Pete!'

'Turn off the engine,' the man shouted. Joanne's hands were shaking so much she couldn't do it. He did it himself, then pushed her across into the passenger seat and got in. Keeping the gun pointed at her he ordered her to lean forward and put her hands behind her back. She started to comply before realising how vulnerable it would leave her, so she refused, only to have the muzzle of the gun pushed against her forehead. Terrified, she obeyed. He looped black electrical cable ties around her wrists and pulled them tight.

The man dragged Joanne roughly out of the Kombi and threw her to the ground. With her hands bound nothing broke her fall. He tried to tie her feet with tape, but it was difficult as she struggled against him. By now Joanne was frightened that something terrible had happened to Peter – and that it was about to happen to her. She started to really fight, lashing out with her feet, inflicting a scratch that cut her attacker deep enough to make him bleed.

'Fucking keep still, you bitch.'

He gave up on the tape, stood up, then leaned down beside her and punched her in the head, almost knocking her out. He dragged her to her feet and pushed her towards his vehicle. Joanne kept struggling as he tried to tape her mouth, so he reached into the covered tray of his 4WD, pulled out a sack and put it over her head. As she was pushed towards the front of the car, she started screaming.

'Pete! Where are you?'

Joanne was shoved into the passenger seat. She managed to shake the sack off her head, losing her hair band in the process, and saw the dog sitting in the driver's seat. In the dim light cast by the vehicle's instruments, it looked brown and white. She started screaming again, calling for help, but they were completely alone. The man was back and pushed her from the front of the car into the covered area at the back. She heard his footsteps on the gravel at the side of the road, then a sound like something was being dragged.

'What do you want with me? Where's Pete? What have you done with Pete?' she called out.

'Be quiet! If you don't I'll fuckin' shoot you.'

'Are you going to rape me?'

Silence.

'Have you shot Pete? Have you shot my boyfriend?'

'No.'

The sound of something being dragged started again, then silence. Joanne thought if she had any chance of escape, this was it. With her hands still tied behind her back, she hung her legs over the tailgate and jumped onto the gravel. She didn't wait to see if her assailant had noticed, she just ran.

Joanne made it to the scrub at the edge of the gravel and kept going, crashing through two- to three-metre-high mulga bushes and clumps of spinifex, stumbling over small fallen branches and debris. In the quiet of the desert night the sound of her flight would surely alert the man to her escape, but she kept going. Twice she fell, struggled to her feet and ran until she could go no further. She found a large mulga bush and went to ground beneath its branches and fine foliage. She curled up under the bush, trying to make herself disappear.

She could see torchlight, flashing through the scrub, coming closer and closer, and soon she could hear the man muttering and cursing. He came so close that she was sure he would see her. But he turned away. The darkness, the strange shapes and shadows cast by the foliage of the mulga had confused his eyes. Yet, as he criss-crossed the scrub, they both knew it could only be a matter of time before he found her. At times, he was so close that she could have reached out and touched him. Indeed, if he'd had any skills as a tracker, he'd have found her in seconds. Fortunately, though, the tricks of light and shadow that had frustrated the search for Azaria Chamberlain at Uluru saved Joanne Lees from her assailant on the roadside north of Barrow Creek.

The man got into his vehicle and turned it around, illuminating the area of scrub where she lay within its powerful lights. Any experienced hunter will tell you that the eyes of every creature in the bush will reflect a spotlight in different colours, depending on the species. Even the eyes of spiders reflect. Yet, he was unable to discern the frightened huddled form of Joanne Lees amid the shadows, branches and tiny points of light.

He turned the vehicle one way and another, but couldn't find her. Then he saw the distant lights of a vehicle, the first that had approached the scene since the attack started, despite the Stuart Highway being the major north–south route through Central Australia.

The driver, Jasper Jimbajimba Haines, and his family were travelling slowly to protect a suspect tyre and to avoid a high-speed encounter with the wildlife of the Northern Territory. They were locals, on their way from visiting relatives eighty kilometres north of Barrow Creek, heading back to their community on the edge of the Tanami Desert, twenty kilometres west of Ti Tree. As they drove by, the sight of a 4WD on the side of the road struck them as strange. A short distance down the road, an apparently abandoned orange Kombi seemed stranger still. But they didn't stop. If you ignore the advice and do drive at night, the next advice is: if you see something strange, don't stop.

The man and his vehicle seemed to have gone so Joanne tried to get free of the cable ties that were binding her hands behind her back. The ties were linked by several loops, which gave her hands some movement, but it would be easier to get them off if her hands were in front. It was impossible to bring her arms over her head without dislocating both shoulders, but maybe she could get them under her bottom and past her legs. Joanne got her hands past her bottom, then pulled her knees up to her chest to shorten her legs. She manoeuvred first one foot then the other past the ties. Getting the ties off her hands was a different problem as they were tight around her wrists. She managed to lift a lip balm out of her pocket and tried to lubricate her wrists, to no avail.

Then she heard footsteps. He must have stopped somewhere up the road and walked back. Joanne froze.

Next she heard the Kombi starting, and being driven a short distance up the road. It sounded like he'd turned the Kombi off the road, into the scrub. The engine stopped and there was a long silence. Then she heard the man's vehicle start, returning to the area where Joanne was hiding. He slowed down, searching the scrub with his headlights, but still couldn't see anything. Then he opened up the throttle and accelerated down the highway, the noise of his vehicle fading south in the direction of Alice Springs.

Alone in the darkness, huddled beneath her mulga tree, Joanne Lees didn't know if the man might come back. She stayed in her hiding place for what seemed like hours, but, knowing that her boyfriend could be lying injured, in need of urgent medical attention, she forced herself back towards the road. Standing there, completely alone on a moonless night, the sky ablaze with stars, she tried to think of what to do next.

On the other side of the road was a patch of long grass. She crossed over and hid in it. From there she could see any vehicles on the road without being seen. A car was approaching from the south. Could it be him again?

She let it pass.

Joanne waited and waited beside the road. Then she heard the distant roar of a road train, a prime mover towing three trailers, fast approaching from the north. That couldn't be him. She left the safety of her hiding place and jumped out on the road, waving her bounds hands in front of her.

The Bulls Transport vehicle was being driven by Vince Millar, with co-driver Rodney Adams sleeping in the bunk behind him. Road trains hurtle through the outback in the dead of night, their massive bullbars and sheer momentum dealing with most things that get in their way, including other traffic, which is another reason why it's safer to drive during the day. When Joanne suddenly appeared Millar managed to swerve to miss her but felt sure that the trailers, not able to change direction as quickly as the prime mover, must have gone straight over her. Millar immediately hit the brakes, but the vehicle still took a kilometre to come to a halt. He grabbed a torch and went back to see if he could find any body parts caught in the wheels of the vehicle. Instead he was confronted by Joanne running towards him, sobbing hysterically. In the lights of his truck, he could see that her hands were tied, and there was duct tape on her legs, in her hair and around her neck.

By then Adams had woken up and climbed down to see what was wrong. The two men cut Joanne free, kept the ties for the police and put her in the truck between them. It was now after midnight on the morning of Sunday, 15 July 2001. They reassured her that she was safe and they did what they could for her cuts and abrasions. She managed to convince them to stop helping her and to look for her boyfriend, who, she told them disjointedly, was still out there, somewhere. The near-hysterical young woman wasn't making much sense, but they unhitched the trailers and drove back up the road, seeing a small pile of dirt beside the road and fresh tyre tracks. They gathered from Joanne that the Kombi might be a little further along the road. Not far past the pile of dirt they came upon a narrow dirt track, which Joanne wanted them to drive down, but the truckies were concerned they'd get bogged.

Then, among the disconnected details Joanne was shakily recollecting, she mentioned the word gun. And the two men realised that an armed and dangerous criminal was potentially lurking in the vicinity. That was enough to convince Millar and Adams, despite Joanne's protests, to get back to the highway and head south to Barrow Creek Roadhouse for assistance.

The roadhouse owner, Les Pilton, was having a party, but the mood soon changed when the truck drivers walked in at one-thirty. Joanne stayed in the truck, terrified that the man might be in the roadhouse. Initially Pilton thought Millar and Adams were joking, then he realised there was not a glimmer of humour in either man and rang the nearest police station. At Ti Tree, ninety kilometres to the south, he got an answering machine, so he rang Alice Springs, 282 kilometres away (Tennant Creek was 249 kilometres north).

Millar and Adams eventually convinced Joanne, who was showing symptoms of shock, to go into the roadhouse, where she was given a cup of sweet tea and some warm clothing. She spoke to police who'd rung the roadhouse back to confirm the call wasn't a hoax.

By the time police arrived it was 4.20 a.m. They photographed Joanne in the clothing she had been wearing during the attack, and an initial examination revealed a hair that may have come from a dog. She gave them a description of the vehicle that was driven by her attacker. They then found her a change of clothes and took her clothing as evidence.

With Millar, the police drove back to the scene, to what was left of the odd pyramid of dirt that had been run over several times by passing vehicles. As dawn broke over Central Australia, the Kombi was located on the side track and the whole area was sealed off as a crime scene. As more police arrived they searched the highway for two kilometres in each direction, hoping to find some sign of Peter Falconio. They used metal detectors but only found bits of debris that had fallen off or been thrown by the passing highway traffic. If Peter had been shot there was no spent cartridge, which there wouldn't be if the weapon was, as Joanne suggested, a revolver. The bullet may or may not have exited the body. If it hadn't, it wouldn't be found unless Peter was. At the mulga tree where Joanne had hidden, the cap of her stick of lip balm was found, but not the balm itself. A request was put in for Aboriginal trackers to attend the scene but there were none available, and police working at the crime scene inevitably obliterated most of the tracks that were present.

At that stage the scene gave police very little to go on. A description of the vehicle involved was broadcast but it matched a large percentage of the vehicles in the Northern Territory, in particular, and the rest of the outback, in general. Joanne hadn't been able to get a licence number, nor the state where the vehicle was registered. In the time since her attack, a determined driver could have reached any state except Tasmania. There was also the possibility that the attacker knew the outback well. If he did, then avoiding police roadblocks wouldn't be a problem.

After returning to the scene with police, Joanne was driven to Alice Springs where interviews with police about what had happened continued into the night, even though she had not slept for nearly forty hours. Joanne also started working with Detective Senior Constable Isobel Cummins on a photofit image of the attacker. The same night police started showing the rough first images around various retail outlets in Alice Springs. At the Shell Truckstop on the northern side of Alice Springs, attendant Andrew Head immediately recognised the picture. Even better, the Truckstop was equipped with video cameras that captured images of both the bowsers and the inside of the shop. It was a slow process extracting the images, but they had recorded both the man and his vehicle.

By the following morning, less than thirty-six hours after the attack, roadblocks were in place on all the main roads out of the Northern Territory. Yet that still gave the attacker ample time to put thousands of kilometres between himself and the scene of the crime. And there were countless minor tracks that criss-crossed the country, little known and even less used. As time went on, the area Joanne and Peter's assailant could have fled to just got bigger and bigger. Soon, it encompassed the entire country.

As it happened, Monday, 16 July, was also the day Prime Minister John Howard was in Alice Springs to turn the first sod in the long-awaited construction of the Alice Springs to Darwin railway. It meant a large media contingent was on hand for the event. Understandably, speeches, handshakes and politicians in Akubra hats couldn't compare with an attack on tourists in the outback, certainly not since the backpacker murders of the early 1990s. Soon reports of the suspected murder and attempted abduction were being filed around the country and then the world. As the body of Peter Falconio had not been found, those who sensed a mystery not unlike that of Azaria Chamberlain twenty years earlier started digging deeper. They also tried to interview the deeply traumatised Joanne Lees.

Meanwhile, the police investigation closely examined the Kombi van and Joanne's clothing. In another connection to the Chamberlain case, the head of the Northern Territory Police Forensic Science Section was Joy Kuhl, whose testing for foetal blood in the Chamberlains' car had contributed to Lindy Chamberlain's conviction, and was later discredited as 'just plain wrong'. She took the initial call to attend the crime scene but as she'd been at a party and had consumed alcohol she sent one of her staff, Carmen Eckhoff, instead.

By Tuesday, Eckhoff was making good progress. She had samples of Joanne and Peter's DNA, plus that of Millar and Adams. She tested bloodstains on Joanne's shirt and found they were all hers. All, that is, except one minute stain on the back of her left sleeve. It didn't match the DNA of Peter, Millar or Adams, either. Then when Eckhoff tested the steering wheel and gearstick of the Kombi, she found more. Not only did it help to corroborate Joanne's story that someone else was there but it gave police vital evidence in identifying a suspect. If they ever managed to track him down.

The media contingent in Alice Springs, meanwhile, was growing bigger and bigger. From the police statements, it was clear that something strange and terrible had happened in the Australian outback, yet again. However, with the scant information provided by the police (who initially made no mention of the Shell Truckstop video or the DNA), the media had very little to go on. Joanne Lees, who'd been attacked, threatened at gunpoint, bound and bashed, then fought with and fled her attacker to hide in terror as he stalked her through the bush, was in a state of shock but trying to hold onto the fragile hope that her boyfriend was still alive. Under pressure from the police to give interviews that might prompt information from the public, she finally relented and gave one, to the Alice Springs local newspaper, the *Centralian Advocate*.

The story was promptly syndicated around the world but it was never going to be enough to satisfy the media. Rather than accept that Joanne wasn't doing interviews because she was deeply distressed by what she'd been through, some media organisations chose to believe there was a more newsworthy reason – she had something to hide. What was to become known as the 'Lindyfication' of Joanne Lees had begun. The isolated outback had provided the setting, and ignorance and fear of this potentially dangerous environment allowed speculation to flourish. Echoes of the Ivan Milat case – backpackers falling prey to evil on lonely highways – stirred the imagination of the public (and from gaol Milat wasn't slow in suggesting Joanne's description of her attacker matched that given by the backpacker-who-got-away, Paul Onions).

The intense search for Peter's body in the immediate vicinity was increased to fifty kilometres north and south of the crime scene, then to a surrounding area of 4800 square kilometres, but it yielded nothing, and media speculated that there was nothing to be found. Yet the 1989 case of a nineteen-year-old Victorian hunter, Dean Robinson, who'd been shot for his guns in similar, isolated outback conditions by two young men, Daniel Luthur Heiss and Peter Michael Kamm, gives some idea of what the police were up against. When Robinson's killers were finally apprehended, even with Kamm's assistance, the police searched for two days before finding his grave under an anthill in the Northern Territory's gulf country.

Nevertheless, at police press conferences the question started being asked: Did police suspect Joanne Lees? To those unfamiliar with the outback, elements of her story didn't ring true. In particular, the notion of a major highway that at that time of night had no passing motorists was impossible to grasp.

Another factor fuelling the growing suspicion was the lack of progress in locating the culprit. The sheer size of the outback certainly made progress extremely difficult but with a good description of both Joanne's attacker and his vehicle someone, somewhere, must have known something. Even taking into account the level of protection given to criminals by friends and associates, detailed in nearly every chapter of this volume, it seemed hard to believe that no one was coming forward with information. Yet every tip that led to a suspect soon turned out to be unfounded.

For the media, finding a suspect posed no such problems. And the less Joanne Lees cooperated with them the more inclined they were to run stories that questioned her innocence. Some openly expressed their desire to 'get Joanne'. Not that the media-shy young woman was doing much to help her cause. When Joanne relented and gave a press conference she allowed just one reporter to be present, plus photographers and camera operators. The collective media submitted fourteen written questions, of which she answered three, flanked by Peter's brother Paul (who'd flown out from England to be with her) and Police Commander Max Pope. The consensus was that she appeared extremely nervous, if not paranoid. Nevertheless, her appearance led to 300 calls from the public, the best input the police had received so far.

On 5 August 2001, a body was found in a rest area sixty

kilometres south of Alice Springs. Police at first thought it was Peter Falconio but tests revealed it to be Alice Springs chef Stuart Rhodes. He could have been another victim of Peter's killer; however, investigations soon linked his death to Andrew Heffernan, who was subsequently apprehended in New South Wales, and didn't match the description given by Joanne Lees.

Also at the beginning of August, Assistant Commissioner John Daulby was sent down from Darwin to take control of the investigation. By then it was apparent that the media suspicions about Joanne Lees were starting to polarise the officers working on the case. Some believed her; others didn't. Daulby acted decisively. The information regarding the discovery of DNA on Joanne's clothing was released, confirming her story, as well as a new identikit picture, showing her attacker with short hair and no moustache. Daulby publicly expressed confidence in Joanne. Behind the scenes, however, he initiated a formal investigation of her story. Only when that was done would she be conclusively excluded as a potential suspect.

The inconsistencies in her story were re-examined in detail. They included the information that: trackers had only found her tracks at the scene (in fact they'd found tracks of her attacker by the road); her description of the dog was like one at Barrow Creek; scrolling on the revolver resembled scrolling on the side of the Kombi; and there didn't appear to be any vehicles that have access from the cabin to the trayback.

After her interview Joanne's statement was sent to several linguistic analysts. They came back with the same response. Joanne was telling the truth but not the whole truth. It was later revealed that Northern Territory police secretly bugged the room where she was staying. They maintained that it was because she might mention something useful to the investigation. Joanne Lees still believes it was because they suspected her of killing Peter Falconio.

It didn't take long to discover the secret behind Joanne's secrecy. When Joanne was visiting an Internet cafe in Alice Springs, her police escort noticed she was sending and receiving emails from a second account. The recipient was someone named Steph. When asked, Joanne admitted that Steph was actually Nick Reilly, a backpacker she'd become involved with while enjoying the vibrant nightlife of Sydney. Her secret was nothing more sinister than the fact that she had been having an affair.

Like the backpacker murders, the Falconio case quickly grew into a major criminal investigation codenamed Taskforce Regulus (after a star in the constellation Leo). It involved searches for vehicles and revolvers, of DNA records around the country and overseas, of criminal records and much more. For the Northern Territory police it was an immense operation that stretched scarce resources over one of the biggest jurisdictions in the world. As the weeks passed, investigators realised the case wasn't going to be cracked in the short term and they started digging in for the long haul.

Several weeks after Peter Falconio's disappearance, Daulby finally decided to release the video from the Shell Truckstop. Police later admitted that not putting it out sooner was a mistake, although they'd spent time having it computer enhanced in the hope that they might be able to make out the licence plate of the vehicle. It didn't, but what the video did do was reveal that the attacker was wearing thongs on his feet. Their almost smooth soles explained why there were so few of his tracks at the crime scene.

As the video elicited a positive response from the public, including information from Toyota that it was one of their vehicles, a 75 Series Toyota Landcruiser cab-chassis, Joanne Lees agreed to another press conference. Continuing her fraught and ill-judged dealings with the media, she turned up in a snug-fitting T-shirt with the words 'cheeky monkey' emblazoned across her chest. According to some accounts she refused to put anything on over it. She now maintains that it was all she had to wear. Paul Falconio, far more at ease with the media, answered all questions, but the pair confirmed that the man in the video was Joanne and Peter's attacker.

Still no one came forward to identify the figure in the video or his vehicle. It was as if he didn't exist. What kind of person were they looking for – a person that no one would identify? Yet someone had to know something. The information from Toyota, meanwhile, gave police the huge but potentially fruitful task of tracking down every owner of a 75 cab-chassis Landcruiser, checking if they looked like the attacker and asking them to account for their movements on the night of 14 July 2001. It was a job of months, if not years.

Three months after the attack, members of Taskforce Regulus decided to revisit the crime scene to refresh their minds and to familiarise those members who had never been there (which was most of them) with the site. At the scene they were shocked to find pieces of tape that had been used to bind Joanne Lees, and, in the place where she had hidden from her attacker, the lip balm that Joanne had claimed she'd used to try and get free of the electrical cable ties. The crime scene was supposed to have been scoured in minute detail by lines of officers crawling slowly forward on their knees. Instead it was like Azaria Chamberlain's missing matinee jacket all over again.

Back in the taskforce office the investigation ground slowly on. Every owner of the relevant model of Landcruiser was tracked down and interviewed in at least a cursory manner. Yet no one immediately sprang to the fore as a suspect.

After a brief stay in Sydney, Joanne Lees flew back to England in November 2001. In March 2002, after saying she would never sell her story, she did an interview on British television with the controversial journalist Martin Bashir for A$120000.

Bashir asked her point blank: 'Did you kill Peter Falconio?' She denied it. Bashir went further, saying that everything – no evidence of a gun, no body, no footprints other than hers – clearly pointed to her as the major suspect.

From the media's perspective, the only people who didn't seem to get it were the police working on Taskforce Regulus. Indeed, they continued slogging their way through unpromising lines of inquiry that hadn't narrowed their suspect down much from 'every mid-forties Caucasian in Australia over 180 centimetres'. Months passed without a breakthrough.

New Zealand-born James Tahi Hepi was certainly not a suspect in the Falconio case when Broome police pulled him over on the outskirts of the West Australian town on 17 May 2002. However, he wasn't completely innocent either. West Australia police had been given an anonymous tip-off and when they searched his vehicle they found four kilograms of cannabis hidden throughout the vehicle. It was more than enough to put him in jail for drug trafficking and supply but Hepi had a very good idea who'd dobbed him in. So when he sat down for questioning with Broome detectives it was payback time. 'I've got some information you might be interested in,' he said. 'It's about that killing up at Barrow Creek.'

The more Hepi talked, the more attention the Broome detectives paid to what he was saying. Evidence of criminals is often discounted when it's given to save themselves but what Hepi said had a ring of truth. Up until December 2001 his partner had been Bradley John Murdoch. They'd had a falling out, in part due to the fact that Murdoch wasn't pulling his weight in the task of transporting drugs from Hepi's property near Sedan, thirty kilometres east of the Barossa Valley in South Australia to Broome. The reason for not making the 4300-kilometre journey across Central Australia was that he kept having modifications done to his 75 Series Toyota Landcruiser cab-chassis. In fact, he'd been modifying it ever since he'd returned from a trip on 16 July 2001, thirty-two hours after the attack on Peter Falconio and Joanne Lees. Rather than drive to the place he and Hepi shared to unload his cargo of marijuana and amphetamines, Murdoch had gone straight to a vehicle workshop and started making extensive modifications to the appearance of his vehicle. He'd also changed his own appearance. Before his trip he'd had a droopy moustache and long hair. When he showed up on 16 July he'd shaved both his moustache and his hair.

Broome police had already paid Murdoch a visit, in November 2001, to ask him about his 75 Series Toyota, but he didn't fit the appearance of the wanted man. He also told the officers he'd been in Broome at the time. Other people had reported Murdoch as resembling the man in the video but when his story checked out, he went back to being just another person Northern Territory police would look into in more detail when they got the chance. Hepi's story, however, moved Bradley John Murdoch up the list of persons of interest. It also explained why no one had come forward with their suspicions about such a potentially strong lead – Murdoch, a drug dealer with a history of weapons-related offences, was not someone to accuse lightly.

By then, the day-to-day operations of Taksforce Regulus were in the hands of Superintendent Colleen Gwynne, reporting to Assistant Commissioner Daulby. In fact, over the months Taskforce Regulus had seen its star wane until it was staffed by only nine officers, slogging through mountains of information. By the end of May 2002, they'd eliminated 2500 persons of interest and 2000 vehicles, plus taken 300 DNA swabs. Gwynne, however, recognised the potential of Hepi's information and asked Broome police to bring Murdoch in for questioning. Unfortunately, when they went to his last known address he'd disappeared. At the end of May a nationwide alert was issued for Bradley John Murdoch.

While police in every state searched for the fugitive, Taskforce Regulus started looking into his background. Murdoch was born on 6 October 1958 in Northampton, Western Australia, 500 kilometres north of Perth, near Geraldton. He'd had a lonely upbringing and grown up wild in the small country town. In a last attempt to get his life on track, his parents moved to Perth when he was twelve. To no avail. He left school at fifteen to work as a mechanic, like his father, and became involved in bikie gangs. He developed into a solidly built 191-centimetre young man with an interest in guns. He eventually moved to Albany, where he married in 1980, aged twenty-one, and had a son. He worked as a bouncer around Albany's nightclubs until he got bored and ended up driving trucks for the next fifteen years. His frequent absences eventually contributed to the breakdown of his marriage.

Over the years he had a number of minor firearm offences but in 1995 he was arrested for shooting at a group of Aboriginal people at Fitzroy Crossing. The rifles involved were a .22 Winchester and .308, both stolen. In his subsequent trial he admitted to being prejudiced towards Aboriginal people. He was sentenced to fifteen months in prison. When he got out of jail he continued in the transport business, except prison had revealed to him a more lucrative line – trafficking drugs. Murdoch eventually settled in Broome, working odd jobs for trucking companies. It was while he was there that Murdoch met and became partners with James Hepi. After they'd split, Murdoch set up in the drug business in competition with Hepi by transporting drugs from South Australia, becoming a dangerous rival to his former partner.

The one thing the police investigation didn't uncover was Murdoch's whereabouts. Through June, July and August 2002 there was no sign of him. In the meantime, Taskforce Regulus had located Murdoch's family. They asked his surviving brother Gary to take a DNA test, and on 14 August he complied. The results were just what the investigators were hoping for. It was a close match, making it likely that a close relative of Gary's was the source of the mystery DNA on Joanne Lees' shirt.

Two weeks later, at the end of August, a young woman and her twelve-year-old daughter walked into a South Australian police station in Port Augusta to report that they'd been raped, abducted and held prisoner for almost a day. They had known their attacker for the previous eighteen months and named him as Bradley Murdoch. Murdoch was driving a white Toyota Landcruiser.

Although the attack had taken place a week earlier an alert was immediately issued throughout South Australia, and it got a result that afternoon. At 4.50 p.m. on Wednesday, 28 August 2002, the vehicle was sighted in a Port Augusta shopping-centre car park. When Murdoch approached his vehicle with two bags of shopping he was confronted by heavily armed police. They ordered him to the ground, cuffed and arrested him for the rape of the two women. A body search revealed a revolver (without the scrolling pattern described by Joanne Lees) in a shoulder holster concealed beneath his clothing. When they searched his vehicle they found significant quantities of drugs and cash, plus a Beretta semi-automatic .38 pistol and a knife.

Murdoch's arrest on the rape charge immediately posed problems. If Murdoch was extradited to the Northern Territory, investigated and then tried for the murder of Peter Falconio, it would be months, possibly years, before the two traumatised rape victims saw their case go to trial. If that happened it would mean reviving their harrowing experience, something that would be especially disturbing for the young girl.

Police, meanwhile, were still unsure whether Murdoch was their man. His legal team, consisting of solicitor Mark Twiggs and barrister Grant Algie (who'd been part of the defence in the Snowtown case), tried to prevent samples of his DNA being sent to the Northern Territory, and then appealed the decision that allowed the transfer. When they lost the appeal the DNA was couriered to the Northern Territory for comparison with the mystery DNA found on Joanne Lees' shirt. On 8 October the forensics lab rang Colleen Gwynne. It was a match.

The result was a real breakthrough, but it was a long way from proving Murdoch had attacked Joanne, and further from proving he'd shot Peter Falconio. However, searches of various properties that Murdoch frequented started to provide evidence that corroborated Joanne's story. At the homestead where the young woman and daughter lived, which Murdoch also used as a base in South Australia, they found Murdoch's dog Jack, a Dalmatian cross (probably with a blue heeler), and took a DNA sample to see if they could get a match with the dog hair found on Joanne's clothing. They also found a black hair tie that Joanne later identified as hers. It was no use to Murdoch, unless he'd kept it as a souvenir. When Joanne was shown a dozen photos of men with similar appearances to Murdoch, she chose Murdoch.

The decision was finally made to try the South Australian rape case first and it went to court late in 2003. The defence attacked the credibility of the mother. She was revealed to be a former escort, her de facto a brothel operator and admitted drug dealer. The defence also suggested that the real motivation for their story was to collect a reward for $250 000 that was being offered for Murdoch's capture. It put enough doubt into the minds of the jury that on 10 November 2003 they took only two hours to arrive at a verdict of not guilty on all charges. Murdoch walked from the court a free man.

However, he didn't get far. He was promptly re-arrested on the charges he was facing in the Northern Territory. Bundled through the media scrum outside the court, he replied to questions about

Peter Falconio with a curt, 'Fuck off.' He was extradited to the Northern Territory and on 14 November charged in Darwin with murder, deprivation of liberty and unlawful assault.

The road to trial was long and convoluted. The committal hearing, before Magistrate Alisdair McGregor, started on 17 May 2004 and had at its disposal 550 witness statements and fifty witnesses. Murdoch was represented by Algie and Twiggs, who were confident they'd get him off just as they'd done in Adelaide. The prosecution was presented by the Northern Territory Director of Public Prosecutions himself, Rex Wild QC.

The prosecution introduced a number of elements of the case that had not previously been made public. It was revealed that DNA had been found on the steering wheel and gearstick, and that it was a probable match with Murdoch; and that Joanne and Peter had stopped and smoked a joint of marijuana while they watched their last sunset together on their fateful journey. Then came the revelation of Joanne's affair with Nick Reilly. There was also a claim from Robert Brown and Melissa Kendall, who worked at a petrol station at Bourke, in the New South Wales outback, that they'd served Peter Falconio a week after he was supposed to have been killed. Their evidence was discredited but not before it made headlines around the world. Finally, though, came evidence from Senior Sergeant Megan Rowe, who had worked on Taskforce Regulus from its very beginning. She revealed that police had found revolvers with scrolling patterns like that described by Joanne Lees, and they'd found vehicles with access from the cab to the chassis area.

After twelve weeks of evidence, the committal hearing finally wound up and on 12 August 2004 Magistrate McGregor decided there was sufficient evidence for Murdoch to stand trial on charges of murdering Peter Falconio, deprivation of liberty and aggravated assault of Joanne Lees. The trial was initially set down for May 2005 but it was subsequently delayed until October.

The reason for the delay was that after the committal hearing further DNA testing was done on the cable ties that had been used to bind Joanne Lees. They were sent to the UK where a new test, Low Copy Number testing (first developed in 1999), was used to identify minute traces of DNA. It was found to be Murdoch's. When the results were revealed, shortly before the trial, the defence demanded more time to conduct their own tests. The trial magistrate, Northern Territory Chief Justice Brian Martin, allowed the request.

The case finally got under way on 17 October 2005. In the Northern Territory, screening of the film *Wolf Creek* was delayed for the duration of the trial to ensure its depiction of the abduction, torture and murder of a group of young tourists didn't influence the jury. The film was inspired by the events of both the Milat and Falconio cases, including Milat's method of paralysing his victims by severing their spinal cords. As the film's assailant put it, he made them 'a head on a stick'. Milat is reputed to have heard about the technique from a Vietnam veteran, as reported by journalists Mark Whittaker and Les Kennedy, authors of the book on the Milat case, *Sins of the Brother*.

Much of the first part of the trial dealt with Joanne's evidence. Joanne had changed considerably in the years since she'd been a frightened tourist unable to deal with the horror of the ordeal she'd been through or with the media attention. Stylishly dressed and speaking with confidence, supported by Peter's family who were there for the trial, she calmly identified her attacker as the accused, Bradley John Murdoch. She offered to demonstrate how she had stepped through the cable ties. Defence barrister Algie declined but the next day Justice Martin asked her to demonstrate. It took her only a few seconds to do what some journalists had declared was physically impossible.

Over the ensuing eight weeks, eighty-two witnesses were called and 350 pieces of evidence were presented. Much of the evidence centred on the DNA evidence that placed Murdoch not only in close proximity to Joanne Lees and her vehicle but also to the cable ties that were used by her attacker. A number of witnesses, including Hepi, testified that it was Murdoch in the Shell Truckstop video and that he'd changed both his appearance and his vehicle before his return to Broome in mid-July 2001.

The case looked strong for the prosecution. No one knew what the defence case might be, but everyone was surprised when Algie called Murdoch as his first witness, and when Murdoch readily admitted to being a drug runner, which was the reason why he changed his appearance, and that of his vehicle, on a regular basis. He said he may have crossed Joanne and Peter's path when he went to a Red Rooster takeaway for a chicken meal in Alice Springs. It was across the road from an auto-parts dealer where he'd purchased some bits and pieces for his vehicle. Other than that, he didn't know how his DNA got on Joanne's shirt. He suspected all the DNA was part of an attempt by the police and/or James Hepi to set him up. He admitted that he was someone who had done bad things but he was no killer. It was a remarkable defence: I'm guilty but not of murder.

Once Algie had finished taking Murdoch through his evidence, it was Rex Wild's turn. His first question was a knockout: 'Mr Murdoch, where did you bury Peter Falconio?'

Not surprisingly, Algie promptly objected but the question set the tone for a tense confrontation between prosecutor and defendant. Wild asked about Hepi's evidence that Murdoch had talked about burying bodies in roadside drains. He challenged him about how long he'd taken to drive from Alice Springs to Broome (1800 kilometres in thirty-five hours) on the dirt track of the Tanami. He tried to get him to admit how many drug runs he'd done, further incriminating himself if he answered. Murdoch denied all Wild's accusations.

After Murdoch left the stand Algie called only four more witnesses. One was the Alice Springs auto-parts dealer who sold Bradley Murdoch the car parts on the day Peter Falconio disappeared. He said that when he'd served Murdoch he was already clean shaven. DNA expert Dr Katrin Both expressed reservations about the validity of Low Copy Number Testing in identifying the DNA on the cable ties. Two biological anthropologists gave their opinions that the person in the Shell Truckstop video wasn't Bradley Murdoch.

The summations reiterated the evidence of the 37-day trial. Algie said his client wasn't the killer and that with no body having been found it was still possible that Peter Falconio had faked his own disappearance. Wild stated that everything pointed to Bradley Murdoch being involved in Peter Falconio's disappearance and in the attack on Joanne Lees. The DNA evidence was compelling, and her eyewitness testimony backed it up.

The jury took just eight hours to arrive at a verdict. Chief Justice Martin had actually called them in to explain that they could return a ten–two verdict when his explanation was interrupted by the news that they'd already arrived at unanimous verdicts on all counts. Martin asked for their verdict on the charge of murder: guilty. On the charge of abduction: guilty. On the charge of assault: guilty.

For the Falconio family and Joanne Lees it was the end of a long and terrible nightmare. For Bradley Murdoch it was the start of a 28-year prison sentence with a non-parole period of twenty-four years. Murdoch still protests his innocence. He has never revealed the whereabouts of Peter Falconio's body, which to date has not yet been found. In 2006, an appeal against Murdoch's conviction was rejected.

Peter Falconio lies somewhere in the vast emptiness of the Australian outback, his lonely grave unmarked, untended and unknown. It's certainly not the only grave, for the outback guards many of its secrets well. However, as Peter's case and others in this volume have shown, the outback's killers can be brought to justice. It's small consolation to those left wondering where their loved ones may be, but it's a glimmer of hope in the red centre's dark heart and it may help the outback's ghosts rest in peace.

SOURCES

Chapter 1: Cannibals

Bonwick, James, *The Bushrangers: Illustrating the Early Days of Van Diemen's Land*, George Robertson, Melbourne, 1856 (facsimile edition, Fullers Bookshop, Hobart, 1967).

Hirst, Warwick, *Great Escapes by Convicts in Colonial Australia*, Kangaroo Press, East Roseville, 1999.

Hobart Town Gazette, editions as noted in the text.

Hughes, Robert, *The Fatal Shore*, The Harvill Press, London, 1987.

Julen, Hans, *The Penal Settlement of Macquarie Harbour*, Mary Fisher Bookshop, Launceston, 1976.

Knopwood, Rev. R., 'The Knopwood Narrative', handwritten manuscripts held in Mitchell Library Sydney and National Library Canberra, circa 1823.

Parks and Wildlife Service Tasmania: http://www.parks.tas.gov.au/wildlife/reptile/snakes.html, as at April 2007.

Report of the Select Committee on Transportation (The Molesworth

Report), House of Commons, London, 1838 (papers and testimony from John Barnes, former surgeon at Macquarie Harbour).

Sprod, Dan, *Alexander Pearce of Macquarie Harbour*, Cat & Fiddle Press, Hobart, 1977.

Chapter 2: The Tyranny of Distance

Adelaide Advertiser, 6 April 1957.

Brisbane Courier, 18 February 1872; 28 February 1872; and undated issues.

Holthouse, Hector, *Up Rode the Squatter*, Angus & Robertson, Sydney, 1970.

McCarthy, Patrick, *The Man Who Was Starlight*, Allen & Unwin, Sydney, 1987.

Matthews, Rachel, *Queensland v. Henry Redford, 11 February 1873 Trial Re-enactment*, published by the author, Roma, 2002.

Walkabout, 1 May 1936.

Warren Herald, 1 June 1901.

Chapter 3: Kelly

Camm, J.C.R. & McQuilton, John (eds), *Australians, A Historical Atlas*, Fairfax, Syme & Weldon Associates, Sydney, 1987.

Jones, Ian, *Ned Kelly: A Short Life*, Lothian, Melbourne, 1995.

Ned Online, the Jerilderie Letter: http://nedonline.imagineering.net.au/Masterframeset.html, as at November 2006.

Chapter 4: Black and White

Clune, Frank, *Jimmy Governor: The True Story*, Horwitz, Sydney, 1959.

Davies, Brian, *The Life of Jimmy Governor*, Ure Smith, Sydney, 1979.

Moore, Laurie, & Williams, Stephan, *The True Story of Jimmy Governor*, Allen & Unwin, Sydney, 2001.

Chapter 5: Bury Me Deep Down Below

Courier-Mail, 6, 8 and 9 January 1941; 3 May 1969.

Johnston, W. Ross, 'Australian Dictionary of Biography': http://www.adb. online.anu.edu.au/biogs/A130221b.htm, as at November 2006.

Main, Jim, *Australian Murders*, BAS Publishing, Melbourne, 2004.

Chapter 6: Pero Raecivich's Apocalypse

Kalgoorlie Miner, 2–6 February; 19–21 March; and 24 March 1942.

Murphy, Sean, ABC Radio News Reports, 2 November 2003; 11 January 2005 (transcripts).

Murphy, Sean, 'Western Australian Bombing Brings Crackdown on Motorcycle Gangs', *7.30 Report*, ABC Television, 3 September 2001 (transcript).

Nott, Holly, 'Police Disappointed by Bikie Verdict', *The Age*, 27 August 2004.

Skehan, Peter, 1942 Boulder and Kalgoorlie Bombings: http:// policewahistory.iinet.net.au/HTML_Pages/Boulder_Bomb.html, as at September 2006.

Sydney Morning Herald, 3 February 1942.

Chapter 7: Manhunt

Harvey, Roy, 'Larry Boy Story', *Northern Territory Police News*, vol. 6, no. 4, September 1983, and vol. 7, no. 1, December 1983.

Idriess, Ion, *Nemarluk*, Angus & Robertson, Sydney, 1941.

Leary, Fr John, 'The Dominant Culture and Tribal Aboriginals', The Bennelong Society, December 2000 Workshop, Aboriginal Policy: Failure, Reappraisal and Reform: http://www.bennelong.com.au/conferences/workshop2000/Leary2000.php, as at April 2007.

Northern Territory News, various issues from September to November 1968.

Wilson, Paul, *A Life of Crime*, Scribe, Newham, 1990.

Chapter 8: Red in Tooth and Claw

Bryson, John, *Evil Angels: The Disappearance of Azaria Chamberlain*, Hodder Headline, Sydney, 2000.

Chamberlain, Lindy, *Through My Eyes: The Autobiography of Lindy Chamberlain*, East Street Publications, Adelaide, 2004.

Harris, Les, 'On the Propensity of Dingoes to Attack Humans': http://www.law.umkc.edu/faculty/projects/ftrials/chamberlain/dingoreport.html, as at 27 October 2006.

Chapter 9: Backpackers

Australian Story, 'Into the Forest', Parts 1 and 2, ABC-TV, transcripts: http://www.abc.net.au/austory/content/2004/s1232032.htm and http://www.abc.net.au/austory/content/2004/s1236866.htm, as at November 2006.

Born to Kill? Ivan Milat, Two Four Productions, 2005.

Whittaker, Mark, & Kennedy, Les, *Sins of the Brother*, Pan Macmillan, Sydney, 1998.

Chapter 10: Motorists

Bowles, Robin, *Dead Centre*, Bantam, Sydney, 2005.

Enough Rope, transcript of an interview with Joanne Lees, ABC-TV, 2006.

Lees, Joanne, *No Turning Back: My Journey*, Hachette Australia, Sydney, 2006.

Williams, Sue, *And Then the Darkness*, ABC Books, Sydney, 2006.

Wills, J., 'Thrill Kill: The Hunting of Dean Robinson', *The Australian Magazine*, May 23–24 1992.